Immigration

**Recent Titles in
Contemporary Debates**

The Affordable Care Act: Examining the Facts
Purva H. Rawal

Climate Change: Examining the Facts
Daniel Bedford and John Cook

IMMIGRATION

Examining the Facts

Cari Lee Skogberg Eastman

Contemporary Debates

An Imprint of ABC-CLIO, LLC
Santa Barbara, California • Denver, Colorado

Library of Congress Cataloging-in-Publication Data

Names: Eastman, Cari Lee Skogberg, 1974– author.
Title: Immigration : examining the facts / Cari Lee Skogberg Eastman.
Description: Santa Barbara, California : ABC-CLIO, [2017] |
    Series: Contemporary debates | Includes index.
Identifiers: LCCN 2016034194 (print) | LCCN 2016049923 (ebook) |
    ISBN 9781440835346 (alk. paper) | ISBN 9781440835353 (ebook)
Subjects: LCSH: United States—Emigration and immigration. |
    United States—Emigration and immigration—Government policy.
Classification: LCC JV6465 .E25 2017 (print) | LCC JV6465 (ebook) |
    DDC 304.8/73—dc23
LC record available at https://lccn.loc.gov/2016034194

ISBN: 978-1-4408-3534-6
EISBN: 978-1-4408-3535-3

21 20 19 18 17   1 2 3 4 5

This book is also available as an eBook.

ABC-CLIO
An Imprint of ABC-CLIO, LLC

ABC-CLIO, LLC
130 Cremona Drive, P.O. Box 1911
Santa Barbara, California 93116-1911
www.abc-clio.com

This book is printed on acid-free paper ∞

Manufactured in the United States of America

Contents

How to Use This Book

Immigration: Examining the Facts is the third volume in ABC-CLIO's *Contemporary Debates* reference series. Each title in this series, which is intended for use by high school and undergraduate students as well as members of the general public, examines the veracity of controversial claims or beliefs surrounding a major political/cultural issue in the United States. The purpose of the series is to give readers a clear and unbiased understanding of current issues by informing them about falsehoods, half-truths, and misconceptions—and confirming the factual validity of other assertions—that have gained traction in America's political and cultural discourse. Ultimately, this series has been crafted to give readers the tools for a fuller understanding of controversial issues, policies, and laws that occupy center stage in American life and politics.

Each volume in this series identifies 30–40 questions swirling about the larger topic under discussion. These questions are examined in individualized entries, which are in turn arranged in broad subject chapters that cover certain aspects of the issue being examined, for example, history of concern about the issue, potential economic or social impact, or findings of latest scholarly research.

Each chapter features 4–10 individual entries. Each entry begins by stating an important and/or well-known **Question** about the issue being studied—for example, "Are immigrants taking the jobs of U.S.

workers?" or "Are immigrants more likely to commit crimes than native-born U.S. citizens?"

The entry then provides a concise and objective one- or two-paragraph **Answer** to the featured question, followed by a more comprehensive, detailed explanation of **The Facts**. This latter portion of each entry uses quantifiable, evidence-based information from respected sources to fully address each question and provide readers with the information they need to be informed citizens. Importantly, entries will also acknowledge instances in which conflicting data exists or data is incomplete. Finally, each entry concludes with a **Further Reading** section, providing users with information on other important and/or influential resources.

The ultimate purpose of every book in the *Contemporary Debates* series is to reject "false equivalence," in which demonstrably false beliefs or statements are given the same exposure and credence as the facts; to puncture myths that diminish our understanding of important policies and positions; to provide needed context for misleading statements and claims; and to confirm the factual accuracy of other assertions. In other words, volumes in this series are being crafted to clear the air surrounding some of the most contentious and misunderstood issues of our time—not just add another layer of obfuscation and uncertainty to the debate.

Introduction

Immigrants are so tightly woven into the fabric of the history, life and culture of the United States that it is nearly impossible to think of one without the other. It was immigrants who built the nation's first roads, schools, and business districts, and immigrants who established the rules and guidelines for governance of the new nation. Immigrants settled the plains and ventured west in search of land and opportunity. Immigrants endured sickness and loss during their journeys to the new land and again once they arrived. In spite of their hardships, those same immigrants, often through sheer grit and determination, forged ahead and built the foundations of what soon became the most powerful country in the world.

Although the United States was built on immigrant ingenuity and labor, and their contributions to the success of the nation continue today, immigrants have not always been welcomed with open arms. Throughout its young history, acceptance and assimilation of newcomers to the United States has often been accompanied by suspicion or rejection of foreigners thought to be threatening in some way to the 'American' way of life. This perceived threat, whether stemming from differences in religion, language, religious beliefs, culture, ethnicity, or skin color (or some combination thereof), has prompted heated debates about what it means to really be American—and whether newcomers to the country's shores are capable of fully integrating into U.S. society.

Recent decades have seen major changes in the nature of U.S. immigration, including the passage of laws that place primary importance on family reunification and highly skilled workers, the arrival of large numbers of unauthorized individuals, rising death tolls in immigrant corridors, and the increase of newcomers from Asia. Some of these trends have resulted in an outcry from U.S. citizens, lawmakers, organizations, and lobbyists who have called for reforms in immigration laws. Some of the proposed reforms would tighten immigration laws and dramatically increase deportation and border security measures, while others would make it easier for immigrants, both lawful and unauthorized, to live in the United States and ultimately become American citizens.

But those reforms remain elusive. For nearly a decade, a partisanship-wracked Congress has repeatedly tried and failed to pass comprehensive immigration reform legislation. In the meantime, immigration has become one of the most polarizing, widely debated topics in the country. The sheer mention of any number of immigration-related issues is likely to produce adamant, emotional, and sometimes angry responses. In the midst of all the social and political rhetoric surrounding immigration-related topics, deciphering fact from fiction can seem an insurmountable task.

"Immigrants are among the most educated in our society."
"Immigrants are among the least educated in our society."
"The southern U.S. border is more secure than ever."
"The southern U.S. border is less secure than ever."
"Illegal immigration is a crisis."
"Illegal immigration is at its lowest level in years."

All of the preceding statements represent mainstream views about immigration in the United States. But how is it that citizens, politicians, and pundits from the same country hold views so divergent from one another?

After hearing both public and private personalities seemingly contradict one another as they make their cases for immigration policy reform, the general public is often left to wonder what to believe.

Immigration: Examining the Facts provides a resource to all who are interested in better understanding the myriad of issues surrounding immigration in the United States. Written as part of a series of books that address controversial current events topics, this work is an effort to empower and equip readers with facts about immigration through the presentation of empirical research and hard data. As it weaves through the presentation of commonly misunderstood immigration myths and realities, this book answers familiar questions with research-driven facts. Ultimately, after examining the complexities of immigration-related issues through facts and figures, it is up to the reader to decide how the data shapes his or her opinions about such topics.

It is hoped that the information gained from this book will stimulate conversations and deeper discussions of these widely misunderstood or misconstrued immigration topics. In contrast to many of the divisive media-driven messages about immigration, the goal of this book is to unite readers through a common font of knowledge that encourages civil discourse and acknowledges diverse views.

This book is written for all who are interested in better understanding the impact of immigrants on U.S. society, from researchers to the general public. Its goal is to stimulate thinking, learning, and the development of sound reasoning for the formation of opinions about this and other controversial topics.

Above all, it is hoped that the information presented in this book will serve as the impetus for action among lawmakers and citizens who wish to see changes made in current immigration policies. Through rich conversations, collaboration, and new insights gained from empirical data, readers will be equipped to inform and act—ready to create a more just and functional system for future immigrants and native-born citizens alike.

1

Who Are We? Demographics, Immigration History, and the Shaping of the United States

Q1. IS THE CURRENT U.S. IMMIGRANT POPULATION THE LARGEST IN THE COUNTRY'S HISTORY, AND ARE UNAUTHORIZED IMMIGRANTS THE LARGEST SHARE OF THIS POPULATION?

Answer: No on both accounts.

The Facts: In a 2014 Ipsos MORI poll, respondents in 14 countries were asked what percentage of their countries' populations were made up of immigrants. In all 14 of the countries surveyed, immigrant populations were overestimated. The disparity between perception and reality in the United States, though, was among the greatest, with respondents estimating that 32.3 percent of the population is made up of immigrants (Ipsos, 2014). In reality, the number of foreign-born persons living in the United States in 2014 was between 42.2 and 42.4 million persons, or just over 13 percent of the population (Brown & Stepler, 2016; Zong & Batalova, 2016). Although these numbers mark a recent high point, they have not surpassed the immigration peak of 1890, when immigrants made up 14.8 percent of the population (Brown, 2015).

Why does the U.S. public tend to overestimate the number of foreign-born within its national borders? Part of the reason may have to do with often-intertwined dialogues about legal and illegal immigration. Sometimes these two different issues are confused by the way in which media and/or politicians have addressed "immigration" by concentrating heavily on problems created by illegal immigration (Estrada, Ebert, & Lore, 2016), or by the way media and public figures have framed immigration-related issues (Lakoff & Ferguson, 2007). At other times, the intersection of issues affecting those with both legal and unauthorized status makes the two difficult to separate. For example, many immigrant families are comprised of both legal and unauthorized individuals, making discussion of "immigrant families" more difficult to accurately categorize.

To be clear, there is no dispute that the United States *is* a popular immigration destination. Although it represents less than 5 percent of the world's population, the United States attracts roughly 20 percent of international migrants from around the globe (Connor & López, 2016; Zong & Batalova, 2015), giving it a larger immigrant population than any other country. Most U.S. immigrants historically have come from Mexico, making this the world's largest migration corridor (Connor & López, 2016). However, when the foreign-born are compared as a *percentage* of the overall population, the USA's immigrant population of roughly 13–14 percent is far lower than that of many other developed countries—both Western and non-Western. As shown in figure 1.1, immigrants make up nearly 17 percent of the population of Sweden, 22 percent of the population of Canada, 28 percent of the population of Australia, 29 percent of the population of Switzerland, 75 percent of the population of Qatar, and 88 percent of the population of the United Arab Emirates (Connor & López, 2016; United Nations, 2015). In fact, there are 64 other countries whose populations have a larger percentage of immigrants than the United States (United Nations, 2015).

What will immigration populations look like in the future? Although no one knows for sure, the Pew Research Center has predicted that 88 percent of the population growth in America between 2015 and 2065 will be due to immigrants (Pew Research Center, 2015). The U.S. Census Bureau predicts that by 2060 foreign-born individuals will make up almost 19 percent of the country's population (Brown, 2015; Colby & Ortman, 2015).

But what about the nation's undocumented population? How many unauthorized persons (or "illegal aliens" as they are also called) live in the United States? Republican presidential candidate Donald Trump asserted that the number is 30–34 million (Sherman, 2015). Conservative

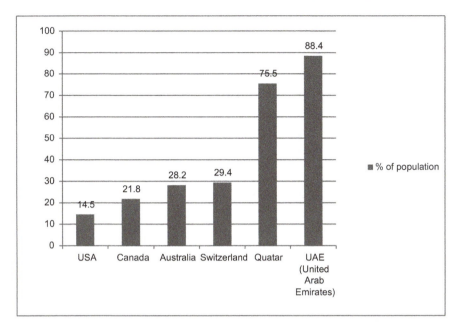

Figure 1.1 Immigrants as a Percentage of the Population of Selected Countries

Source: Adapted from United Nations Department of Economic and Social Affairs, Population Division, "International Migration, 2015."

columnist Ann Coulter claims there are 30 million (Coulter, 2015, p. 72). Former talk show host Lou Dobbs argued as far back as 2006 that some estimates put the number as high as 20 million (Dobbs, 2006). Opponents of immigration have sometimes characterized this flow as an existential threat to the country. "If we don't do something effective and workable," said U.S. Representative James Sensenbrenner (R-WI) to Dobbs in 2006, "we're going to have 20 million more illegal aliens in the next 10 years, according to a demographic study I've seen. They'll flood our schools. Our health care system will collapse. And our social services system will end up being overtaxed. And we've got to get control of our borders because if we don't, we're going to see our economy collapse" (ibid.).

Are these estimates accurate? No. There is no valid documentation to support any of these claims. While Trump says he has heard the figure 30 million "from other people" and he has "seen it written in newspapers" (Sherman, 2015) and Coulter defends her higher figures based on "common sense" and the assumption that Census figures (upon which most research is partially based) are incorrect (Boyle, 2015), all of the preceding statements have been refuted by population researchers and demographers. Trump's claim, in fact, received a "pants on fire" rating by Politifact.com (Sherman, 2015). Numerous government agencies, think tanks, educational institutions, demographers, and independent research groups (including the Center for Migration Studies, Center for Immigration Studies, Pew Research Center, and U.S. Department of Homeland Security) have all placed the U.S. unauthorized population somewhere between 10.9 and 12 million, or around 3.5 percent of the overall U.S. population.

Steven Camarota, director of research for the Center for Immigration Studies (a center that advocates for reduced immigration), said illegal immigration levels have not changed much in recent years because the number of individuals leaving or achieving legal status is nearly equal to the number arriving (Camarota, 2015). Robert Warren, a former demographer for the U.S. Census Bureau and the Immigration and Naturalization Service and current fellow at the Center for Migration Studies, said that margins of error could account for "maybe plus or minus a million" but that "there is virtually no evidence that the real number could be even a few million higher than 11 million" (Sherman, 2015).

Therefore, allegations that both legal and unauthorized immigrant populations have reached unprecedented levels are unfounded. Although future immigration levels may eventually reach and surpass historic highs, possibly as early as 2025 (Brown, 2015), current levels have not yet done so.

FURTHER READING

Baker, B. & Rytina, N. (2013, March). *Estimates of the unauthorized immigrant population residing in the United States: January 2012.* Washington, DC: Department of Homeland Security Office of Immigration Statistics. Retrieved from https://www.dhs.gov/sites/default/files/publications/ois_ill_pe_2012_2.pdf

Boyle, M. (2015, May 26). *Jorge Ramos admits to Ann Coulter: Bring all of Mexico to live here.* Breitbart.com. Retrieved from http://www.breitbart.com/big-government/2015/05/26/jorge-ramos-admits-true-feelings-to-ann-coulter-no-limit-to-number-of-mexicans-allowed-into-america%E2%80%A8/

Brown, A. (2015, March 9). *U.S. immigrant population expected to rise, even as share falls among Hispanics, Asians.* Washington, DC: Pew Research Center. Retrieved from http://www.pewresearch.org/

fact-tank/2015/03/09/u-s-immigrant-population-projected-to-rise-even-as-share-falls-among-hispanics-asians/

Brown, A. & Stepler, R. (2016, April 19). *Statistical portrait of the foreign-born population in the United States*. Washington, DC: Pew. Retrieved from http://www.pewhispanic.org/2016/04/19/statistical-portrait-of-the-foreign-born-population-in-the-united-states-key-charts/

Camarota, S. A. (2015, July). *2.5 million join illegal population under Obama*. Washington, DC: Center for Immigration Studies. Retrieved from http://cis.org/2.5-Million-Join-Illegal-Population-under-Obama

Colby, S. L. & Ortman, J. M. (2015, March). *Projections of the size and composition of the U.S. population: 2014 to 2060*. Washington, DC: U.S. Department of Commerce, Census Bureau. Retrieved from http://www.census.gov/content/dam/Census/library/publications/2015/demo/p25-1143.pdf

Connor, P. & López, G. (2016, May 18). *5 facts about the U.S. rank in worldwide migration*. Washington, DC: Pew Research Center. Retrieved from http://www.pewresearch.org/fact-tank/2016/05/18/5-facts-about-the-u-s-rank-in-worldwide-migration/

Coulter, A. (2015, June 1). *¡Adios, America! The Left's plan to turn our country into a third world hellhole*. Washington, DC: Regnery Publishing.

Dobbs, L. (2006, March 27). *Lou Dobbs Tonight: Guest worker plan approved by Senate Judiciary Committee; Interview with Congressman James Sensenbrenner* [Transcript]. Atlanta, GA: CNN.com. Retrieved from http://transcripts.cnn.com/TRANSCRIPTS/0603/27/ldt.01.html

Estrada, E. P., Ebert, K., & Lore, M. H. (2016). Apathy and antipathy: Media coverage of restrictive immigration legislation and the maintenance of symbolic boundaries. *Sociological Forum* (doi: 10.1111/socf.12262).

Ipsos MORI. (2014, November 1). The perils of perception: Americans fail on all measures of "perceptions versus facts" in unique sociodemographic knowledge test; Places 13th of 14 countries surveyed. Ipsos.com. Retrieved from http://ipsos-na.com/news-polls/pressrelease.aspx?id=6657#

Krogstad, J. M. & Passel, J. S. (2015, November 19). *5 facts about illegal immigration in the U.S.* Washington, DC: Pew Research Center. Retrieved from http://www.pewresearch.org/fact-tank/2015/11/19/5-facts-about-illegal-immigration-in-the-u-s/

Lakoff, G. & Ferguson, S. (2007, September 24). The framing of immigration. *The Rockridge Institute Journal*. Retrieved from http://afrolatinoproject.org/2007/09/24/the-framing-of-immigration-5/

Passel, J. S. & Cohn, D. (2015, July 22). *Unauthorized immigrant population stable for half a decade*. Washington, DC: Pew Research Center. Retrieved from http://www.pewresearch.org/fact-tank/2015/07/22/un authorized-immigrant-population-stable-for-half-a-decade/

Passel, J. S., Cohn, D., Krogstad, J. M., & Gonzalez-Barrera, A. (2014, September 3). *As growth stalls, unauthorized immigrant population becomes more settled*. Washington, DC: Pew Research Center's Hispanic Trends Project. Retrieved from http://www.pewhispanic.org/files/2014/09/2014-09-03_Unauthorized-Final.pdf

Pew Research Center. (2015, September 28). *Modern immigration wave brings 59 million to U.S., driving population growth and change through 2065*. Washington, DC: Pew Research Center. Retrieved from http://www.pewhispanic.org/2015/09/28/modern-immigration-wave-brings-59-million-to-u-s-driving-population-growth-and-change-through-2065/

Sherman, A. (2015, July 28). Donald Trump wrongly says the number of illegal immigrants is 30 million or higher. *Politifact.com, Politifact Florida*. Retrieved from http://www.politifact.com/florida/statements/2015/jul/28/donald-trump/donald-trump-says-number-illegal-immigrants-30-mil/

United Nations. (2015). *International migration 2015 (Wall chart)*. United Nations Department of Economic and Social Affairs, Population Division. Retrieved from http://www.un.org/en/development/desa/population/migration/publications/wallchart/docs/MigrationWall Chart2015.pdf

Warren, R. (2016). U.S. undocumented population drops below 11 million in 2014, with continued declines in the Mexican undocumented population. *Journal on Migration and Human Society*, 4(1), 1–15. New York: Center for Migration Studies. Retrieved from http://jmhs.cmsny.org/index.php/jmhs/article/view/58

Zong, J. & Batalova, J. (2016, April 14). *Frequently requested statistics on immigrants and immigration in the United States*. Washington, DC: Migration Policy Institute. Retrieved from http://www.migra tionpolicy.org/article/frequently-requested-statistics-immigrants-and-immigration-united-states/

Zong, J. & Batalova, J. (2015, February 26). *Frequently requested statistics on immigrants and immigration in the United States*. Washington, DC: Migration Policy Institute. Retrieved from http://www.migra tionpolicy.org/article/frequently-requested-statistics-immigrants-and-immigration-united-states-4

Q2. ARE MOST IMMIGRANTS IN THE UNITED STATES FROM MEXICO?

Answer: Yes, but probably not for long. Mexicans currently make up the majority of the immigrants in the United States of America. However, recent years have been marked by high levels of Asian immigration. If these trends continue, Mexico may not hold this distinction much longer.

The Facts: Conservative pundit Ann Coulter charged that one of the problems with the current immigration system is that it brings immigrants who make the USA "a lot poorer and a lot more Latin" (Coulter, 2015). Coulter subsequently made the claim that "America has already taken in one-fourth of Mexico's entire population" (ibid.). To support her assertion, Coulter pointed to a Pew Research Study that found in 2011, 33.5 million people of Mexican origin were living in the United States (Brown & Patten, 2013).

While Mexican nationals do make up the greatest percentage of unauthorized persons in the United States, Coulter's statement neglected to account for the fact that that approximately 20 million of the 33.5 million individuals of Mexican origin claim Mexican heritage but have never lived in Mexico. Only 8,822 of those individuals in the study were noncitizens (information that was also included in the report) (Brown & Patten, 2013). Coulter's statement earned a "pants on fire" rating from PunditFact (Cabaniss, 2015).

Most late 19th century and early 20th century immigrants came from Europe, whereas today's immigrant population is much more diverse. The 1965 Immigration and Nationality Act (INA) eliminated a national origins quota system that heavily favored European immigrants, stressing instead family reunification and skilled workers. In the wave of immigration that has occurred since the passage of that act, over half (51 percent) of immigrants have come from Latin America and a quarter from Asia (Pew Research Center, 2015). The number of immigrants from Africa is also growing. While still small at only 4.4 percent of the total immigrant population, this figure represents a large increase since 1970 when Africans made up only 0.8 percent of America's immigrant population (Anderson, 2015).

In 2014, Mexicans and other Latin Americans together made up 51.6 percent of the immigrants residing in the United States. Mexico still remains the largest source of immigrants, with Mexicans comprising 28 percent of the foreign-born U.S. population (Zong & Batalova, 2016). Mexicans make up five times more of the total foreign-born population in the United States than China, the next-closest sending country (Frey, 2016). However, a rapid growth in Asian immigration and simultaneous slowing of Latin American migration is changing historical trends. During and after the Great Recession in the USA, immigration from Latin America (Mexico in particular) dropped significantly. In fact, from the end of the Recession in mid-2009 to 2015, more Mexicans exited than entered the United States (Gonzalez-Barrera, 2015).

During that same period, Asian immigration increased, particularly from China and India, and the number of Asian immigrants surpassed that of Latino immigrants for the first time in over a century (Brown & Stepler, 2016; Frey, 2016). Since 2011, Asia has been the largest source of newly arrived immigrants, accounting for more than half of the 1 million new immigrants who arrived between 2013 and 2014 (Frey, 2016). This increase in immigration makes Asians the U.S. fastest-growing racial group (Pew Research Center, 2013, 2015). In 1960, Asians made up only 5 percent of the country's foreign-born population, but by 2014 they comprised 30 percent of U.S. immigrants (Zong & Batalova, 2016). In 2013, both China and India individually surpassed Mexico in the number of immigrants sent to the United States (Jensen, 2015).

Although the greatest immigration gains of recent years have been made by Asians, this trend may also change in the not-so-distant future. Based on current population trends, the U.S. Census Bureau predicts that by 2060 the total share of foreign-born Asians and Hispanics will fall and the share of blacks and whites from foreign nations will double (Colby & Ortman, 2015).

FURTHER READING

Anderson, M. (2015, November 2). *African immigrant population in U.S. steadily climbs*. Washington, DC: Pew Research Center, Fact Tank. Retrieved from http://www.pewresearch.org/fact-tank/2015/11/02/afri can-immigrant-population-in-u-s-steadily-climbs/

Brown, A. & Patten, E. (2013, June 19). *Hispanics of Mexican origin in the United States, 2011*. Washington, DC: Pew Research Center. Retrieved from http://www.pewhispanic.org/2013/06/19/hispanics-of-mexican-origin-in-the-united-states-2011/

Brown, A. & Stepler, R. (2016, April 19). *Statistical portrait of the foreign-born population in the United States*. Washington, DC: Pew Research Center. Retrieved from http://www.pewhispanic.org/2016/04/19/statistical-portrait-of-the-foreign-born-population-in-the-united-states-key-charts/

Cabaniss, W. (2015, July 2). 5 myths about immigration. *Punditfact*. Retrieved from http://www.politifact.com/punditfact/article/2015/jul/02/5-myths-about-immigration/

Colby, S. L. & Ortman, J. M. (2015, March). *Projections of the size and composition of the U.S. population: 2014 to 2060*. Washington, DC: U.S. Department of Commerce, Census Bureau. Retrieved from http://www.census.gov/content/dam/Census/library/publications/2015/demo/p25-1143.pdf

Coulter, A. (2015, May 27). Ramos can stay, but Matt Lauer has to go. [column] *Ann Coulter*. Retrieved from http://www.anncoulter.com/columns/2015-05-27.html

Frey, W. H. (2016, January 1). Asian Surprise. *The Milken Institute Review, First Quarter 2016*. Retrieved from http://assets1c.milkeninstitute.org/assets/Publication/MIReview/PDF/05-07MR69.pdf

Gonzalez-Barrera, A. (2015, November 19). *More Mexicans leaving than coming to the U.S.* Washington, DC: Pew Research Center. Retrieved from http://www.pewhispanic.org/2015/11/19/more-mexicans-leaving-than-coming-to-the-u-s/

Jensen, E. (2015, May 1). *China replaces Mexico as the top sending country for immigrants to the United States*. Washington, DC: U.S. Census Bureau. Retrieved from http://researchmatters.blogs.census.gov/2015/05/01/china-replaces-mexico-as-the-top-sending-country-for-immigrants-to-the-united-states/

Pew Research Center. (2013, April 4). *The rise of Asian Americans*. Washington, DC: Pew Research Center, Social & Demographic Trends Project. Retrieved from http://www.pewsocialtrends.org/2012/06/19/the-rise-of-asian-americans/

Pew Research Center. (2015, September 28). *Modern immigration wave brings 59 million to U.S., driving population growth and change through 2065*. Washington, DC: Pew Research Center. Retrieved from http://www.pewhispanic.org/2015/09/28/modern-immigration-wave-brings-59-million-to-u-s-driving-population-growth-and-change-through-2065/

Zong, J. & Batalova, J. (2016, January 6). *Asian immigrants in the United States*. Washington, DC: Migration Policy Institute. Retrieved from http://www.migrationpolicy.org/article/asian-immigrants-united-states/

Q3. HAS THE UNITED STATES ALWAYS WELCOMED IMMIGRANTS WHO ARRIVE LEGALLY?

Answer: No. Immigration history in the United States is full of instances of discrimination against "unwanted" individuals.

The Facts: The United States has the largest immigrant population of any country in the world. Currently, 45 million immigrants live in the United Sates, making up between 13 and 14 percent of the population. Over half of the nation's population growth in the past 50 years can be attributed to immigrants (Pew Research Center, 2015). However, discriminatory laws and policies against "undesirable" immigrants can be traced all the way back to the first decade of this country's existence.

Historians emphasize that the United States was built on the labor of immigrants, and that the contributions of immigrants over the course of more than 200 years have quite literally shaped the identity of the nation. As a result, the idea that immigrants have always been welcome on U.S. shores seems to pervade much of the public discourse on immigration, particularly discourse about illegal immigration. Take, for example, the following excerpts from news articles and interviews:

- "When you've got immigrants who are coming here legally, we've never in the history of this country passed any laws or done anything based on race or religion [to stop them]."—South Carolina Governor Nikki Haley (Pitts, 2016).
- "America has always welcomed immigrants with open arms, especially the most downtrodden."—Columnist for *The Delaware County Daily Times* (Friend, 2015).
- "Those people came in and became 200 percent Americans, but that's not the class of people coming in now."—Eagle Forum founder Phyllis Schlafly, contrasting immigrants of previous generations with those coming today (Bremmer, 2014).
- "With only a very few exceptions, America has always welcomed immigrants who come to this country honestly, with their work ethic and appreciation of liberty, seeking the promises and opportunities of the American Dream."—Heritage Foundation (Spalding, 2006).
- "America has always welcomed immigrants with very diverse backgrounds, languages, cultures and religions. All we ask is that they obey our laws and treat their fellow Americans with respect."—U.S. Border Control, a Washington, D.C., lobbyist group (Nelson, 2010).

While the idea of previous generations of immigrants arriving on U.S. shores to welcome arms is a comforting one, it is not accurate. Not all who made the journey have been welcomed, even when they followed legal pathways to come. On the contrary, throughout U.S. history immigrants have faced discrimination and rejection for racial, ethnic, or social reasons.

To be sure, immigration to the United States in the 18th and early 19th centuries was largely open to anyone able to survive the long passage by ship to the new country. Even beyond the first settlers, most of those who arrived to U.S. shores were granted permission to enter and build lives in the young nation. Under the Naturalization Act of 1790, citizenship was granted to any "free white persons" of "good moral character" after a two-year residency requirement (Muhlenberg, Adams, & Washington, 1790).

That is not to say, however, that everyone escaped scrutiny of federal authorities who did not deem all fit for naturalized citizenship. In 1798, when the country was preparing for a possible war with France, the Alien and Sedition Acts were passed. Primarily directed at newcomers, these acts increased residency requirements for citizenship from 5 to 14 years, ensuring that new arrivals who favored the Democratic-Republican Party would not be allowed to vote for at least the first 14 years of their residence. The legislation, among other things, also allowed President John Adams to deport anyone deemed dangerous to the peace or safety of the country (Warne, 1916).

In 1854 anti-immigrant sentiment became more specific with the rise of the Know-Nothings. The primary goal of this nativist political party was to restrict immigration of the Irish, who had arrived on American shores in large numbers after the Potato Famine of 1845–1851. Protestants were afraid that too much immigration growth from Catholic Ireland would result in Papal control over the new nation.

As more and more immigrants arrived in the United States, discontent and suspicion of the newcomers grew, even though the bulk of the established population was made up of newcomers themselves. By the late 19th and early 20th centuries, new laws and regulations restricted entry of persons considered undesirable, including "lunatics" and people likely to become public charges (1882), the diseased, persons convicted of "crimes involving moral turpitude" and polygamists (1891), and anarchists and political extremists (1901). The Dillingham Commission, a joint House-Senate committee formed in 1907, released a report in 1911 that concluded immigrants from Southern and Eastern Europe threatened American society and culture, and recommended that their numbers be severely restricted. Sponsors of the quota acts of the 1920s, which placed the first numerical limits on immigration, relied heavily on the Dillingham Commission's report (Dillingham, 1911; Ewing, 2012). These quota acts were subsequently designed to favor immigrants from Western Europe and limit the numbers of immigrants from other countries (Mexico and Canada were exempted from these quotas).

The Immigration Act of 1917 had contributed many more categories of undesirables that would not be allowed to immigrate, including "idiots, imbeciles, epileptics, alcoholics, poor, criminals, beggars, any person suffering attacks of insanity, those with tuberculosis, and those who have any form of dangerous contagious disease, aliens who have a physical disability that will restrict them from earning a living in the United States . . ., polygamists and anarchists, those who were against the organized government or those who advocated the unlawful destruction of property and those who advocated the unlawful assault of killing of any officer." Decades later, Communists would be added to the list with the passage of the 1950 Internal Security Act. This legislation created grounds not only for immigration restriction but also for deportation of past or present members of the Communist Party or any other totalitarian political party (McCarran, 1950).

Even seemingly unlikely groups were targets of early anti-immigration sentiment in the United States. Benjamin Franklin warned about the damaging effects of the Germans on U.S. society (1753). During the Civil War General Ulysses S. Grant issued an expulsion order for all Jews within the parts of territory he controlled (1862). The largest single mass lynching in U.S. history took place in New Orleans in 1891 when 11 Sicilians (who had been accused of a murder but had been found *not* guilty) were attacked by an angry mob of 10,000 people. New immigrants from many racial or ethnic groups often struggled to make a place for themselves in America amid public sentiment that portrayed them as dirty, criminally inclined, unhealthy, or otherwise undesirable.

The Chinese experienced an especially large degree of discrimination in the late 1800s and early 1900s. They were legally and socially excluded from the mainstream of American life and business for years, in spite of their extensive contributions to the U.S. mining industry and their seminal role in construction of the Transcontinental Railroad. Anti-Chinese laws included (but are not limited to) the following:

- The "Anti-Coolie" Act of 1862 discouraged Chinese immigration and imposed a tax on Chinese individuals or the employers of Chinese workers.

- The Chinese Exclusion Act of 1882 placed a 10-year ban on Chinese immigration to the United States.
- The Geary Act of 1892 extended the Chinese Exclusion Act immigration ban for another 10 years and required Chinese residents to carry identification.
- The Chinese Exclusion Act was renewed in 1902 without any provision for an ending date, thus making Chinese immigration permanently illegal. The Chinese Exclusion Act was not repealed until 1943.

Asians in general were largely restricted from immigrating to the United States and from integrating fully into society once they did arrive. In 1907 passports were not issued for Japanese laborers under an informal "Gentlemen's Agreement" between the U.S. and Japanese governments. The Naturalization Act of 1870 limited naturalization to whites and persons of African descent, thus excluding Asians. Asians were not granted citizenship until 1898. A 1917 literacy law passed by Congress also prohibited immigration from Asia, with the exception of Japan and the Philippines. Perhaps most impactful were the Immigration Act of 1917, which limited Asian immigration through creation of an "Asiatic Barred Zone," and the Oriental Exclusion Act (a provision of the Johnson-Reed Act) of 1924, which again prohibited nearly all immigration from Asia, including Japan. Additionally, the Supreme Court ruled in 1923 that Indians from the Asian subcontinent could not become U.S. citizens. After the bombing of Pearl Harbor in 1942, Japanese internment or "relocation" camps were used to detain roughly 120,000 persons of Japanese descent until the end of World War II, even though about two-thirds of those detained were U.S. citizens (Daniels, 2004).

Mexicans had been traveling back and forth across the border long before an official border between the United States and Mexico was established. With the establishment of a Border Patrol in 1924, their movement was more restricted, as was their acceptance in the eyes of the populace. They were exempted, however, from quotas, largely because U.S. agricultural employers made extensive use of their labor to harvest the crops in their fields.

Mexicans were encouraged to enter the United States to fill labor needs left vacant by active servicemen during World War I. In the 1930s, however, the travails of the Great Depression led the U.S. government to deport between 300,000 and 500,000 Mexican workers in order to provide greater job opportunities for white U.S. citizens. This cycle repeated itself during World War II, when millions of American men joined the armed forces. As factories became desperate for workers, Mexicans were encouraged to come to the United States as *Braceros*, or temporary workers. Many did, and so did a number of undocumented workers who were readily employed. Then, in the mid-1950s the government made an effort to remove those undocumented workers through a widespread enforcement and public relations campaign called Operation Wetback. From 1954 to 1958, 3.8 million people of Mexican descent were deported. Among them were both legal immigrants and U.S. citizens of Mexican descent who were caught up in the massive federal sweeps (Calavita, 1992; Ewing, 2012).

THE FACE OF IMMIGRATION TODAY

In 1965 Congress amended the original 1952 Immigration and Nationality Act (INA), which significantly changed the face of immigration to the United States. Prior to this, immigration policy had been driven by a national origins quota system that favored individuals from Western Europe. The INA replaced this system with a policy that emphasized skilled immigrants and family reunification. President Lyndon B. Johnson praised the passage of the legislation, remarking that under the old system, "only 3 countries were allowed to supply 70 percent of all the immigrants" (Johnson, 1965).

Between 1965 and 2015 approximately 59 million immigrants arrived in the United States, more than the total of the primarily European arrivals during the 19th and early 20th centuries (Pew Research Center, 2015). The new immigrants contributed to a more diverse populace, with 51 percent of post-INA immigrants coming from Latin America and one-quarter coming from Asia (ibid.).

However, these immigrants also faced many obstacles as they tried to assimilate and begin new lives in the United States. After the terrorist attacks of September 11, 2001, on American soil, Muslim immigrants became targets of federal investigations that led to the arrest and detention of persons later not found to have any connections with the terrorists (Bernstein, 2006). Hate crimes against Muslim Americans also rose exponentially after the attacks, and in 2015 remained at levels five times higher than those before 9/11 (Ingraham, 2015).

Hispanics, too, have faced increasing scrutiny and discrimination, particularly in recent decades as illegal immigration and border security have become widely debated topics on a national stage. People of Hispanic descent, both citizens and noncitizens, have found themselves subject to hateful rhetoric, racial discrimination, and anti-immigration sentiment, particularly in states like Arizona where state and local authorities fed up with federal responses to immigration-related problems have taken matters into their own hands (Fox, 2014; Pew Research Center, 2010). For example, in 2011, Maricopa County, Arizona sheriff Joe Arpaio, famous for his unyielding efforts to find and arrest "illegals," was found guilty of systematic racial profiling. In 2014 he was found guilty again—this time of ignoring a federal judge's orders to stop singling out and violating the constitutional rights of Latinos (Santos, 2014).

Debates about national security, terrorist threats, and social welfare spending and the perceived connection between these issues and porous borders and/or "anchor babies" have also taken center stage in recent congressional, gubernatorial, and presidential campaigns. Public discourse is highly polarized and is often filled with negative assertions of the ways immigrants (both legal and unauthorized) are harming the country.

FURTHER READING

The Alien Act. (1798, July 6). Fifth Congress; Enrolled Acts and Resolutions; General Records of the United States Government; Record Group 11; National Archives. Retrieved from http://www.ourdocu ments.gov/doc.php?flash=true&doc=16

Bernstein, N. (2006, January 23). Held in 9/11 net, Muslims return to accuse U.S. *The New York Times*. Retrieved from http://www.nytimes .com/2006/01/23/nyregion/23detain.html?pagewanted=all&_r=0

Bremmer, P. (2014, November 21). Schlafly: Obama's election strategy for Ferguson flops. *WorldNetDaily*. Retrieved from http://www.wnd .com/2014/11/schlafly-obamas-election-strategy-for-ferguson-flops/

Calavita, K. (1984). *US immigration law and the control of labor: 1820–1924*. London, Orlando: Academic Press.

Calavita, K. (1992). *Inside the state: The Bracero Program. Immigration, and the I.N.S.* New York: Routledge.

California's Anti-Coolie Act of 1862 [Document]. Retrieved from http:// www-rohan.sdsu.edu/dept/polsciwb/brianl/docs/1862Californiaanti coolieact.pdf

Daniels, R. (2004). *Prisoners without trial: Japanese Americans in World War II*. New York: Hill and Wang.

Dillingham Commission. (1911). *Dillingham Commission (1907–1910)*. Overview provided by Harvard University, *Immigration to the United States, 1789–1930*. Retrieved from http://ocp.hul.harvard.edu/immi gration/dillingham.html

Ewing, W. A. (2012, January). Opportunity and exclusion: A brief history of U.S. immigration policy. Immigration Policy Center. Washington, DC: American Immigration Council. Retrieved from http://www.immigrationpolicy.org/sites/default/files/docs/Opportunity_Exclusion_011312.pdf

Fox, L. (2014, July 24). Anti-immigrant hate coming from everyday Americans. *U.S. News and World Report*. Retrieved from http://www.usnews.com/news/articles/2014/07/24/anti-immigrant-hate-coming-from-everyday-americans

Franklin, B. (1753). Letter to Peter Collinson. [Document]. Retrieved from http://teachingamericanhistory.org/library/document/letter-to-peter-collinson/

Friend, C. (2015, September 15). Chris Friend: Easy answers to tough immigration dilemmas. *The Delaware County Daily Times*. Retrieved from http://www.delcotimes.com/opinion/20150915/chris-freind-easy-answers-to-tough-immigration-dilemmas

Grant, U. S. (1862, December 17). General orders No. 11 [Original text]. Retrieved from http://americanjewisharchives.org/exhibits/aje/_pdfs/S_120.pdf

Harvard University. (n/d). *Immigration to the United States, 1789–1930; Timeline, key dates and landmarks in United States immigration history*. Retrieved from http://ocp.hul.harvard.edu/immigration/timeline.html

Immigration Act of 1917. (1917). [Text]. Retrieved from http://library.uwb.edu/static/USimmigration/39%20stat%20874.pdf

Ingraham, C. (2015, February 11). Anti-Muslim hate crimes are still five times more common today than before 9/11. *The Washington Post*. Retrieved from https://www.washingtonpost.com/news/wonkblog/wp/2015/02/11/anti-muslim-hate-crimes-are-still-five-times-more-common-today-than-before-911/

Johnson, L.B. (1965, October 3). Remarks at the signing of the immigration bill, Liberty Island, New York. Retrieved from http://www.lbjlib.utexas.edu/Johnson/archives.hom/speeches.hom/651003.asp

McCarran, P. (1950, September 23). McCarran Internal Security Act [1950]. [Text]. Retrieved from http://www.historycentral.com/documents/McCarran.html

Muhlenberg, F. A., Adams, J., & Washington, G. (1790, March 26). *Congress of the United States: At the second session*. [Copy of Naturalization Act of 1790]. Cambridge, MA: Harvard University Library. Retrieved from http://pds.lib.harvard.edu/pds/view/5596748

Nelson, E. (2010, November 16). Washington, DC: U.S. Border Control. Retrieved from http://www.usbc.org/national-security/enemy-within/for-immediate-release/comment-page-1/

Pew Research Center. (2010, April 29). Hispanics and Arizona's new immigration law: Fact sheet. Washington, DC; Pew Research Center. Retrieved from http://www.pewhispanic.org/2010/04/29/hispanics-and-arizonas-new-immigration-law/

Pew Research Center. (2015, September 28). *Modern immigration wave brings 59 million to U.S., driving population growth and change through 2065.* Washington, DC: Pew Research Center. Retrieved from http://www.pewhispanic.org/2015/09/28/modern-immigration-wave-brings-59-million-to-u-s-driving-population-growth-and-change-through-2065/

Pitts Jr., L. (2016, January 17). Opinion: U.S. immigration fantasies live on. *The Lawrence Journal-World.* Retrieved from http://www2.ljworld.com/news/2016/jan/17/opinion-us-immigration-fantasies-live/

Santos, F. (2014, March 24). Angry judge says sheriff defied order on Latinos. *The New York Times.* Retrieved from http://www.nytimes.com/2014/03/25/us/judge-says-arpaio-defied-order-on-profiling-latinos.html

Spalding, M. (2006, March 16). *Making citizens: The case for patriotic assimilation.* Washington, DC: The Heritage Foundation. Retrieved from http://www.heritage.org/research/reports/2006/03/making-citizens-the-case-for-patriotic-assimilation

United States Department of State Office of the Historian. (n/d). Milestones 1921–1936: The Immigration Act of 1924 (The Johnson-Reed Act). Retrieved from https://history.state.gov/milestones/1921-1936/immigration-act

U.S. Supreme Court. (1923, February 19). *United States v. Bhagat Singh Thind,* 261 U.S. 204 (1923). Retrieved from https://supreme.justia.com/cases/federal/us/261/204/case.html

Warne, F. (1916). *The tide of immigration.* New York: D. Appleton. Retrieved from http://pds.lib.harvard.edu/pds/view/3885768?n=248

Q4. GIVEN THE WELL-KNOWN DANGERS OF ILLEGAL BORDER CROSSINGS, WHY DON'T UNAUTHORIZED IMMIGRANTS "STAND IN LINE" TO ENTER LEGALLY?

Answer: For most of the individuals trying to enter illegally, there is no line to stand in.

The Facts: In 2014 *CNN* noted that "in the debate over immigration, there's a common refrain from people who oppose a path to residency for undocumented immigrants: 'Why don't they get in line?' But don't tell that to Yesenia. She has been waiting in line for a green card for 17 years" (Basu, 2014).

This idea that would-be border crossers should just "get in line" and wait for their turn is a popular phrase among politicians speaking out against illegal immigration. The idea, rephrased and repeated in various forms, has been a common sentiment in both private and political circles. As Senator Orrin Hatch (R-UT) told the Utah State Legislature, "If we provide a pathway for people who come into our country illegally . . . most of us believe they have got to go to the back of the line just like everybody else and play by the rules" (Montero & Davidson, 2013). And in a discussion over comprehensive immigration reform, Senator Rand Paul (R-KY) said, "I'm the bridge between people who won't consider it at all to people who want it. I'm in the middle such that I'll vote for it if I think it'll do the right job and it creates border security, doesn't create a new pathway to citizenship, and allows people to get in an existing line, the same way someone in Mexico City would get in line" (O'Brien, 2013).

For many would-be migrants, however, the line referenced earlier by Hatch and Paul does not exist. U.S. immigration laws have evolved over the years in ways that have excluded some groups and provided preferential treatment for others. What began as a system of naturalization with relatively few restrictions evolved into a national-origin, quota-based immigration system. Eventually that, too, was changed in favor of contemporary policies focused primarily on attracting highly skilled workers and reuniting families.

There are currently three basic legal means of obtaining lawful permanent residency in the United States:

1. A family member living legally in the United States can petition to bring other family members from abroad.
2. Political asylum or refugee status is available to those who qualify.
3. Highly skilled or specialized workers can be sponsored by a U.S.-based employer to come live and work legally in the United States.

However, most of the unauthorized persons currently living in the United States would not qualify to come legally under any of those provisions. Many do not have family members already living legally in the United States. Even for those who do, the visa backlogs for certain categories of family members (especially siblings or children of U.S. citizens) can be decades long. In November 2015, the wait time to bring a sibling from the Philippines was 23 years; for Mexico it was 17 years

(United States Citizenship and Immigration Services [USCIS], 2015). On top of that, annual caps are established for most visa categories, and there is a 7 percent per-country limit on the number of visas issued. Overwhelmingly, demand exceeds supply in the majority of those categories. In 2015, for example, the per-country visa limit was 25,900, but there were 1,323,978 applicants from Mexico alone (U.S. Department of State [USDOS], 2014).

Most currently undocumented individuals in the United States would not qualify for political asylum or refugee status, as both designations are extremely difficult to attain. The refugee admissions ceiling (maximum number that can be admitted) in 2013 was 70,000, and refugee status was given to 69,909 people (Martin & Yankay, 2014). Those figures remain steady; in 2015 the United States resettled 69,933 refugees (Zong & Batalova, 2015). Asylum-seekers must prove persecution or fear of persecution in their home countries to qualify. Although poverty is one of the driving factors of illegal immigration, the United States grants only political, not economic asylum. Asylum status in 2014 (the most recent figures available) was granted to 23,533 individuals (Mossad, 2016).

The top three countries of nationality for refugee arrivals in 2014 were Iraq, Burma, and Somalia, respectively, and the top three countries of nationality for asylees that same year were People's Republic of China, Egypt, and Syria (ibid.). Mexico was not in the top five countries of nationality for either category.

Finally, employer-sponsored visas are another option, but most current undocumented immigrants would not qualify. These types of visas are reserved for immigrants with special skills and for those who do qualify, employer-sponsored visas are also subject to annual quotas. For example, priority worker visas (E1) are reserved for persons with a special ability in the arts or sciences, education, business, or athletics; outstanding researchers or professors; or multinational managers or executives (USDOS, n/da). In contrast, only 13 percent of the unauthorized population in the United States in 2013 had a bachelor's, graduate, or professional degree (Migration Policy Institute, 2013). Another employment-based category (E5) is reserved for foreign nationals who invest $1 million (or $500,000 in high-unemployment or rural areas) in a qualifying commercial enterprise (USDOSb, n/db). A large share of those who come to the United States illegally, however, struggle financially. About two-thirds of the unauthorized population in the United States had a family income below 200 percent of the poverty level (roughly $44,000 for a family of four) (Migration Policy Institute, 2013).

For children seeking to escape violence and persecution in their home countries, opportunities to enter the United States legally are extremely limited. These children lack the education, resources, and eligibility requirements to apply for refugee status or special visas through traditional means in their home countries. (The difference between a refugee and asylee is that a refugee lives outside his or her country and is afraid to return home because of persecution or fear of persecution. The refugee applies for status from outside the United States, while asylum seekers (who meet the same criteria as a refugee) are individuals already at the U.S. port of entry.

During fiscal year 2014, an unprecedented 68,541 unaccompanied alien children (UACs) made a long journey northward and were apprehended along the Southwest U.S. border. In 2015 the number dropped, but was still 39,970 (U.S. Customs, 2015). Most of the children were from Mexico, Guatemala, El Salvador, and Honduras (ibid.). A study of these UACs by the United Nations High Commissioner for Refugees found that 58 percent were forcibly displaced and qualified for some type of international protection (2014). A separate study by the Congressional Research Service showed that 48 percent of the children were victims of societal violence and 21 percent were victims of domestic abuse (Kandel et al., 2014). In reality, however, relatively few of these children were granted asylum, special immigrant juvenile status, or other types of legal status (Special Immigrant Juveniles [SIJ] status is designed for children who have experienced abuse, abandonment, or neglect. Those who receive the status can never petition for a green card for their parents, and they cannot petition for a green card for a sibling until the age of 21). Only a small number of these children were granted formal relief. The majority were granted informal relief, meaning they were allowed to remain in the United States, but without legal status.

To address the need of these Central American children for protection and reduce the number of children making the dangerous journey to the United States, the Obama administration created a new program called the Central American Minors (CAM) Refugee/Parole Program. This program provides in-country refugee processing to children affected by violence in Central America who have a parent living lawfully in the United States with whom they can legally reunite (Hipsman & Meissner, 2015).

Legal immigration to the United States today is a very complicated process that requires very specific resources or requirements for eligible applicants. For many of the poor or disadvantaged who come seeking economic opportunities, there simply is no legal way to enter the United States.

FURTHER READING

Basu, M. (2014, September 9). Waits for immigration status—the legal way—can be long and frustrating. *CNN.com*. Retrieved from http://www.cnn.com/2014/09/08/us/immigration-visa-long-waits/index.html

Hipsman, F. & Meissner, D. (2015, August). *In-country refugee processing in Central America: A piece of the puzzle*. Washington, DC: Migration Policy Institute. Retrieved from http://www.migrationpolicy.org/research/country-processing-central-america-piece-puzzle

Kandel, W. A., Bruno, A., Meyer, P. J., Ribando Seelke, C., Taft-Morales, M., & Wasem, R. E. (2014, July 3). *Unaccompanied alien children: Potential factors contributing to recent immigration* (CRS R43628). Congressional Research Service Report. Washington, DC: Congressional Research Service.

Martin, D. C. & Yankay, J. E. (2014, August). *Refugees and asylees: 2013* [Annual flow report]. Office of Immigration Statistics. Washington, DC: Department of Homeland Security. Retrieved from http://www.dhs.gov/sites/default/files/publications/ois_rfa_fr_2013.pdf

Migration Policy Institute (MPI). (2013). *Profile of the unauthorized population: United States*. Washington, DC: Author. Retrieved from http://www.migrationpolicy.org/data/unauthorized-immigrant-population/state/US

Montero, D. & Davidson, L. (2013, February 20). Hatch warns Utahns of economic disaster, talks immigration. *The Salt Lake Tribune*. Retrieved from http://archive.sltrib.com/story.php?ref=/sltrib/politics/55866916-90/hatch-immigration-percent-reform.html.csp

Mossad, N. (2016, April). *Refugees and asylees, 2014* [Annual flow report]. Office of Immigration Statistics. Washington, DC: Department of Homeland Security. Retrieved from https://www.dhs.gov/sites/default/files/publications/Refugees%20%26%20Asylees%20Flow%20Report%202014_508.pdf

O'Brien, M. (2013, May 13). 2016 Republicans might have to run immigration gauntlet in Iowa. *NBC News*. Retrieved from http://firstread.nbcnews.com/_news/2013/05/13/18232235-2016-republicans-might-have-to-run-immigration-gauntlet-in-iowa?lite

Pierce, S. (2015, October). Unaccompanied child migrants in U.S. communities, immigration court, and schools. [Issue Brief]. Washington,

DC: MPI. Retrieved from https://assets.documentcloud.org/docu-ments/2460908/uac-integration-finalweb.pdf

United Nations High Commissioner for Refugees (UNHCR). (2014, March). *Children on the run: Unaccompanied children leaving Central America and Mexico and the need for international protection.* Washington, DC: UNHCR Regional Office for the United States and the Caribbean.

United States Citizenship and Immigration Services (USCIS). (2015, November). When to file your adjustment of status application for family sponsored or employment-based preference visas: November 2015. Washington, DC: USCIS. Retrieved from http://www.uscis.gov/visabulletin-nov-15

United States Customs and Border Protection (USCBP). (2015). South-west border unaccompanied alien children. Washington, DC: Depart-ment of Homeland Security. Retrieved from http://www.cbp.gov/news room/stats/southwest-border-unaccompanied-children

U.S. Department of State (USDOS). (2014). Annual report of immigrant visa applicants in the family-sponsored and employment-based prefer-ences registered at the National Visa Center as of November 1, 2014. Washington, DC: Author. Retrieved from http://travel.state.gov/content/dam/visas/Statistics/Immigrant-Statistics/WaitingListItem.pdf

U.S. Department of State (USDOS). (n/da). *Employment-based immigrant visa.* Washington, DC: Author. Retrieved from http://travel.state.gov/content/visas/en/immigrate/employment.html

U.S. Department of State (USDOS). (n/da). Immigrant investor visas. Washington, DC: Author. Retrieved from http://travel.state.gov/con tent/visas/en/immigrate/Immigrant-Investor-Visas.html

Zong, J. & Batalova, J. (2015, October 28). *Refugees and asylees in the United States.* Migration Policy Institute. Washington, DC: Author. Retrieved from http://www.migrationpolicy.org/article/refugees-and-asylees-united-states/

Q5. ARE OBAMA'S EXECUTIVE ACTIONS ON IMMIGRATION RESPONSIBLE FOR THE INCREASE IN UNAUTHORIZED CHILDREN AND FAMILIES LIVING IN THE UNITED STATES?

Answer: Yes and no. Obama has used his executive power to enact pol-icies that would allow certain unauthorized children and their unautho-rized parents to remain in the United States, although many of his efforts to date have been blocked by judicial rulings and see little chance of implementation before the end of his presidency. However, the primary factors that led to increased settlement of unauthorized families in the United States were in play long before Obama took office.

The Facts: The estimated population of unauthorized resident aliens in the United States has increased significantly in the past 30 years. From 1986 to 2000 the numbers jumped by 5 million, and from 2000 to 2007 they increased 3.3 million more for an estimated total of 12.4 million unauthorized persons living in the United States (Hoefer, Rytina, & Baker, 2008; Passel & Kohn, 2008). By 2014, that number had declined to an estimated 11.3 million (Krogstad & Passel, 2015).

While a number of factors have contributed to the general increase in the unauthorized population, a great deal of conservative rhetoric has pointed to President Obama's executive actions as a primary motivator for illegal immigration. Opponents of the president's efforts say the measures he enacted created confusion about U.S. immigration policy and encouraged unauthorized migrants to come, thinking they would be granted legal status. Primary among their criticisms was a program meant to give temporary relief to individuals brought to the United States as youth.

On June 15, 2012, President Obama used his executive authority to implement a program offering deportation relief to certain individuals who had come to the United States as children. The program, Deferred Action for Childhood Arrivals (DACA), did not offer legal status, but rather provided two years of deferred action against removal as well as authorization to work in the United States (United States Citizenship and Immigration Services [USCIS], 2015). To be eligible, applicants:

- Must have arrived in the United States before their 16th birthday
- Must have continuously resided in the United States from June 15, 2007 through June 15, 2012
- Must be under the age of 31 as of June 15, 2012
- Must never have held lawful immigration status prior to implementation of DACA, or any lawful immigration status or parole prior to that date must have expired
- Must currently be in school, have completed high school, have obtained a GED, or have been honorably discharged from the Coast Guard or Armed Forces of the United States
- Must not have a felony conviction, significant misdemeanor, or three or more misdemeanors
- Must not be a threat to national security

- Must be physically present in the United States on June 15, 2012, and at the time of submitting application for the DACA program (ibid.)

In the first two and a half years of the program 787,068 requests were approved and 38,668 were rejected (USCIS, 2015).

Most Republicans were angered by Obama's executive implementation of DACA, and numerous conservative leaders claimed the program was responsible for a surge in the number of unauthorized children and families crossing the border. Mike Needham, chief executive officer of the Heritage Foundation, said, "When the president used his pen to sign the Deferred Action for Childhood Arrivals, or DACA, memorandum on June 15, 2012, he effectively rolled out the welcome mat to those abroad seeking to immigrate illegally" (2014, July 30). Senator John McCain linked the DACA program to the huge surge of unaccompanied minors crossing the border in recent years. "That triggered a mass movement into the United States of America," he asserted (Kasperowicz, 2014). Arizona Governor Jan Brewer wrote a letter to Congress complaining about the surge of children and stating, "It has become clear that the administration has encouraged this massive influx and intends to continue ignoring the states' calls to end this policy" (2014).

However, what was missing from these arguments was the fact that DACA only applied to children or youth *already in the United States*, not foreign arrivals. Youth who have not lived in the United States continuously since June 15, 2007, do not qualify. Additionally, the huge flows of migrant children actually began in 2011, a year before the implementation of DACA, thus discrediting arguments that the migrant children misunderstood the program as a "free pass" and that served as their motivation for coming north. Most studies have concluded that it was violence and poverty, not a hope of being covered under DACA, that prompted the children's migration to the United States (Kandel et al., 2014; UNHCR, 2014).

President Obama also attempted to use executive power in 2014 to enact a similar program that would have granted temporary deportation relief to parents of U.S. citizen children or lawful permanent residents. The Deferred Action for Parents of Americans and Lawful Permanent Residents (DAPA) program (as well as an extended DACA program) was announced in November 2014. Since then, implementation of the programs has been stymied by a lawsuit filed by 26 right-leaning states, a subsequent injunction ordered by U.S. District Judge Andrew S. Hanen, and a split ruling of the case in 2016 by the U.S. Supreme Court. The inability of the Supreme Court to issue a decision on the matter upheld the ruling of the lower courts and thus blocked implementation of the programs (Iyengar & Rhodan, 2015; Park & Parlapiano, 2016).

What has more likely contributed to increased numbers of unauthorized immigrants planting roots in the United States over the past two decades was a series of immigration policies enacted in the late 1980s and 1990s. These enforcement-based policies called for greater numbers of border patrol agents, construction of a wall along parts of the Southwestern U.S. border, and use of technology to aid in the location and apprehension of unauthorized migrants (Andreas, 2009). The goal of these policies was to deter and prevent illegal entry, but instead of doing so they simply shifted migrant flows. Prior to this border enforcement push, migration patterns were marked by circular flows of target wage earners who came to the United States for a period of time (usually to earn a predetermined amount of money) and then returned to Mexico until the need arose to return north once again. Estimates from 1965 to 1985 indicate that 86 percent of undocumented entries were offset by departures (Massey & Singer, 1995). These migrants most often entered through traditional border crossing points—places like Tijuana/San Diego and Ciudad Juárez/El Paso. The ramping up of border enforcement, however, forced would-be border crossers into more remote and dangerous crossing areas such as the Sonoran Desert of northern Sonora/ southern Arizona. The result was riskier, more expensive crossings that required the hiring of a "coyote," or human smuggler. It soon was no longer cost-effective for these migrants to return home after completing a job in the United States, so many opted to stay in the United States and send for family members. Additionally, laborers from Mexico and Central America began to branch out from their traditional agricultural work and seek employment in a broader range of economic sectors that required longer stays in the United States (Fitzgerald, 2008). The result was family immigration that replaced what was once a male-dominated circular pattern of migration (Massey, Durand, & Malone, 2003). The unintended consequences of increased border enforcement, not presidential executive actions, were arguably among the most influential factors contributing to the arrival and/or reunification of unauthorized immigrant families in the United States.

FURTHER READING

Andreas, P. (2009). *Border games: Policing the U.S.-Mexico divide*. Ithaca, NY: Cornell University Press.

Brewer, J. (2014, June 12). [Letter to Speaker Boehner and Majority Leader Reid]. Retrieved from https://docs.google.com/viewer?url=https://media.azpm.org/master/document/2014/6/12/pdf/brewer-letter-to-congress ional-leaders-061214–1.pdf

Fitzgerald, D. (2008, August). Focus migration: Mexico. Hamburg Institute of International Economics. Hamburg, Germany. Retrieved from http://focus-migration.hwwi.de/typo3_upload/groups/3/focus_ Migration_Publikationen/Laenderprofile/Cp_14_Mexico.pdf

Hoefer, M., Rytina, N., & Baker, B.C. (2008). Estimates of the unauthorized immigrant population residing in the United States: January 2007. Washington, DC: Office of Immigration Statistics, Policy Directorate, U.S. Department of Homeland Security. Retrieved from http://www.dhs.gov/xlibrary/assets/statistics/publications/ois_ill_pe_2007.pdf

Iyengar, R. & Rhodan, M. (2015, February 17). Judge approves injunction against Obama's executive action on immigration. *Time*. Retrieved from http://time.com/3711551/texas-judge-obama-immigration-executive-action-injunction-dapa/

Kandel, W. A, Bruno, A., Meyer, P. J., Ribando Seelke, C., Taft-Morales, M., & Wasem, R. E. (2014, July 3). *Unaccompanied alien children: Potential factors contributing to recent immigration* (CRS R43628). Congressional Research Service Report. Washington, DC: Congressional Research Service.

Kasperowicz, P. (2014, June 10). GOP: Blame Obama for border crisis. *The Blaze*. Retrieved from http://www.theblaze.com/blog/2014/06/10/gop-blame-obama-for-border-crisis/

Krogstad, J. M. & Passel, J. S. (2015, November 19). *5 facts about illegal immigration in the U.S.* Washington, DC: Pew Research Center. Retrieved from http://www.pewresearch.org/fact-tank/2015/11/19/5-facts-about-illegal-immigration-in-the-u-s/

Massey, D. S., Durand, J., & Malone, N. J. (2003). *Beyond smoke and mirrors: Mexican migration in an era of economic integration*. New York: Russell Sage Foundation.

Massey, D. S. & Singer, A. (1995, May). New estimates of undocumented Mexican migration and the probability of apprehension. *Demography*, 32(2), 203–213.

Needham, M. (2014, July 30). Obama's self-made border crisis. *The Daily Signal*. Retrieved from http://dailysignal.com/2014/07/30/obamas-self-made-border-crisis/?utm_source=heritageaction&utm_medium= email&utm_campaign=comm-press&utm_content=

Park, H. & Parlapiano, A. (2016, June 23). Supreme Court's decision on immigration case affects millions of unauthorized immigrants. *The New York Times*. Retrieved from http://www.nytimes.com/interactive/

2016/06/22/us/who-is-affected-by-supreme-court-decision-on-immi
gration.html?_r=0

Passel, J. S. & Cohn, D. (2008, October 2). *Trends in unauthorized immigration: Undocumented inflow now trails legal inflow.* Pew Hispanic Center.
Retrieved from http://www.pewhispanic.org/files/reports/94.pdf

United Nations High Commissioner for Refugees (UNHCR). (2014,
March). *Children on the run: Unaccompanied children leaving Central
America and Mexico and the need for international protection.* Washington,
DC: UNHCR Regional Office for the United States and the Caribbean.

United States Citizenship and Immigration Services (USCIS). (2015,
February 12). Deferred action for childhood arrivals process (through
fiscal year 2015, 1st Qtr.). Washington, DC: USCIS. Retrieved from
http://www.uscis.gov/sites/default/files/USCIS/Resources/Reports%20
and%20Studies/Immigration%20Forms%20Data/All%20Form%20
Types/DACA/I821d_performancedata_fy2015_qtr1.pdf

Q6. GIVEN EXISTING IMMIGRATION TRENDS, WILL HISPANICS SOON OVERTAKE WHITES TO BECOME THE MAJORITY POPULATION IN THE UNITED STATES?

Answer: No. Projections based on extensive study of historical and
contemporary immigration data indicate that while the percentage of
Hispanics, Asians, and blacks will rise during the next 50 years, no single
racial or ethnic group will make up a majority of the U.S. population.

The Facts: When census figures came out in 2006 stating that almost
half of all children in the United States under the age of five were racial or
ethnic minorities, some conservative lawmakers, think tanks, and media
figures reacted with alarm. They warned that rising Hispanic populations
would change the political and cultural landscape of the country. Some
went so far as to say that Hispanics would soon overtake whites as the
majority population. For example, John Gibson of Fox News stated, "You
know what that means? Twenty-five years and the majority of the population is Hispanic." Gibson went on to encourage his viewers to "make
more babies" (Gibson, 2006).

Conservative commentator Ann Coulter made the following comments about ethnic trends:

In 1960, whites were 90 percent of the country. The Census
Bureau recently estimated that whites already account for less than

two-thirds of the population and will be a minority by 2050. Other estimates put that day much sooner.

One may assume the new majority will not be such compassionate overlords as the white majority has been. If this sort of drastic change were legally imposed on any group other than white Americans, it would be called genocide. Yet whites are called racists merely for mentioning the fact that current immigration law is intentionally designed to reduce their percentage in the population.

We needed to have "more discussion" about Iraq for nearly two years before finally invading. When will we be allowed to begin discussion of a government policy enacted by stealth 40 years ago specifically intended to decimate one particular ethnic group in our own country? (Coulter, 2007)

Even popular culture entered discussion on this topic. On a 2012 episode of the hit television show *Glee*, singer Ricky Martin plays a Spanish teacher who tells his class, "Do you know that the U.S. Census believes that by 2030 the majority of Americans will use Spanish as their first language?" While this is a statement about the use of the Spanish language, not the percentage of the Hispanic population, the implication of a Hispanic majority is clear.

That particular *Glee* statement earned a "Pants on Fire" rating from PolitiFact Florida (Sherman, 2012). First, the Census Bureau does not record projected language use. However, two experts from the agency who had written a paper on the topic said the statement from *Glee* was "blatantly wrong" with no evidence to support the claim (ibid.). Second, the Census projection for Hispanics as a percentage of the population in 2030 was 23 percent—far from a majority.

Statements such as the ones made by Gibson and Coulter are also not only factually incorrect (no official data projects a Hispanic majority by 2031) but also have been criticized for inspiring fear and/or nativism and misconstruing public perceptions about minority and/or immigrant populations. A 2014 survey found the U.S. public thinks immigrants make up 32 percent of the population, when the actual number is only a little more than 13 percent (Ipsos MORI, 2014). Groups such as the Leadership Conference on Civil and Human Rights, a coalition of more than 200 national organizations, have called on public figures to tone down the rhetoric on immigration and engage in more civil dialogue, citing a corresponding rise between FBI statistics on hate crimes against Latinos and escalation in the level of media-based anti-immigrant messages (Leadership Conference on Civil Rights Education Fund, 2009).

The fact is Hispanics have been the nation's largest minority group for over a decade, currently comprising 17 percent of the overall population (Clemetson, 2003; U.S. Census, 2014). As of 2012, one in ten Mexican-born individuals worldwide lived in the United States (Passel, Cohn, & Gonzalez-Barrera, 2012). For decades the Hispanic population in America saw tremendous growth, from 9.1 million in 1970 to 53 million in 2012 (Krogstad & Lopez, 2014). While immigration drove much of that expansion, a decline in Mexican migration to the United States since 2000 has resulted in native births accounting for most Hispanic population growth. By 2012, the share of foreign-born Hispanics among the total Hispanic population decreased nearly 5 percent from a decade earlier (ibid.).

In a few individual states, however, Hispanics have already become the plurality, meaning their numbers are not more than half the population (majority), but they make up the largest percentage of any racial or ethnic group. Hispanics make up 47 percent of the population of New Mexico and 38.6 percent in Texas, while in California (the state with the largest numbers of Hispanics in the country) they became the largest racial/ethnic group in 2014 with 39 percent of the state's population (Lopez, 2014; U.S. Census, 2015a). California actually became a majority-minority state in 2000, meaning that non-Hispanic whites make up less than 50 percent of the population and therefore no racial or ethnic group is in the majority (Baldassare, 2000). There are currently four majority-minority states: New Mexico, Texas, California, and Hawaii (which has a 77.1 percent minority population consisting largely of Asian and native Hawaiian groups). Additionally, the District of Columbia is majority-minority according to 2012 U.S. Census data. The U.S. Census Bureau predicts that the U.S. population as a whole will become majority-minority in 2044 (U.S. Census, 2015b). However, non-Hispanic whites are expected to remain the largest single group. Even by 2060 Census Bureau projects the non-Hispanic White population will be 43.6 percent of the overall population, much higher than the projected 28.6 percent for Hispanics (Colby & Ortman, 2015). The Pew Research Center estimated in 2015, meanwhile, that based on adjusted Census data, the Hispanic population in 2065 will be only 24 percent of the total U.S. population (Pew Research Center, 2015).

FURTHER READING

Baldassare, M. (2000, September 7). California's majority-minority milestone: What lies ahead? *San Diego Union Tribune*. Retrieved from http://www.ppic.org/main/commentary.asp?i=227

Clemetson, L. (2003, January 22). Hispanics now largest majority, Census shows. *The New York Times*. Retrieved from http://www.nytimes .com/2003/01/22/us/hispanics-now-largest-minority-census-shows .html

Colby, S.L. & Ortman, J.M. (2015, March). *Projections of the size and composition of the U.S. population: 2014 to 2060*. Census.gov. Washington, DC: United States Census Bureau. Retrieved from https://www.census .gov/content/dam/Census/library/publications/2015/demo/p25-1143.pdf

Coulter, A. (2007, June 6). Bush's America: Roach motel [Copyrighted column]. Distributed by Universal Press Syndicate, Kansas City, MO. Retrieved from http://www.anncoulter.com/columns/2007-06-06.html

Gibson, J. (2006, May 11). Procreation not recreation [transcript]. *The Big Story*. [News program]. FoxNews.com. Retrieved from http://www .foxnews.com/story/2006/05/11/procreation-not-recreation.html

Ipsos MORI. (2014, November 1). The perils of perception: Americans fail on all measures of "perceptions versus facts" in unique sociodemographic knowledge test; Places 13th of 14 countries surveyed. Ipsos.com. Retrieved from http://ipsos-na.com/news-polls/pressrelease .aspx?id=6657#

Krogstad, J. M. & Lopez, M. H. (2014, April 29). *Hispanic nativity shift: U.S. births drive population growth as immigration stalls*. Washington, DC: Pew Research Center. Retrieved from http://www.pewhispanic .org/2014/04/29/hispanic-nativity-shift/

Leadership Conference on Civil Rights Education Fund. (2009, June). Confronting the new faces of hate: Hate crimes in America 2009. Washington, DC: The Leadership Conference on Civil and Human Rights. Retrieved from http://www.civilrights.org/publications/hate crimes/

Lopez, M. H. (2014, January 24). In 2014, *Latinos will surpass whites as largest racial/ethnic group in California*. Washington, DC: Pew Research Center. Retrieved from http://www.pewresearch.org/fact-tank/2014/01/24/in-2014-latinos-will-surpass-whites-as-largest-ra cialethnic-group-in-california/

Passel, J. S., Cohn, D., & Gonzalez-Barrera A. (2012, April 23). *Net migration from Mexico falls to zero—and perhaps less*. Pew Research Center, Hispanic Trends. Retrieved from http://www.pewhispanic.org/2012/04/23/ net-migration-from-mexico-falls-to-zero-and-perhaps-less/

Pew Research Center. (2015, September 28). Modern immigration wave brings 59 million to U.S., driving population growth and change through 2065. Washington, DC: Pew. Retrieved from http://www.pewhispanic .org/2015/09/28/modern-immigration-wave-brings-59-million-to-u-s-driving-population-growth-and-change-through-2065/

Richards, V. (2014, October 30). Muslims, immigration, and teenage pregnancy; British people are ignorant about almost everything. *Independent (UK)*. Retrieved from http://www.independent.co.uk/news/ uk/muslims-immigration-and-teenage-pregnancy-british-people-are-ignorant-about-almost-everything-9825116.html

Sherman, A. (2012, February 14). 'Glee' says the Census Bureau projects the majority of Americans will use Spanish by 2030. PolitiFact Florida. Retrieved from http://www.politifact.com/florida/statements/2012/ feb/14/glee/ricky-martins-character-tv-show-glee-says-us-censu/

U.S. Census Bureau. (2014, September 8). *Facts for features: Hispanic Heritage Month 2014: Sept. 15–Oct. 15*. Washington, DC: Author. Retrieved from http://www.census.gov/newsroom/facts-for-features/2014/ cb14-ff22.html

U.S. Census Bureau. (2015a, October 14). *State & county quick facts: Texas*. Retrieved from http://quickfacts.census.gov/qfd/states/48000 .html

U.S. Census Bureau. (2015b, March 3). *New Census Bureau report analyzes U.S. population projections*. Washington, DC: Author. Retrieved from https://www.census.gov/newsroom/press-releases/2015/cb15-tps 16.html

2

❖

Labor, Employment, and Economics of Immigration

Q7. ARE IMMIGRANTS TAKING THE JOBS OF U.S. WORKERS?

Answer: Generally, no. There *are* specific segments of the U.S. labor force in which unauthorized immigrants may compete with native labor pools, but because employment is not a zero-sum game, most immigrants don't compete directly with U.S. citizens for jobs. Research shows that immigration actually helps create jobs and sometimes boosts wages for native workers, and that immigrant labor is particularly necessary for STEM (science, technology, engineering, mathematics) jobs because there are not enough U.S.-born applicants to fill those positions.

   The Facts: The notion that "immigrants are taking American jobs" has become a cornerstone of anti-immigration rhetoric. It is a concept that has been repeated numerous times over the years, as evidenced by a 2004 Coalition for the Future American Worker ad that compares Iowa workers to punching bags for "greedy corporations and politicians" who import foreign workers, or a subsequent ad by the Coalition showing unemployed workers descending in an elevator while the narrator warns "with millions jobless, our government is still bringing in a million-and-a-half foreign workers a year to take American jobs" (Coalition for the Future American Worker, 2009).

Politicians in recent years have recirculated the assertion, calling for reductions in the number of legal immigrants as well as deportation of unauthorized immigrants, saying they threaten economic prospects of American workers. Republican congressman Mo Brooks of Alabama said that he would deport all DREAM Act kids, and that would just be a start. "There are 8 million jobs in America now held by illegal aliens," he said. "That's 8 million job opportunities taken from American citizens" (Benin, 2014). Former Senator Rick Santorum (R-PA) furthered the idea that immigrants replace U.S. workers, stating there have been 6 million new jobs created in the United States since 2000 and "all of them" are held by immigrants (Santorum, 2015).

These assertions, however, are not accurate for a number of reasons. First, Santorum was citing a 2014 Center for Immigration Studies report that, except in a footnote, left out significant employment gains made by native workers over the age of 65 (Zeigler & Camarota, 2014). In fact, because of these gains, 2.6 million more natives of all ages were working in 2014 than in 2000 (Robertson, 2015). Additionally, when looking specifically at the first quarter of 2010 to the first quarter of 2014, native-born workers of all ages gained 4.4 million jobs, while immigrants gained only 2.5 million (ibid.).

Brooks, on the other hand, spoke about employment as a zero-sum endeavor—the idea that only a limited number of jobs are available to fill and once they are filled there are no further opportunities (U.S. Chamber of Commerce, 2013). On the contrary, the number of jobs available is not finite, and as economist Giovanni Peri said, "There is not a zero-sum tradeoff between natives and immigrants" (Zumbrun & Stiles, 2014). Employment growth and the growth of the U.S. economy overall depend largely on the resources and entrepreneurial ability of individuals who establish businesses and hire labor. As immigrants (even unauthorized immigrants) move into communities, they not only establish their own new businesses which then create jobs (Fairlie, 2012) but also increase demand for housing, food, services, and other forms of labor. Therefore, while increasing the supply of labor as workers themselves, immigrants are also—through new businesses and through their very presence—increasing overall demand for labor in their communities.

A recent study by the National Bureau of Economic Research indicates that as a result of this increase in consumer demand, each immigrant creates 1.2 jobs for local workers, most of which go to the native-born (Hong & McLaren, 2015). In contrast to much of the rhetoric surrounding the issue, immigrants are not "stealing jobs" any more than high school or college graduates are "stealing jobs" when they enter the job market (Davidson, 2015). Instead, they help to create them.

The impact of immigrant labor on native jobs also depends largely on where that labor is applied. Debating the impact of immigration on U.S.-born workers by using generalities does not address the diversity of labor markets and their very different labor needs. In other words, referring to a "loss of American jobs" to immigrants does not account for the fact that employment of a low-wage agricultural worker will not affect the employment prospects of a highly skilled industrial technology worker.

This is not to say, however, that immigration does not create competition in the job market at all. There has been great debate regarding whether immigrants have a negative impact on specific sectors of the labor pool. Those who affirm the negative impact say poor natives with low levels of education are the most likely to be affected by immigrant labor (Camarota, 2015; Camarota & Zeigler, 2009). A 2010 study led by Harvard economist George Borjas found that an increase in immigrant labor was correlated with a reduction in employment and wages of low-skilled black men between 1960 and 2000 (Borjas, Grogger, & Hanson, 2010). Another similar study specifically connected Latino immigration to unemployment among blacks (Shihadeh & Barranco, 2010). And earlier research by Borjas concluded that between 1980 and 2000 unauthorized Mexican workers had a negative impact on native male high school dropouts (Borjas, 2005).

These studies have been challenged by research concluding that, overall, immigrant labor either has minimal negative effects or provides more benefits than harm. A 2009 National Bureau of Economic Research study concluded "inflow of immigrants since 1980 has had a small impact on the relative wages of native-born workers in different skill groups" (Card, 2009). Two different 2009 studies found no significant correlation between employment of immigrants and blacks (Jaynes, 2009; Paral, 2009). A 2010 Congressional Research Report that reviewed the literature on immigrant competition to native workers stated, "More recent national studies have estimated the adverse wage effect of immigration in the short run to be much smaller, even among the least skilled" (Levine, 2010).

Various other studies by a wide variety of economic organizations and researchers have also determined that immigrant labor has a positive effect on the overall economy and labor market of local communities, and of the country in general. A 2011 American Enterprise Institute and Partnership for a New American Economy study found that "overall, when looking at the effect of all immigrants on employment among U.S. natives, there is no evidence that immigrants take jobs from U.S.-born workers" (Zavodny, 2011, p. 11). Likewise, a 2010 Economic Policy Institute study found "little evidence that immigration negatively impacts native-born workers" (Shierholz, 2010). A leading Federal Reserve Bank economist stated that "evidence is scant that immigrants diminish the employment opportunities of U.S.-born workers" (Peri, 2010). And an IZA World of Labor study concluded, "Whether high- or low-skilled, migrants rarely substitute directly for native workers. Instead, migrants often complement native workers or accept jobs that natives don't want or can't do" (Constant, 2014).

An analysis of employment data shows that as a general rule, immigrants come to the job market with different skill sets than most native workers. Because the two groups specialize in different areas, their labor is most often complimentary, not competitive (Congressional Budget Office, 2010; Peri, 2010). Some observers also assert that immigrants' distinct cultural backgrounds also enable them to think differently, fostering creativity and bringing fresh ideas to the work setting (Stadler, 2015).

One new conclusion drawn in more recent literature is that the people most adversely affected by immigrant labor are earlier immigrants, not native workers (Costa, Cooper, & Shierholz, 2014). This may be because the two groups are competing for very similar positions, whereas immigrants and native workers have different skill sets and generally are not in competition with one another for the same jobs (U.S. Chamber of Commerce, 2013). Additionally, immigrants help boost wages by "stimulating investment and promoting specialization," both of which grow the economy's productive capacity (Peri, 2010).

FILLING LABOR SHORTAGES

Immigrants have also filled important jobs in U.S. industries facing labor shortages. For example, immigrants in the health-care industry are more likely than natives to be doctors, surgeons and home health aides, thus filling projected job shortages in these areas as the U.S. population ages (Singer, 2012). Highly skilled immigrants are also filling important roles in the information technology industry, taking jobs such as computer programmers and managers that are not even on the list of primary IT occupations for natives. Although some politicians have raised concerns about technology jobs being given to foreign workers over Americans (Nazarian, 2015), studies show there are almost twice as many STEM jobs available as there are U.S.-born, college-educated professionals to fill them (Change the Equation, 2016).

Finally, it still holds true that immigrants also do the work that Americans just don't want to do, although some argue that U.S.-born workers won't do those jobs in part because immigrants are willing to do them for a lesser wage. One example is the role of immigrant labor in agriculture. In spite of intensive efforts to recruit workers in recent years—even in areas with high unemployment rates—farmers across the United States watched their crops rot in the fields because they could not find enough labor to complete the harvest (Serrano, 2012). In Georgia, agriculture is the state's largest industry. But after legislators passed strict laws designed to drive unauthorized immigrants from the state, farmers lost millions of dollars of produce because they could not recruit enough labor to pick the crops in time (Mataconis, 2011). Many in the agriculture industry have lobbied Congress in favor of comprehensive immigration reform, saying they depend on migrant labor, and reliance on H-2A visas (temporary worker visas for agriculture) is insufficient to meet their needs (Hoffelt, 2011). One farmer commented, "[The immigrant workers] are not taking the best jobs; they're filling the niches that are the hardest to fill" (ibid.). Others have emphasized that in addition to the direct, time-sensitive labor these immigrants perform, they create additional packaging, shipping and marketing jobs for the products they harvest.

Immigrants and native-born workers are not competing for the same set of finite jobs. The U.S. economy is flexible and able to expand where demand for labor is added. Both native and foreign workers bring unique skills and education to the workforce, further reducing the likelihood that they regularly compete for the same jobs. In contrast to the idea that "immigrants replace American labor", research shows overwhelmingly that immigrants help to create jobs and often in the process boost wages of native workers. Their intellectual, economic and physical contributions to the U.S. labor market serve to both strengthen and expand it.

FURTHER READING

Benin, S. (2014, August 4). The House's GOP immigration plan: "Deport 'em all." *The Rachel Maddow Show*, msnbc.com. Retrieved from http://www.msnbc.com/rachel-maddow-show/the-house-gops-immigration-plan-deport-em-all

Borjas, G. J. (2005, April). *The evolution of the Mexican-born workforce in the United States*. Cambridge, MA: National Bureau of Economic Research.

Borjas, G. J., Grogger, J., & Hanson, G. H. (2010, April). Immigration and the economic status of African-American men. *Economica*, 77(306), 255–282.

Camarota, S. A. (2015, January 6). Unskilled workers lose out to immigrants. *The New York Times*. Retrieved from http://www.nytimes.com/

roomfordebate/2015/01/06/do-immigrants-take-jobs-from-american-born-workers/unskilled-workers-lose-out-to-immigrants

Camarota, S. A., & Zeigler, K. (2009, August). *Jobs Americans won't do? A detailed look at immigrant employment by occupation.* Washington, DC: Center for Immigration Studies. Retrieved from http://cis.org/illegalImmigration-employment

Card, D. (2009, January). *Immigration and inequality* [Working paper 14683]. Cambridge, MA: National Bureau of Economic Research.

Change the Equation. (2016). *STEM help wanted.* Washington, DC: Change the Equation. Retrieved from http://changetheequation.org/stemdemand

Coalition for the Future American Worker. (2004, January). Ad1 [Punching bag television ad]. Retrieved from http://www.americanworker.org/iowa_ad1.html and https://www.gwu.edu/~action/2004/ads04/iaimmad0104.html

Coalition for the Future American Worker. (2009). "Elevator" [Television ad]. Baltic Productions. Retrieved from http://americanworker.org/

Congressional Budget Office (CBO). (2010, July). *The role of immigrants in the U.S. labor market: An update.* Washington, DC: CBO. Retrieved from https://www.cbo.gov/publication/21656

Constant, A. (2014, May). Do migrants take the jobs of native workers? *IZA World of Labor,* 10. Retrieved from http://wol.iza.org/articles/do-migrants-take-the-jobs-of-native-workers.pdf

Costa, D., Cooper, D., & Shierholz, H. (2014, August 12). *Facts about immigration and the U.S. economy.* Economic Policy Institute. Retrieved from http://www.epi.org/publication/immigration-facts/

Davidson, A. (2015, March 24). Debunking the myth of the job-stealing immigrant. *The New York Times.* Retrieved from http://www.nytimes.com/2015/03/29/magazine/debunking-the-myth-of-the-job-stealing-immigrant.html

Fairlie, R. W. (2012). *Open for business: How immigrants are driving small business creation in the United States.* The Partnership for a New American Economy. Retrieved from http://www.renewoureconomy.org/sites/all/themes/pnae/openforbusiness.pdf

Hoffelt, J. (2011, December 29). Agriculture Coalition for Immigration Reform dedicates a decade of support to migrant workers. *Agri-view.* Retrieved from http://www.agriview.com/news/dairy/agriculture-coalition-for-immigration-reform-dedicates-a-decade-of-support/article_72a542fa-326d-11e1-a30d-0019bb2963f4.html

Hong, G., & McLaren, J. (2015, April). *Are immigrants a shot in the arm for the local economy?* [Working paper 21123]. Cambridge, MA: The National Bureau of Economic Research. Retrieved from http://www.nber.org/papers/w21123

Jaynes, G. D. (2009, July). *The economic effects of immigration on African Americans*. Washington, DC: Immigration Policy Center. Retrieved from http://www.immigrationpolicy.org/sites/default/files/docs/Gerald%20Jaynes%20071409.pdf

Levine, L. (2010, April 13). *Immigration: The effects of low-skilled and high-skilled native-born workers*. Washington, DC: Congressional Research Service. Retrieved from http://www.au.af.mil/au/awc/awcgate/crs/95-408.pdf

Mataconis, D. (2011, June 22). Georgia's new immigration law leading to crops rotting in farmers' fields. Outsidethebeltway.com. Retrieved from http://www.outsidethebeltway.com/georgias-new-immigration-law-leading-to-crops-rotting-in-farmers-fields/

Nazarian, A. (2015, March 18). Senate committee warned: H-1B visas could eliminate STEM jobs for Americans. Breitbart.com. Retrieved from http://changetheequation.org/stemdemand

Paral, R. (2009, May). *Immigration and native-born unemployment across racial/ethnic groups*. Washington, DC: Immigration Policy Center. Retrieved from http://www.immigrationpolicy.org/sites/default/files/docs/Part%202%20-%20Unemployment%20Race%20Disconnect%2005-19-09.pdf

Peri, G. (2010, August 30). *The effect of immigrants on U.S. employment and productivity*. Federal Reserve Bank of San Francisco. Retrieved from http://www.frbsf.org/economic-research/publications/economic-letter/2010/august/effect-immigrants-us-employment-productivity/

Robertson, L. (2015, January 30). All U.S. jobs did not go to immigrants. FactCheck.org. Retrieved from http://www.factcheck.org/2015/01/all-u-s-jobs-did-not-go-to-immigrants/

Santorum, R. (2015, January 24). Iowa Freedom Summit, Rick Santorum [video]. *C-SPAN*. Retrieved from http://www.c-span.org/video/?323834-11/iowa-freedom-summit-rick-santorum

Serrano, A. (2012, September 21). Bitter harvest: U.S. farmers blame billion-dollar losses on immigration laws. Time.com. Retrieved from http://business.time.com/2012/09/21/bitter-harvest-u-s-farmers-blame-billion-dollar-losses-on-immigration-laws/

Shierholz, H. (2010, February 4). *Immigration and wages: Methodological advancements confirm modest gains for native workers* [Briefing paper #255]. Washington, DC: Economic Policy Institute. Retrieved from http://epi.3cdn.net/7de74ee0cd834d87d4_a3m6ba9j0.pdf

Shihadeh, E. S., & Barranco, R. E. (2010). Latino employment and black violence: The unintended consequence of U.S. immigration policy. *Social Forces*, 88(3), 1393–1420.

Singer, A. (2012, March 15). *Immigrant workers in the U.S. labor force*. Brookings Institute and the Partnership for a New American Economy.

Retrieved from http://www.brookings.edu/research/papers/2012/03/15-immigrant-workers-singer

Stadler, C. (2015, September 8). 5 reasons why immigrants make great entrepreneurs to boost an economy. *Forbes*. Retrieved from http://www.forbes.com/sites/christianstadler/2015/09/08/5-reasons-why-immigrants-make-great-entrepreneurs-to-boost-an-economy/#f21e6217b6f2

U.S. Chamber of Commerce. (2013, October 24). *Immigration myths and facts*. Retrieved from https://www.uschamber.com/sites/default/files/documents/files/Immigration_MythsFacts.pdf

Zavodny, M. (2011, December). *Immigration and American jobs*. The American Enterprise Institute for Public Policy Research and Partnership for a New American Economy. Retrieved from http://www.aei.org/wp-content/uploads/2011/12/-immigration-and-american-jobs_144002688962.pdf

Zeigler, K., & Camarota, S. A. (2014, June). *All employment growth since 2000 went to immigrants*. Washington, DC: Center for Immigration Studies. Retrieved from http://cis.org/all-employment-growth-since-2000-went-to-immigrants

Zumbrun, J., & Stiles, M. (2014, May 22). Skilled foreign workers a boon to pay, study finds. *The Wall Street Journal*. Retrieved from http://www.wsj.com/articles/SB10001424052702303749904579578461727257136

Q8. WHAT IMPACT DOES IMMIGRATION HAVE ON THE U.S. ECONOMY AND ECONOMIC GROWTH?

Answer: Most studies indicate that immigrant labor has helped to strengthen the economy and drive American economic growth.

The Facts: The effect of immigrants on the U.S. economy has been hotly debated for many years. While most economists agree that immigrants in general provide the economy with a small net gain, the public has tended to view immigrants—and unauthorized immigrants in particular—more skeptically (Campo-Flores, 2010). In a 2010 *The New York Times/CBS News* poll, 74 percent of respondents said illegal immigrants weakened the economy because they don't all pay taxes, yet can use public services (*The New York Times*, 2010).

In reality, the U.S. economy benefits greatly from immigrant labor, tax contributions, and spending. Because many immigrants arrive in the United States with the intention of seeking work, there is a higher proportion of working-age adults in U.S. immigrant populations than there is in the country's population overall (Zallman, 2014). In 2012, more than 66 percent of the foreign-born were working compared to 63.2 percent of native-born citizens (ibid.). As a result, immigrant populations have a lower ratio of elderly beneficiaries to working-age adults, and they therefore contribute a greater proportion than they receive in federal program benefits (ibid.). Their contributions have helped sustain federal programs such as Social Security and Medicare.

As the U.S. population ages and baby boomers reach retirement age, there is a need to replenish the workforce and contribute to social and retirement programs. The Census Bureau estimates that by 2030 the working-age population will decline to roughly 57 percent, but almost 80 percent of immigrants will be of working age (Ortman, Velkoff, & Hogan, 2014). Those new immigrants entering the workforce prevent labor productivity from becoming stagnant and help to ensure economic growth (Chang, 2015). In 2015, foreign-born individuals made up 16.7 percent of the U.S. labor force; nearly half of those foreign-born were Hispanic and almost a quarter were Asian (Bureau of Labor Statistics, 2016).

In addition to filling important labor roles, immigrant entrepreneurs create jobs. Immigrants are twice as likely as native-born individuals to start a business (Fairlie et al., 2015). In 2008, 17 percent of all new businesses in the United States were started by immigrants (Fairlie, 2008), but by 2015, immigrant entrepreneurs were responsible for 28.5 percent of the country's new businesses (Fairlie et al., 2015). Collectively, immigrant-owned businesses have created 4 million existing U.S. jobs according to one research study (Fairlie, 2012).

The impact of these jobs on the American economy is significant. New immigrant business owners in the United States had a net income of $121 billion, or 15 percent of all net business income in the United States, from 2006 to 2010 (Fairlie, 2012). As an example, Google, cofounded by Russian immigrant Sergey Brin, made $66 billion in revenue in 2014 and employed over 42,000 workers (Fortune, 2014; Martonik, 2015). Immigrants have made a particularly strong contribution to the high-tech sector. Between 2006 and 2012, 43.9 percent of Silicon Valley companies had at least one key founder who was foreign-born (Wadhwa, Saxenian, & Siciliano, 2012). Other immigrant-founded U.S. business mammoths include Bank of America, eBay, Yahoo!, AT&T, Kohl's, Comcast, Kraft foods, Pfizer, and Procter & Gamble. More than 40 percent of the 2010 Fortune 500 companies were established by immigrants or their children, and 7 of the world's 10 most valuable brands came from companies in the United States founded by immigrants or their children (Partnership for a New American Economy, 2011). Immigrants are also three times more likely than native U.S. citizens to file patents (Greenstone & Looney, 2010), and more than half of the United States' $1 billion start-up companies had at least one immigrant founder (Anderson, 2016).

In addition to creating jobs, many immigrants bring unique educational backgrounds and skills that have helped to boost productivity and pay not only for themselves but for higher-skilled natives as well (Peri, Shih, & Sparber, 2014). According to one study, the income growth generated by immigrant-owned businesses between 2000 and 2010 (60 percent) outpaced the business income growth of native-owned companies (14 percent during the same period). Although the average payroll of immigrant businesses is lower than that of native-owned companies, they collectively pay out $126 billion in payroll each year (Fairlie, 2012).

Immigrant advocates also warn against measuring the value of immigrant populations only by the extent of their economic contributions. Doing so, they say, leaves out many other important ways that immigrants shape and improve U.S. society—socially, culturally, and politically.

FURTHER READING

Anderson, S. (2016, March). *Immigrants and billion dollar startups.* Arlington, VA: National Foundation for American Policy (Policy Brief). Retrieved from http://nfap.com/wp-content/uploads/2016/03/Immigrants-and-Billion-Dollar-Startups.NFAP-Policy-Brief.March-2016.pdf

Bureau of Labor Statistics. (2016, May 19). Foreign-born workers: Labor force characteristics – 2015. (USDL-16-0989) Washington, DC: U.S. Department of Labor. Retrieved from http://www.bls.gov/news.release/pdf/forbrn.pdf

Campo-Flores, A. (2010, May 13). Why Americans think immigration hurts the economy. *Newsweek.* Retrieved from http://www.newsweek.com/why-americans-think-immigration-hurts-economy-72909

Chang, S. (2015, August 7). 6 things Donald Trump doesn't know about immigration. *MarketWatch.* Retrieved from http://www.marketwatch.com/story/6-things-donald-trump-doesnt-know-about-immigration-2015-08-07?page=2

Fairlie, R. W. (2008). *Estimating the contribution of immigrant business owners to the U.S. economy.* Washington, DC: U.S. Small Business Administration, Office of Advocacy.

Fairlie, R. W. (2012). *Open for business: How immigrants are driving small business creation in the United States.* The Partnership for a New

American Economy. Retrieved from http://www.renewoureconomy
.org/sites/all/themes/pnae/openforbusiness.pdf

Fairlie, R. W., Morelix, A., Reedy, E. J., & Russell, J. (2015). *The Kauffman Index: Startup activity, national trends.* Kansas City, MO: The
Ewing Marion Kauffman Foundation. Retrieved from http://www
.kauffman.org/~/media/kauffman_org/research%20reports%20
and%20covers/2015/05/kauffman_index_startup_activity_national_
trends_2015.pdf

Fortune. (2014). 100 best companies to work for. *Fortune.* Retrieved from
http://archive.fortune.com/magazines/fortune/best-companies/2014/
list/?iid=BC14_sp_full

Greenstone, M., & Looney, A. (2010, September). *Ten economic facts
about immigration.* Washington, DC: The Hamilton Project. Retrieved
from http://www.brookings.edu/~/media/research/files/reports/2010/9/
immigration%20greenstone%20looney/09_immigration#page=13

Kerr, W. R. (2013, August). *U.S. high-skilled immigration, innovation, and
entrepreneurship: Empirical approaches and evidence* [Working paper
19377]. Cambridge, MA: National Bureau of Economic Research.

Martonik, A. (2015, January 29). *Google posts earnings: $66 billion reve-
nue for 2014, $18 billion in Q4 alone.* Androidcentral.com. Retrieved
from http://www.androidcentral.com/google-posts-q4–2014-earnings-
66-billion-revenue-2014-18-billion-q4

The New York Times and CBS News. (2010, April 28–May 2). *New
York Times/CBS News poll.* Retrieved from http://s3.amazonaws.com/
nytdocs/docs/330/330.pdf

Ortman, J. M., Velkoff, V. A., & Hogan, H. (2014, May). *An aging nation:
The older population in the United States.* Washington, DC: The U.S.
Census Bureau. Retrieved from http://www.census.gov/prod/2014pubs/
p25-1140.pdf

Partnership for a New American Economy. (2011, June). The "New
American" Fortune 500 [Report]. Retrieved from http://www.renewour
economy.org/wp-content/uploads/2013/07/new-american-fortune-
500-june-2011.pdf

Peri, G., Shih, K.Y., & Sparber, C. (2014, May). *Foreign STEM workers
and native wages and employment in U.S. cities.* Cambridge, MA: The
National Bureau of Economic Research. Retrieved from http://www
.nber.org/papers/w20093

Stadler, C. (2015, September 8). 5 reasons why immigrants make great entrepreneurs to boost an economy. *Forbes.* Retrieved from http://www.forbes
.com/sites/christianstadler/2015/09/08/5-reasons-why-immigrants-
make-great-entrepreneurs-to-boost-an-economy/#f21e6217b6f2

Wadhwa, V., Saxenian, A., & Siciliano, F. D. (2012, October). *Then &
now: America's new immigrant entrepreneurs, Part VII.* Kansas City, MO:
The Ewing Marion Kauffman Foundation. Retrieved from http://www
.kauffman.org/~/media/kauffman_org/research%20reports%20
and%20covers/2012/10/then_and_now_americas_new_immigrant_
entrepreneurs.pdf

Zallman, L. (2014, August). *Staying covered: How immigrants have prolonged the solvency of one of Medicare's key trust funds and subsidized care
for U.S. seniors.* Partnership for a New American Economy. Retrieved
from http://www.renewoureconomy.org/wp-content/uploads/2014/08/
pnae-medicare-report-august2014.pdf

Q9. ARE IMMIGRANTS PRIMARILY EMPLOYED IN THE AGRICULTURAL SECTOR?

Answer: No. While U.S. agriculture has always depended largely on
immigrant labor, many other industries rely on foreign workers as well.
In fact, in recent years immigration has declined in the agricultural sector
due to a combination of factors that have made it difficult for workers to
get to the fields where their labor is needed. At the same time, immigration rates have grown in high-tech sectors.

The Facts: Historically, immigrants from Mexico made up a large
share of agricultural workers in the United States. Beginning in 1942,
many came under legal guest worker (Bracero) programs; others crossed
the border without official authorization to fill labor demands, often
in the fields. Both groups generally followed circular migration patterns, returning home when the work was finished or when public anti-
immigrant sentiment drove them out of the country (Calavita, 1992).
These circular migration cycles that often followed agricultural seasons
were replaced by more permanent settlement patterns with the militarization of the border that began in the late 1980s (Massey, Durand, &
Pren, 2016).

Over the decades the once-agriculture-based migrant labor also diversified, largely because of immigration laws that encouraged the legal
entrance of specialized, highly educated workers. Today's recent immigrants are more likely to be Asian than Hispanic, they are better educated
than immigrants were 50 years ago, and roughly half work in manage-
rial, professional, and sales and administrative support positions (Pew
Research Center, 2015).

Immigrants have also found a niche in technology-related fields. In places where the high-tech industry is thriving, immigration rates are rising. An analysis of census data reveals that from 2010 to 2015, the 10 U.S. counties with the greatest immigration gains were all centers with education or technology at their core—places such as Middlesex County, Massachusetts (home of Massachusetts Institute of Technology and Harvard University), San Diego County, California (hub of numerous technology corporations), and King County, Washington (home to Seattle and numerous technology companies) (Henderson, 2016).

In fact, a quarter of all U.S. engineering and technology-related companies founded between 1995 and 2005 had a minimum of one immigrant founder (American Immigration Council, 2015). However, the immigrants coming to work in these jobs are not Mexicans, traditionally the largest group of immigrants to the United States. Instead, the majority of the new immigrants are coming from Asia on skilled worker visas (Henderson, 2016).

While technology is drawing immigrants to Seattle, particularly from south India, the agriculturally dependent counties surrounding the area are struggling to find workers to harvest crops. From 2010 to 2015 there was a 50–90 percent drop in immigration in the 11 counties surrounding Seattle compared to 10 years prior (Henderson, 2016).

For those immigrants who *are* still employed in agricultural industries, their farm-related jobs have a big impact outside the fields. According to the Ag Workforce Coalition, "Each of the 1.6 million hired farm employees working on American farms and ranches supports 2–3 full-time jobs further down the value chain in food processing, transportation, farm equipment, marketing and retail and other sectors" (2014).

Today, half of all U.S. dairy farm workers are immigrants (Adcock, Anderson, & Rosson, 2015). Dairy owners say it is difficult to find native workers who are willing to do the smelly, messy work of milking cows multiple times a day (ibid.). Fruit-growers in states like California still rely heavily on migrant labor to harvest their crops, although a decline in available laborers has forced them to consider technological alternatives (Jacoby, 2015).

In 2012 *unauthorized* immigrants made up 3.5 percent of the U.S. population (Passel & Cohn, 2015) but 5.1 percent of the U.S. labor force, with 8.1 million individuals either working or looking for work (Krogstad & Passel, 2015). These employees are most likely to be young, working-age individuals, thus explaining their large share of the labor force compared to that of native U.S. citizens (ibid.). However, the nature of unauthorized labor has changed greatly in recent decades. While U.S. agriculture

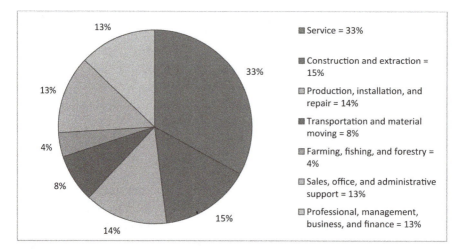

Figure 2.1 Percentage of unauthorized immigrant workers in the United States in major occupations, 2012

Source: Pew Research Center, Hispanic Trends.

still depends largely on immigrant labor—in most states, farming is the workforce with the highest share of unauthorized workers—only 4 percent of unauthorized workers currently are employed in farming-related jobs (Passel & Cohn, 2015). (Farmers now rely more heavily on authorized workers and temporary labor through H-2A seasonal agricultural work visas.) As shown in Figure 2.1, the largest percentage of unauthorized immigrants today are employed in the service industry (33 percent), followed by construction and extraction (15 percent); production, installation, and repair (14 percent); sales, office, and administrative support (13 percent); professional, management, business, and finance (13 percent); and transportation and material moving (8 percent) (ibid.).

DANGEROUS WORK

Over the years, Hispanic workers have been disproportionately represented in higher-risk, lower-wage jobs, resulting in higher rates of fatal occupational injury among that population. This is especially true of foreign-born Hispanics. As far back as 2004, the fatality rate for *native-born* Hispanic workers was actually below the overall national average, but the rate among *foreign-born* Hispanic laborers was 44 percent higher than the national average (Richardson, 2005).

In 2013 there were 804 fatal work injuries among Hispanic or Latino workers in the United States, the highest death toll since 2008. Sixty-six percent of these deaths involved foreign-born workers. While the most actual deaths occurred in the construction industry, the agriculture, forestry, fishing, and hunting industries together recorded the highest fatal injury *rate* of any sector that year, with 22.2 fatal injuries per 100,000 full-time employees (Bureau of Labor Statistics, 2016).

FURTHER READING

Aadcock, F., Anderson, D., & Rosson, P. (2015, August). *The economic impacts of immigrant labor on U.S. dairy farms.* Texas A&M University, Center for North American Studies. Retrieved from http://www.nmpf.org/files/immigration-survey-090915.pdf

Ag Workforce Coalition and Partnership for a New American Economy. (2014, February). #1 farm immigration: Immigration reform to advance America's agriculture industry. Iamimmigration.org. Retrieved from http://www.agworkforcecoalition.org/wp-content/uploads/2014/06/10-iFarm-Briefing-Book.pdf

American Immigration Council. (2015, December). *Giving the facts a fighting chance: Addressing common questions on immigration.* Washington, DC: American Immigration Council. Retrieved from http://www.immigrationpolicy.org/sites/default/files/docs/giving_the_facts_a_fighting_chance_addressing_common_questions_on_immigration.pdf

Bureau of Labor Statistics. (2016, April 21). *Injuries, illnesses, and fatalities: Revisions to the 2014 Census of Fatal Occupational Injuries (CFOI).* Washington, DC: U.S. Department of Labor. Retrieved from http://data.bls.gov/cgi-bin/print.pl/iif/cfoi_revised14.htm

Calavita, K. (1992). *Inside the state: The Bracero program, immigration, and the I.N.S.* New York: Routledge.

Henderson, T. (2016, May 4). *Immigration: Down in farm country, up in some cities.* Stateline. Philadelphia, PA: The Pew Charitable Trusts. Retrieved from http://www.pewtrusts.org/en/research-and-analysis/blogs/stateline/2016/05/04/immigration-down-in-farm-country-up-in-some-cities

Jacoby, J. (2015, April 29). Strawberry field hands forever? Probably not. *Boston Globe.* Retrieved from http://www.jeffjacoby.com/16506/strawberry-field-hands-forever

Krogstad, J. M., & Passel, J. S. (2015, July 24). *5 facts about illegal immigration in the U.S.* Washington, DC: Pew Research Center.

Retrieved from http://www.pewresearch.org/fact-tank/2015/07/24/5-facts-about-illegal-immigration-in-the-u-s/

Massey, D. S., Durand, J., & Pren, K. A. (2016, March). Why border enforcement backfired. *American Journal of Sociology*, 121(5), 1557–1600.

Passel, J. S., & Cohn, D. (2015, March 26). *Share of unauthorized immigrant workers in production, construction jobs falls since 2007*. Washington, DC: Pew Research Center, Hispanic Trends. Retrieved from http://www.pewhispanic.org/2015/03/26/share-of-unauthorized-immigrant-workers-in-production-construction-jobs-falls-since-2007/

Pew Research Center. (2015, September 28). *Modern immigration wave brings 59 million to U.S., driving population growth and change through 2065*. Washington, DC: Pew. Retrieved from http://www.pewhispanic.org/files/2015/09/2015-09-28_modern-immigration-wave_REPORT.pdf

Richardson, S. (2005, October). *Occupational safety and health: Fatal work injuries among foreign-born Hispanic workers* [Monthly Labor Review]. Washington, DC: Bureau of Labor Statistics, Office of Compensation and Working Conditions.

Q10. DO UNDOCUMENTED OR "ILLEGAL" IMMIGRANTS PAY TAXES?

Answer: Undocumented immigrants do pay a number of taxes, including sales and excise taxes, property taxes (directly through homeownership or indirectly through rent payments), and in many cases personal income taxes. Their effective tax rate is also higher than that of U.S. citizens.

The Facts: During a 2010 episode of *The O'Reilly Factor*, host Bill O'Reilly implied to *CNN* personality Lou Dobbs that unauthorized immigrants "dodge taxes." When Dobbs responded that "amnesty advocates say that illegal immigrants are already paying taxes," O'Reilly replied, "No, that's all talk. You know it's crap" (Uwimana, 2010).

According to a 2016 Institute on Taxation and Economic Policy (ITEP) report, undocumented immigrants pay an estimated $11.64 billion a year in sales and excise taxes, property taxes, and personal income taxes (Gee, Gardner, & Wiehe, 2016). Even if they do not directly own property, those property taxes are added in and paid through their rent. Undocumented individuals also have a higher effective tax rate (the percentage of their incomes paid in taxes) than U.S. citizens. They pay an average of 8 percent of their incomes in state and local taxes—nearly $12 billion in 2012 (Gee, Gardner, & Wiehe, 2016; Williams et al., 2015). In contrast, the top 1 percent of U.S. taxpayers pays an average nationwide effective tax rate of 5.4 percent of their incomes (Gee, Gardner, & Wiehe, 2016).

If Congress were to create a path to citizenship and legal means of obtaining work for the 11 million currently unauthorized immigrants in the United States, their current state and local tax contributions would increase by more than $2.1 billion per year (ibid.). Furthermore, implementation of President Obama's plan to provide temporary immigration relief for 5 million qualifying Deferred Action for Childhood Arrivals and Deferred Action for Parents of Americans and Lawful Permanent Residents individuals would produce a gain of more than $805 million per year in state and local tax contributions, with the greatest increase coming from personal income tax (ibid.). These executive actions are currently suspended as the result of a lawsuit and divided Supreme Court decision on the matter.

In addition, the ITEP report disproved the notion that unauthorized immigrants do not pay income taxes. According to the best evidence available, ITEP says at least *half* of undocumented immigrants file income tax returns using Individual Tax Identification Numbers (ITINs) (Gee, Gardner, & Wiehe, 2016). ITINs were created to provide foreign nationals not eligible for a Social Security number a means to pay the taxes they are legally required to pay (American Immigration Council, 2016). Because they were designed as a tax compliance tool and not an immigration enforcement tool, unauthorized individuals may obtain ITINs without fear of the Internal Revenue Service sharing their private information with immigration enforcement agencies (ibid.). In some states, the ITIN is accepted in place of a Social Security number for purposes of opening a bank account, obtaining a driver's license, or providing proof of residency. ITIN holders are also eligible for the Child Tax Credit but are not eligible for Social Security benefits or the Earned Income Tax Credit as long as they are unauthorized (ibid.).

The chief actuary for the Social Security Administration estimates that 3.1 million unauthorized individuals have contributed taxes to the federal treasury through use of fake or expired Social Security numbers (Germano, 2014). Their contributions to the Social Security Trust Fund alone over the past decade are estimated to be $100 billion (ibid.). And even among undocumented individuals who do not file tax returns, those who are payroll employees still have taxes automatically deducted from their paychecks like any other employee (Gee, Gardner, & Wiehe, 2016).

FURTHER READING

American Immigration Council. (2016, April 5). *The facts about the Individual Tax Identification Number (ITIN)*. Washington, DC: American Immigration Council. Retrieved from http://www.immigrationpolicy .org/just-facts/facts-about-individual-tax-identification-number-itin

Gee, L. C., Gardner, M., & Wiehe, M. (2016, February). *Undocumented immigrants' state and local tax contributions*. Washington, DC: The Institute on Taxation & Economic Policy. Retrieved from http://www.itep .org/pdf/immigration2016.pdf

Germano, R. (2014, August 4). Unauthorized immigrants paid $100 billion into Social Security over last decade. *Vice News*. Retrieved from https://news.vice.com/article/unauthorized-immigrants-paid-100-billion-into-social-security-over-last-decade

Uwimana, S. (2010, March 10). *O'Reilly, Dobbs wrong that undocumented immigrants don't pay taxes*. Media Matters for America. Retrieved from http://mediamatters.org/research/2010/03/10/oreilly-dobbs-wrong-that-undocumented-immigrant/161434

Williams, E., Leachman, M., Wallace, M., & Albares, N. (2015, October 29). *For states, inclusive approach to unauthorized immigrants can help build better economies*. Washington, DC: Center on Budget and Policy Priorities. Retrieved from http://www.cbpp.org/research/state-budget-and-tax/for-states-inclusive-approach-to-unauthorized-immigrants-can-help

Q11. DO IMMIGRANTS RECEIVE MORE AID THROUGH GOVERNMENT-FUNDED PROGRAMS THAN THEY PAY IN TAXES?

Answer: Generally, no, although there are exceptions. The impact of immigrants—both legal and unauthorized—on many federal public assistance programs is a net positive; they contribute more than they extract from these programs. Overall impact on state and local budgets is less clear because unauthorized immigrants tend to use more services at this level, but they also pay a higher percentage of their incomes in state and local taxes than the native population. The general conclusion is that net impact is modest. Cost of education of unauthorized children—funded through both federal and state governments—is debatable. While it is difficult to estimate the overall cost of education for unauthorized immigrant children compared to their eventual contributions back to society throughout adulthood, most experts agree that money invested in education will lead to significant returns in the form of higher-paying jobs and greater tax revenue than would be received from noneducated populations.

The Facts: One of the most common assertions among conservatives calling for immigration restrictions is that use of government-funded programs by immigrants (particularly those without legal status) costs U.S. taxpayers dearly. During efforts to promote its bipartisan comprehensive immigration reform bill, the Senate's "Gang of 8" received a letter from conservative leaders concerned with "the long-term costs that will be imposed on taxpayers once millions of illegal immigrants eventually become eligible not only for our nation's major entitlements but approximately 80 different means-tested welfare and low-income assistance programs" (United States Senate, 2013). The letter also stated, "Once the present illegal population receives green cards, they will be eligible under current law for a wide array of federal welfare programs including food stamps, Supplemental Security Income, Temporary Assistance for Needy Families, and Medicaid. . . . The long-term costs, and the strain on resources for low-income Americans, could be enormous."

Or consider this more specific claim from an editorial in *Investor's Business Daily*: "Welfare programs make up a significant share of federal and state spending—$670 billion at the federal level alone—and illegals who receive it pay little or no income tax to help defray those costs" (2015).

This assertion is not entirely true, however. Not only do unauthorized workers pay taxes, including, in many cases, income taxes which help fund federal welfare and social programs, but their tax contributions actually help to sustain a number of these programs.

Immigrants with legal status pay in just the same as native citizens do, while those without documentation pay sales and property taxes like any other citizen. However, depending on how they are compensated for their work (in cash vs. being on a payroll), perhaps as many as half of undocumented workers do not file income tax returns. It is estimated that the remaining 50 percent of undocumented workers use Individual Tax Identification Numbers to file income tax returns (Gee, Gardner, & Wiehe, 2016).

The federal government gains the most from immigrant tax contributions, particularly those of unauthorized immigrants who are unlikely to reap the benefits of the money they contribute through taxes to programs like Social Security and Medicare, but also because of lower use of federal programs among immigrant families than among native families. (Some studies contest this conclusion, but a further explanation and deeper discussion of those discrepancies is given later in the chapter.)

Immigrants' impact on state and local governments is somewhat controversial, but most economists agree they generally have a positive overall impact on their state and local economies. A Congressional Budget Office report on the topic issued in 2007 said that most studies from the prior two decades show that "in aggregate and over the long term, tax revenues of all types generated by immigrants—both legal and unauthorized—exceed the cost of the services they use" (Congressional Budget Office, 2007, p. 1). It also notes that because the federal government requires state and local governments to provide certain services for individuals regardless of their immigration status, the state and local governments bear most of the burden for providing those services (e.g., education, health care, and law enforcement) but that overall costs to provide them to unauthorized immigrants specifically were small (ibid.).

A report by economists from the Federal Reserve Bank of Dallas highlighted the fact that immigrant labor has been concentrated at both the high and low ends of skill distribution. High-skilled immigration, particularly in the high-tech sector, has had a positive fiscal impact, while large-scale unauthorized immigration and its accompanying lower-skilled labor force "has had modest adverse fiscal and labor market effects on taxpayers and U.S.-born workers" (Orrenius & Zavodny, 2013).

Because of the significant overall positive social and economic impacts of immigrants, numerous individual states have welcomed and attempted to attract foreign-born populations. For example, communities in Iowa have rolled out welcoming initiatives for immigrants, who have revitalized dying towns and contributed significantly to the state's innovation economy (American Immigration Council, 2013a). In Florida, almost a quarter of the state's 2010 net business revenue ($13.3 billion) came from new immigrant business owners (American Immigration Council, 2013b). Denver's foreign-born population has contributed more than $673 million in state and local taxes. In 2013 they paid $1 billion to Social Security and $256 million to Medicare (Partnership for a New American Economy, 2015). And the increased immigration that has powered Detroit's economic recovery has been called "the single great urban revitalization strategy in modern-day America, and it's one that doesn't cost tax dollars" (American Immigration Council, 2013c).

The impact of *unauthorized* immigrants on state and local government budgets remains more inconclusive—some studies cite deficits, while others indicate net positive inputs. Some research indicates that unauthorized immigrants use more in state and local services than they pay for in taxes. As mentioned, the Congressional Budget Office (CBO), after reviewing 29 reports on the issue, concluded that state and local governments often incur the brunt of the costs associated with unautho-rized populations, namely education, health care, and law enforcement. In general, tax revenues generated by unauthorized immigrants do not fully offset the costs of services provided to them. Most unauthorized fam-ilies earn less than native citizens and other groups of immigrants and are therefore taxed at a lower rate. As a result, they end up paying a smaller portion of their income in taxes, and their smaller sum of earnings also means less disposable income to spend on other purchases. The report also concluded, however, that costs to state and local governments were modest and that in most cases "spending for unauthorized immigrants accounted for less than 5 percent of total state and local spending for these services" (p. 3).

In 2016 the Institute on Taxation and Economic Policy (ITEP) issued a report showing the nationwide average effective tax rate of undocumented immigrants is now higher than that of the general population (Gee, Gard-ner, & Wiehe, 2016). The percentage of their paychecks that goes to taxes (primarily state and local) is estimated at 8 percent. In comparison, the average nationwide effective tax rate of the top 1 percent of taxpayers in the country is just 5.4 percent (ibid.). In California, undocumented immigrants contribute more than $3.2 billion in state and local taxes. Researchers estimate state and local tax contributions of the unauthorized would increase by over $2 billion per year if they were granted legal status and thus legal authorization to work (California Legislature, 2015).

Finally, some have argued that because they use roads, parks, and city infrastructure, unauthorized persons put an additional strain on public funds and services (Rector & Richwine, 2013). However, as previously mentioned, the ITEP concluded that unauthorized immigrants, with a higher nationwide average effective tax rate, make a significant tax impact at the state and local levels (Gee, Gardner, & Wiehe, 2016). Through the money paid in sales, property, and income and other taxes, unauthorized immigrants, just like native citizens and immigrants with legal status, are contributing to the state and local governments that fund such services.

IMMIGRANT IMPACT ON SOCIAL SECURITY, MEDICARE, AND HEALTH CARE OVERALL

A common argument against immigration, unauthorized immigration in particular, is that immigrants are draining U.S. social welfare programs by taking more out of them by dollar value than they contribute. A 2013 report by the Heritage Foundation explicitly stated, "Unlawful immigrants, on average, are always tax consumers; they never once generate a 'fiscal surplus' that can be used to pay for government benefits elsewhere in society" (Rector & Richwine, 2013). This report, however, was criticized—even by some fellow conservatives—for what they said was flawed methodology and inaccurate assumptions (Avila & Marshall, 2013; National Immigration Forum, 2013; Nowrasteh, 2013). More significantly, statistics disprove the Heritage Foundation's assertion. Not only have unauthorized immigrants generated a fiscal surplus for certain government programs, but that surplus has helped keep those government programs alive as well.

Contributions by unauthorized individuals, for example, have helped to bolster Social Security. The Social Security Administration stated that according to projections, "the presence of unauthorized workers in the United States has, on average, a positive effect on the financial status of the Social Security Program" (Goss et al., 2013). As mentioned in the previous section, experts believe unauthorized workers paid $100 billion into the Social Security fund over the past decade, money that they are unlikely to ever receive back in benefits because of their legal status (Germano, 2014). In 2010 (the most recent data available), undocumented workers paid $12 billion in net excess tax revenue to the Social Security Trust Funds that they are highly unlikely to ever receive back in benefits. Officials state that while unauthorized workers as a whole are less likely to report their income as taxable, they are "even less likely to be credited for future benefit entitlement" (Goss et al., 2013, p. 2).

Medicare, too, has benefited from the contributions of immigrants. Partnership for a New American Economy, a coalition of businesses leaders and mayors advocating for comprehensive immigration reform, says immigrants (both citizen and noncitizen) have heavily subsidized Medicare's Hospital Insurance Trust Fund (the program's core trust fund), contributing $182.4 billion more than they received in benefits between 1996 and 2011 (Zallman, 2014). During each year of the 16 years studied, immigrants generated a surplus to the trust fund—even during Recession years when U.S.-born individuals generated sizable net deficits, taking out far more in benefits than they contributed in payroll contributions. Over the 15 years that immigrants contributed a net of $182.4 billion to the fund, "the U.S.-born population generated a deficit of $68.7 billion" (p. 2). Without the annual average of $11.4 billion in surplus money that immigrants generated between 1996 and 2011, Medicare's core trust fund was expected to become insolvent in 2027—three years earlier than the current projection of 2030 (ibid.). Authors of the study state explicitly that their report "uses hard data to show that instead of being a drain on the Medicare program, immigrants are instead arguably a key reason why the Medicare's Hospital Insurance

Trust Fund will remain solvent through the next decade and able to adequately cover care" (p. 2).

Another study, conducted by Harvard University, determined that from 2002 to 2009 immigrants paid $115.2 billion more into the Medicare trust fund than they took out (Zallman et al., 2013). The largest group of immigrant contributors was noncitizens, which includes legal permanent residents (or "green card" holders), conditional permanent residents, refugees, asylees, victims of human trafficking, and unauthorized individuals. As an example of their impact, in 2009 immigrants contributed a net surplus of $13.8 billion to the trust fund, while U.S.-born individuals generated a deficit of $30.9 billion (ibid.). The study concluded, "Policies that restrict immigration may deplete Medicare's financial resources" (p. 1). Authors noted that a path to citizenship for immigrants who are currently unauthorized would increase revenue from payroll taxes but would also increase expenditures for those immigrants as they reach the age of eligibility for Medicare. Therefore, authors stressed, it is important over the coming years to attract young immigrants who can offset the expenditures of an aging U.S. population (ibid.).

A study analyzing health-care spending from 2000 to 2009 by using Medical Expenditure Panel Survey data found that as a whole, immigrants (of all types) spent slightly less for health care than U.S. natives. The average yearly health-care expense for immigrants was $95.6 billion compared to just over $1 trillion for U.S. natives (Stimpson, Wilson, & Su, 2013). *Unauthorized* immigrants spend less on health care overall than legal residents, naturalized citizens, and U.S. natives. Within any given 12-month period, 60 percent of unauthorized immigrants had health-related expenses (of any kind) compared to 87 percent of U.S. natives. This lower spending is attributed by some to good health among recent migrants (called the healthy immigrant effect) (Kennedy et al., 2015), but other research suggests that immigrants generally simply seek medical care less often than the overall population (Ku, 2009; Stimpson Wilson, & Eschbach, 2010) because of obstacles such as lack of access to insurance, language barriers, differing local policies on public health care, or immigration status (Derose, Escarce, & Lurie, 2007). As a result, a higher percentage of diseases are left undiagnosed among recent migrants (Stimpson, Wilson, & Su, 2013).

However, the study pointed out that unauthorized immigrants were also twice as likely as U.S. natives to receive care for which the provider was never compensated. It is estimated that providers are not reimbursed for the care of 5.9 percent of unauthorized individuals, compared to 2.8 percent of U.S. natives (Stimpson, Wilson, & Su, 2013). Authors attribute this primarily to the lack of medical care options currently available to unauthorized immigrants (ibid.).

IMMIGRANT IMPACT ON WELFARE/ NUTRITION ASSISTANCE

Since passage of the Personal Responsibility and Work Opportunity Reconciliation Act (PRWORA) of 1996, unauthorized immigrants have been automatically ineligible for federal government welfare programs and the benefits they provide, with the exception of

1. emergency Medicaid treatment,
2. emergency disaster relief services (noncash and short term),
3. immunizations and testing/treatment for communicable diseases,
4. community-based services or assistance, as determined by the attorney general (e.g., local soup kitchen),
5. limited housing or community development assistance for those who were already receiving it in 1996.

Programs requiring proof of immigration status for which unauthorized immigrants (as well as other nonqualified immigrants such as students, tourists, and asylum seekers) are *not* eligible include Supplemental Nutrition Assistance Program (formerly food stamps), Temporary Assistance for Needy Families, Supplemental Security Income (SSI), nonemergency Medicaid, and the Affordable Care Act (FactCheck.org, 2016; National Conference of State Legislatures, 2014; Wasem, 2014).

Even for immigrants who are in the country legally, public benefits from the aforementioned programs are not automatic. Since enactment of the PRWORA in 1986, most immigrants who are lawful permanent residents must wait five years before they become eligible for federal government programs such as nutrition assistance, Medicaid, or cash assistance for families with children (Wasem, 2014). There are certain exceptions to the five-year wait for public-benefit programs. Federal agencies and some states have allowed more immediate assistance for refugees, asylees and other immigrants exempt on humanitarian grounds, veterans and their families, and members of the military (Assistant Secretary for Planning and Evaluation, 2012; Wasem, 2014).

Another common argument that has surfaced in recent discourse about unauthorized individuals' impact on federal funds is they actually drain more from the welfare system than it first appears because many benefit from the welfare eligibility of their U.S.-citizen children. A Center for Immigration Studies (CIS) report argues that U.S.-citizen children of unauthorized individuals must be included in welfare statistics because "it is the low income of immigrant parents that makes the children eligible. It is the parents who signed the children up for the programs, and the parents clearly benefit by having taxpayers provide for their children" (Camarota, 2013).

A 2015 report from CIS, an organization describing itself as "low-immigration, pro-immigrant," states that immigrant households (of all types) use welfare programs at a significantly higher rate than native households (Camarota, 2015). The study claims to be the most accurate representation of immigrant welfare use because it is based on data from the Census Bureau's Survey of Income and Program Participation (SIPP) rather than the more commonly used Census Bureau Current Population Survey. According to SIPP data, says the report, immigrant households use welfare programs at a rate of 21 percentage points higher than native households. Based on 2012 data, it concludes that 51 percent of households headed by immigrants (irrespective of legal status) utilized at least one welfare program that year (a Medicaid, cash, food, or housing program) compared to only 30 percent of native-headed households.

This CIS study was widely cited and discussed by media outlets upon its release, but it has been criticized by various scholars and research organizations who assert that it employs flawed methodology. By using households rather than individuals as the unit of analysis, critics say, the number of immigrants using welfare is inflated (Nowrasteh, 2015; Reston, 2015). As long as one of the heads of a household is an immigrant, the entire family is counted as an "immigrant household." Therefore, even if the member of the family who qualifies for a welfare program is a U.S. citizen spouse or child, the entire group is counted statistically as an immigrant household utilizing a welfare program. As one progressive critic noted, a family would be considered an immigrant household using welfare even if it was their U.S.-citizen child who qualified for a subsidized school lunch program (Reston, 2015).

Another analysis pointed out that the CIS report does not correct for income and as a result ends up making comparisons of welfare usage among rich versus poor populations rather than comparing poor immigrants to poor natives. It also does not mention the dollar value of the benefits received and does not include the two largest programs in the welfare state, Social Security or Medicaid, in its analysis. A researcher from the libertarian CATO Institute said of the report, "Simply put, the CIS study does not compare apples to apples but rather apples to elephants" (Nowrasteh, 2015).

CATO research found, in contrast to the CIS report, that welfare use is less common among low-income, noncitizen adults and children than among poor, native-born citizen adults and children (Ku & Bruen, 2013). Furthermore, when poor noncitizens (immigrants) do use Medicaid, the Children's Health Insurance Program (CHIP), nutrition assistance and SSI programs, the dollar amount for the benefits received is lower than the amount used by poor native-born citizens (ibid.). For example, in 2010 low-income immigrant children consumed an average of $465 in Medicaid/CHIP expenditures, while low-income citizen children consumed an average of $1,030 (p. 3). The exception to this trend was the amount of cash assistance granted; dollar values for cash assistance programs were nearly equal for low-income adult immigrants and low-income adult natives (pp. 4–6).

A 2013 study came to a similar conclusion. Researchers found that immigrant families did use welfare at higher rates than the native population until the mid-1990s. However, when analyses were conducted in 1995, 2000, and 2005, children in poor immigrant families were *less* likely to use welfare than children in poor native-born families, and in 2010 the two groups had nearly equal rates of use (Joo & Kim, 2013). Furthermore, welfare assistance is not assumed to benefit only the primary recipient. While welfare programs are designed to assist U.S. citizens living in poverty, the government's overarching goal is to maintain the health and well-being of all children and their families (Child Welfare Information Gateway, 2015). By being able to better provide for their children's needs, families as a whole benefit. This is true of any family receiving assistance, whether the family has legal status or not. As U.S. citizens, advocates argue, children of immigrant parents or of mixed-status families (one parent is unauthorized and another is not) can receive government assistance just like any other child whose parents qualify.

EDUCATION

The 1982 Supreme Court ruling in *Plyler v. Doe* established that all children in the United States, regardless of their legal status, have the right to a free public education. In its decision, the Court cited the equal protection clause (Fourteenth Amendment) of the Constitution and added that "by denying these children a basic education we deny them the ability to live within the structure of our civic institutions, and foreclose any realistic possibility that they will contribute in even the smallest way to the progress of our Nation" (United States Supreme Court, 1982). The

Court also explained that minors should not be held accountable for the actions of their parents and thus should not be denied the right to an education.

In spite of this ruling, various groups have lobbied against the education of "illegal aliens," citing the cost of educating unauthorized children as a major taxpayer burden. The Young Conservatives Web site, for example, features an article titled "This Is How Much Your State Has to Pay for Illegal Aliens to Go to School" followed by a U.S. map listing each state's expenditures (Riddle, 2014). A section below the map reads:

> Click on the photo above to enlarge. As you can see, a lot of tax dollars will be going to school illegal aliens.
> Meanwhile, our veterans are dying in waiting rooms. #priorities

The cost of educating noncitizen children is also frequently addressed by the Federation for American Immigration Reform, which has published numerous reports documenting the cost of education for unauthorized children. While calculating the dollar amounts spent each year per pupil in their public school systems is relatively easy, it is more difficult to determine what the eventual payback or benefit of that education will be once the students become adults and begin to work. Many of the arguments decrying the high costs of educating unauthorized children either assume those children will eventually be employed in low-skill sectors for low wages or altogether dismiss their contributions as future taxpayers.

However, doing so does not fairly consider the abilities and potential of these youth to be not just eventual contributors to U.S. society but to contribute as skilled or highly skilled workers. Two such undocumented youth made headlines in 2016 when, after graduating as valedictorians of their high school classes, they revealed their unauthorized status. One had earned a 4.5 grade point average and received a full scholarship to the University of Texas; the other was accepted to Yale. Both, however, faced immediate backlash on social media because of their immigration status (Ross, 2016). Their stories are not unique, nor are their goals or talents. Researchers at City University of New York found undocumented students were as well prepared for college as their U.S.-citizen counterparts, and they outperformed native students in terms of grades and completion of associate degrees (Conger & Chellman, 2013).

What is not as difficult to determine is the *added* cost society will bear if these children do not receive an education, or if they are kept from pursuing a higher education because of legal status or costs. According to the CBO, "To a considerable extent, educational attainment determines the role of foreign-born workers in the labor market" (Congressional Budget Office, 2010). The higher the level of education immigrant children receive, advocates say, the more likely they will be to find well-paying jobs and contribute larger dividends back to society. As one undocumented immigrant student stated, "I don't see us as risks; I think of us as smart investments" (Educators for Fair Consideration, n.d.).

Another current argument is that the recent waves of unaccompanied minors from Central America are draining schools' resources and damaging the quality of public education. Fox Business Network's Brenda Buttner warned parents about "a surge of up to 60,000 illegal kids in their classrooms" in 2014 (Buttner, 2014). The "surge" of unaccompanied minors being discussed actually was a group of roughly 60,000 children, widely dispersed across the United States, that made up "just over one-tenth of 1 percent of all public school children." Even the states that sheltered the largest numbers of these unaccompanied children would see only tiny increases in their enrollment (Center for American Progress, 2014).

Even the CIS, which advocates for lower immigration levels, agrees that education is critical to economic success later in life, saying "Education is the single best predictor of income, welfare use, and socioeconomic status" (Camarota, 2013). A CIS report, asserting that uneducated immigrants are the group most likely to use welfare, says that in 2011 "28 percent of immigrants (ages 25 to 65) had not graduated from high school, compared with 7 percent of natives." This statistic seems a counterpoint to the Economic Policy Institute estimate that 46 percent of immigrants have at least some college education (Costa, Cooper, & Shierholz, 2014), but both types of data support the idea that providing a solid education for immigrant children, regardless of their legal status, will reap major benefits for the U.S. economy in the long run. In the words of the Supreme Court, "The long-range costs of excluding any children from the public schools may well outweigh the costs of educating them" (United States Supreme Court, 1982).

FURTHER READING

American Immigration Council (AIC). (2013a, July 19). *Iowa: Immigrant entrepreneurs, innovation, and welcoming initiatives.* Washington, DC: AIC. Retrieved from http://www.immigrationpolicy.org/just-facts/iowa-immigrant-entrepreneurs-innovation-and-welcoming-initiatives

American Immigration Council. (2013b, July 24). *Florida: Immigrant entrepreneurs, innovation, and welcoming initiatives in the Sunshine State.*

Washington, DC: AIC. Retrieved from http://www.immigrationpolicy
.org/just-facts/florida-immigrant-entrepreneurs-innovation-and-
welcoming-initiatives-sunshine-state

American Immigration Council. (2013c, July 26). *How states and local
economies benefit from immigrants.* Washington, DC: AIC. Retrieved
from http://immigrationimpact.com/2013/07/26/how-states-and-local-
economies-benefit-from-immigrants/

AOL.COM. (2015, September 3). Report: Most immigrant households
rely on public assistance. *AOL.COM News.* Retrieved from http://
www.aol.com/article/2015/09/03/report-most-immigrant-households-
rely-on-public-assistance/21231149/

Assistant Secretary for Planning and Evaluation (ASPE). (2012, March 27).
Overview of immigrants' eligibility for SNAP, TANF, Medicaid and CHIP.
Washington, DC: ASPE, Department of Health and Human Services.
Retrieved from https://aspe.hhs.gov/basic-report/overview-immigrants-
eligibility-snap-tanf-medicaid-and-chip

Avila, J., & Marshall, S. (2013, May 7). Immigration cost: Statistically sound data or biased research? abcnews.com. Retrieved from
http://abcnews.go.com/Politics/conservatives-cite-flaws-study-
touting-costs-immigration-reform/story?id=19120147

Buttner, B. (2014, August 10). Bulls and Bears [News program]. *Fox Business Network.* Embedded video retrieved from http://mediamatters
.org/embed/static/clips/2014/08/13/36400/fnc-bb-20140813-
refugeesebolaschools

California Legislature. (2015, June 2). Senate Bill No. 10; Introduced
by Senator Lara [Amended in Senate June 2, 2015]. Retrieved from
http://leginfo.ca.gov/pub/15-16/bill/sen/sb_0001-0050/sb_10_bill_
20150602_amended_sen_v98.html

Camarota, S. A. (2013, February). *The cost of cheap labor.* Washington, DC: Center for Immigration Studies. Retrieved from http://cis
.org/OpedsandArticles/Cato-Use-Public-Assistance-Benefits-
Citizens-Non-citizen-Immigrants-United-States

Camarota, S. A. (2015, September). *Welfare use by immigrant and native
households.* Washington, DC: Center for Immigration Studies. Retrieved
from http://cis.org/Welfare-Use-Immigrant-Native-Households

Center for American Progress. (2014, August 8). *Putting the child refugees
in context.* Washington, DC: Author. Retrieved from http://theyoung
center.org/wp-content/uploads/2014/08/Putting-the-Central-American-
Children-in-Context1.pdf

Child Welfare Information Gateway. (2015). *Immigration and child welfare.* Washington, DC: Department of Health and Human Services,
Children's Bureau.

Conger, D., & Chellman, C. C. (2013, Summer). Undocumented college students in the United States: In-state tuition not enough to ensure four-year degree completion. *Education, Finance, and Policy*, 8(3), 364–377.

Congressional Budget Office (CBO). (2007, December). *The impact of unauthorized immigrants on the budgets of state and local governments*. Washington, DC: CBO. Retrieved from http://www.cbo.gov/sites/ default/files/cbofiles/ftpdocs/87xx/doc8711/12-6-immigration.pdf

Congressional Budget Office (CBO). (2010, July). *The role of immigrants in the U.S. labor market: An update*. Washington, DC: CBO. Retrieved from https://www.cbo.gov/publication/21656

Costa, D., Cooper, D., & Shierholz, H. (2014, August 12). *Facts about immigration and the U.S. economy*. Washington, DC: Author. Retrieved from http://www.epi.org/publication/immigration-facts/

Derose, K. P., Escarce, J. J., & Lurie, N. (2007, September). Immigrants and health care: Sources of vulnerability. *Health Affairs*, 26(5), 1258–1268.

Devlin, F. R., & Wolff, H. (2015, October 14). Welfare: Who's on it, who's not? [Web site]. Retrieved from http://www.amren.com/ features/2015/10/welfare-whos-on-it-whos-not/

Educators for Fair Consideration. (n.d.). The case for undocumented students in higher education. Retrieved from http://e4fc.org/images/ E4FC_TheCase.pdf

FactCheck.org. (February 7, 2016). FactChecking the eighth GOP debate. FactCheck.org. Retrieved from http://www.factcheck.org/2016/02/ factchecking-the-eighth-gop-debate

Gee, L. C., Gardner, M., & Wiehe, M. (2016, February). *Undocumented immigrants' state and local tax contributions*. Washington, DC: Institute on Taxation & Economic Policy (ITEP). Retrieved from http://www .itep.org/pdf/immigration2016.pdf

Germano, R. (2014, August 4). Unauthorized immigrants paid $100 billion into Social Security over last decade. *Vice News*. Retrieved from https://news.vice.com/article/unauthorized-immigrants-paid-100-billion-into-social-security-over-last-decade

Gomez, A. (2015, September 2). Report: More than half of immigrants on welfare. *USA Today*. Retrieved from http://www.usatoday. com/story/news/nation/2015/09/01/immigrant-welfare-use-report/ 71517072/

Goss, S., Wade, A., Skirvin, J. P., Morris, M., Bye, K. M., & Huston, D. (2013, April). *Effects of unauthorized immigration on the actuarial status of the Social Security Trust Funds*. Baltimore, MD: Social Security

Administration, Office of the Chief Actuary. Retrieved from https://www.ssa.gov/OACT/NOTES/pdf_notes/note151.pdf

Investor's Business Daily. (2015, August 28). U.S. taxpayers bear weight of anchor babies [Editorial]. *Investor's Business Daily*. Retrieved from http://www.investors.com/politics/editorials/us-taxpayers-bear-weight-of-anchor-babies/

Joo, M., & Kim, J. (2013, September). Net effects of poverty on welfare use and dependency among children by family immigration and citizenship statuses. *Children and Youth Services Review, 35*(9), 1556–1565.

Kennedy, S., Kidd, M. P., McDonald, J. T., & Biddle, N. (2015, May). The healthy immigrant effect: Patterns and evidence from four countries. *Journal of International Migration and Integration, 16*(2), 317–332.

Ku, L. (2009). Health insurance coverage and medical expenditures of immigrants and native-born citizens in the United States. *American Journal of Public Health, 99*(7), 1322–1328.

Ku, L., & Bruen, B. (2013, March 4). Poor immigrants use public benefits at a lower rate than poor native-born citizens. *CATO Institute Economic Development Bulletin, 17*. Retrieved from http://object.cato.org/sites/cato.org/files/pubs/pdf/edb17.pdf

May, C. (2015, September 2). Report: Immigrant households using welfare at vastly higher rate than native-born households. Breitbart.com. Retrieved from http://www.breitbart.com/big-government/2015/09/02/report-immigrant-households-using-welfare-at-vastly-higher-rate-than-native-born-households/

National Conference of State Legislatures (NCSL). (2014, February 24). *Federal benefits available to unauthorized immigrants*. Denver, CO, and Washington, DC: NCSL. Retrieved from http://www.ncsl.org/research/immigration/federal-benefits-to-unauthorized-immigrants.aspx

National Immigration Forum. (2013, May 7). *Conservative responses to May 6, 2013, Heritage Foundation report*. Washington, DC: Author. Retrieved from http://immigrationforum.org/wp-content/uploads/2015/04/Reaction_to_Heritage_Study.pdf

Nowrasteh, A. (2013, May 7). *Heritage's flawed immigration analysis*. Washington, DC: CATO Institute. Retrieved from http://www.cato.org/blog/heritages-flawed-immigration-analysis

Nowrasteh, A. (2015, September 2). Center for Immigration Studies report exaggerates immigrant welfare use. Washington, DC: CATO Institute. Retrieved from http://www.cato.org/blog/center-immigration-studies-exaggerates-immigrant-welfare-use

Orrenius, P. M., & Zavodny, M. (2013, September). *Immigrants in the U.S. labor market*. Federal Reserve Bank of Dallas. Retrieved from

https://www.dallasfed.org/assets/documents/research/papers/2013/
wp1306.pdf

Partnership for a New American Economy. (2015, October). New Americans in Denver. Retrieved from http://www.renewoureconomy.org/
wp-content/uploads/2015/10/DENVER-METRO-Factsheet.pdf

Rector, R., & Richwine, J. (2013, May 6). *The fiscal cost of unlawful immigrants and amnesty to the U.S. taxpayer*. Washington, DC: Heritage Foundation. Retrieved from http://www.heritage.org/research/
reports/2013/05/the-fiscal-cost-of-unlawful-immigrants-and-amnesty-
to-the-us-taxpayer

Reston, L. (2015, September 3). Immigrants don't drain welfare. They fund it. *New Republic*. Retrieved from https://newrepublic.com/
article/122714/immigrants-dont-drain-welfare-they-fund-it

Riddle, J. (2014, September 4). This is how much your state has to pay for illegal immigrants to go to school [Web site post]. YoungConservatives.com. Retrieved from http://www.youngcons.com/this-is-how-
much-your-state-has-to-pay-for-illegal-immigrants-to-go-to-school/

Ross, J. (2016, June 12). What's happening to two undocumented Texas valedictorians says it all about the immigration debate. *The Washington Post*. Retrieved from https://www.washingtonpost.com/news/
the-fix/wp/2016/06/12/whats-happening-to-two-undocumented-texas-
valedictorians-says-it-all-about-the-immigration-debate/

Stimpson, J. P., Wilson, F. A., & Eschbach, K. (2010). Trends in health care spending for immigrants in the United States. *Health Affairs*, 29(3), 544–550.

Stimpson, J. P., Wilson, F. A., & Su, D. (2013, July). Unauthorized immigrants spend less than other immigrants and U.S. natives on health care. *Health Affairs*, 32(7), 1313–1318.

Team Fix. (2016, February 6). Transcript of the New Hampshire GOP debate, annotated. *The Washington Post*. Retrieved from https://www
.washingtonpost.com/news/the-fix/wp/2016/02/06/transcript-of-the-
feb-6-gop-debate-annotated/

United States Senate. (2013, April 18). *How the gang of 8 proposal would impact U.S. taxpayers*. Washington, DC: United States Senate Committee on the Budget. Retrieved from http://www.budget
.senate.gov/newsroom/budget-background/how-the-gang-of-eight-
proposal-would-impact-us-taxpayers

United States Supreme Court. (1982, June 15). *Plyler v. Doe* (No. 80-1538). Retrieved from http://caselaw.findlaw.com/us-supreme-court/457/202
.html

Wasem, R. E. (2014, September 24). *Noncitizen eligibility for federal public assistance: Policy overview and trends.* Washington, DC: Congressional Research Service [RL 33809]. Retrieved from https://www.fas.org/sgp/crs/misc/RL33809.pdf

Zallman, L. (2014, August). *Staying covered: How immigrants have prolonged the solvency of one of Medicare's key trust funds and subsidized care for U.S. seniors.* Partnership for a New American Economy. Retrieved from http://www.renewoureconomy.org/wp-content/uploads/2014/08/pnae-medicare-report-august2014.pdf

Zallman, L., Woolhandler, S., Himmelstein, D., Bor, D., & McCormick, D. (2013, June). Immigrants contributed an estimated $115.2 billion more to the Medicare Trust Fund than they took out in 2002–09. *Health Affairs, 32*(6), 1153–1160.

3

❖

Unauthorized Immigration, Refugees, and Asylees

Q12. ARE MOST IMMIGRANTS IN THE UNITED STATES "ILLEGAL/UNAUTHORIZED" IMMIGRANTS?

Answer: No. The overwhelming majority of U.S. immigrants came to the country through proper legal channels. However, the degree of attention given to the issue of illegal immigration has overshadowed that of legal immigrants in recent years, and this has had negative implications for legal immigrants as well.

The Facts: The total foreign-born immigrant population (both legal and unauthorized) in the United States in 2014 was estimated at just over 42 million, or slightly more than 13 percent of the total population of the country (Brown & Stepler, 2016; U.S. Census Bureau, 2016). Among the foreign-born, somewhere between 10.9 and 11.3 million, just 3.4–3.5 percent of the nation's population comprised unauthorized immigrants (sometimes called "illegal" immigrants) (Krogstad & Passel, 2015; Warren, 2016).

In reality, the current population of unauthorized immigrants in the United States is somewhat speculative. Because of the very nature of unauthorized immigration and the fact that most individuals who enter the United States without permission try to avoid being located or identified by authorities, it is nearly impossible to know the exact number of unauthorized persons living in the country. However, based on a wide variety of studies and data sources including the Census Bureau's American Community Survey, researchers and scholars tabulate annual estimates that aid in identifying the number and nature of unauthorized persons in the United States. The estimates hovering around 11 million are based on those studies.

In recent years, public discourse surrounding immigration reform has focused heavily on illegal immigration. The result has been a tendency to talk about "immigrants" and issues related to those immigrants without distinguishing between authorized and unauthorized individuals. This has led to misunderstandings among the general public about issues affecting both groups. As rhetoric about immigration has become more heated, politicians and activists have spoken out strongly against the problems caused by immigrants, sometimes failing to distinguish between authorized and unauthorized immigrants and at times purposely blurring the two identities. For example, during the 2010 U.S. Senate race in Nevada, Republican Sharron Angle ran an ad using a picture of three young boys who appeared to be Latino but contained no other identifying information. The words "ILLEGAL ALIENS" were printed across the image. However, it was discovered that the three young boys were actually photographed in Mexico, not the United States, and there was no evidence that they had ever crossed illegally into the United States (Bell, 2010). The implication was clear that just looking Latino was enough reason to suspect someone of being in the United States illegally and that Angle would be tough on the problem of "illegal aliens" (Chavez, 2008).

Given that for many years the largest percentage of unauthorized persons entering the United States have been from Mexico, this blurring of the conversation about "immigration" in general has had severe repercussions for U.S. citizens of Mexican descent. Mexican American respondents of one study said they fear that "the nativism Mexican immigrants attract leads to status degradation of all people of Mexican origin" (regardless of legal status) (Jiménez, 2007, p. 601). This has been problematic in Arizona, for example, where increasing hostility toward Latinos placed Mexican Americans at greater risk before law enforcement based on their supposed "Mexicanness"—inferred from skin color, bilingualism, or physical presence in largely Latino neighborhoods (Romero, 2006). Many found themselves on the receiving end of immigration law enforcement practices that included racial profiling, stops and searches without probable cause, harassment, intimidation, and abuse (ibid.). In 2013 Sheriff Joe

Arpaio of Maricopa County, Arizona, was found guilty of racial profiling and widespread civil rights violations, a ruling that was challenged but upheld (Cassidy, 2015). Two years later, Arpaio faced a contempt of court case in which he acknowledged violations of court orders—specifically allowing his officers to continue immigration patrols for 18 months after the federal judge had ordered them stopped.

Therefore, while the vast majority of immigrants to the United States come to the country through proper legal channels, many of those "legal immigrants" have felt subject to the negative effects of generalized anti-immigrant rhetoric.

FURTHER READING

Bell, M. (2010, October 8). Sharron Angle, David Vitter's illegal aliens not quite illegal, photographer says [Blog post]. *The Washington Post.* Retrieved from http://voices.washingtonpost.com/blog-post/2010/10/sharon_angle_david_vitters_ill.html

Brown, A., & Stepler, R. (2016, April 19). *Statistical portrait of the foreign-born population in the United States.* Washington, DC: Pew Research Center. Retrieved from http://www.pewhispanic.org/2016/04/19/statistical-portrait-of-the-foreign-born-population-in-the-united-states-key-charts/

Cassidy, M. (2015, April 15). Court largely upholds racial-profiling ruling against Sheriff Joe Arpaio. *The Arizona Republic.* Retrieved from http://www.azcentral.com/story/news/local/phoenix/2015/04/15/arpaio-loses-appeal-melendres/25823671/

Chavez, L. (2008). *The Latino threat: Constructing immigrants, citizens, and the nation.* Stanford, CA: Stanford University Press.

Jiménez, T. (2007, September). Weighing the costs and benefits of Mexican immigration: The Mexican-American perspective. *Social Science Quarterly, 88*(3), 599–618. Retrieved from https://www.researchgate.net/publication/4791059_Weighing_the_Costs_and_Benefits_of_Mexican_Immigration_The_Mexican-American_Perspective

Krogstad, J. M., & Passel, J. S. (2015, November 19). *5 facts about illegal immigration in the U.S.* Washington, DC: Pew Research Center. Retrieved from http://www.pewresearch.org/fact-tank/2015/11/19/5-facts-about-illegal-immigration-in-the-u-s/

Romero, M. (2006). Racial profiling and immigration law enforcement: Rounding up of usual suspects in the Latino community. *Critical Sociology, 32*(2–3), 447–473.

U.S. Census Bureau. (2016, February 28). *American fact finder: Selected characteristics of the native and foreign-born populations. 2010–2014 American Community Survey 5-year estimates*. Washington, DC: Author.

Warren, R. (2016). U.S. undocumented population drops below 11 million in 2014, with continued declines in the Mexican undocumented population. *Journal on Migration and Human Society*, 4(1), 1–15. New York: Center for Migration Studies. Retrieved from http://jmhs.cmsny.org/index.php/jmhs/article/view/58

Q13. HOW ACCURATE ARE TERMS LIKE "ILLEGAL ALIEN" AND "ILLEGAL IMMIGRANT" IN DESCRIBING PEOPLE ENTERING THE UNITED STATES WITHOUT AUTHORIZATION?

Answer: Although it has been used as a legal term for decades, the phrase "illegal alien" has been challenged because of the implication that the person, and not that person's actions, is illegal. Opponents say this term, as well as the phrase "illegal immigrant," is simply not accurate because no human being is illegal. Additionally, opponents argue, the phrases incorrectly lump all those without documented legal status into the category of "illegal" when there are many legitimate cases in which individuals have applied but have not yet achieved or been granted full legal status.

The Facts: Across the United States, a "war of words" is being waged over how to describe someone who enters the United States without proper documentation. While newsrooms have historically used phrases like "illegal alien" and "illegal immigrant" to describe individuals who enter without legal status, critics charge that such terms are both insensitive and inaccurate (Guskin, 2013; Vargas, 2012).

The term "alien" has been utilized in the United States since the late 1800s to refer to someone who is in the country as a foreigner or outsider, and use of the term "illegal alien," still used by U.S. government agencies, appeared in newspapers as far back as 1926 to describe a foreigner who entered the country without first going through inspection (Hudson, 2012). "Alien" is currently defined by the U.S. Citizenship and Immigration Services (USCIS) as "[a]ny person not a citizen or national of the United States" (USCIS, n.d.).

Today, the phrases "illegal alien" and "illegal immigrant" are still widely utilized by many politicians, researchers, media outlets, and members of the public. Those who employ the terms often point to the fact that the phrase "illegal alien" has been used in official U.S. documents since the Naturalization Act of 1790 (Liberty Ellis Foundation, n.d.). They also state that if someone is in the country illegally, referring to them as "illegal aliens" or "illegal immigrants" is perfectly acceptable because those expressions factually refer to the individuals in terms of their nonlegal actions. Arguments against the expressions, they say, show the extremity of political correctness at the expense of fact.

Critics argue that the term "illegal alien," when used as a noun to describe individuals in the United States without proper authorization, dehumanizes and criminalizes the individual rather than his or her purported actions. Immigration advocates frustrated with the use of this language often borrow from Elie Wiesel's famous quote that "no human being is illegal." One immigration lawyer points out: "I'm not aware of any other circumstance in our common vernacular where a crime is considered to render the individual—as opposed to the individual's actions—as being illegal. We don't even refer to our most dangerous and vile criminals as being "illegal" (Haque-Hausrath, 2009).

Another common phrase used in media and public discourse that has been challenged is "illegal immigrant." Neither the term "immigrant" nor "illegal immigrant" appears in USCIS glossary, but the Internal Revenue Service defines an immigrant as "an alien who has been granted the right by the USCIS to reside permanently in the United States and to work without restrictions in the United States" (Internal Revenue Service, 2016). Under this definition, then, an immigrant is one who has already been granted legal status, so the term "illegal immigrant" makes no sense. Critics of the language also point out that *entering* the United States without inspection is a federal misdemeanor, not a criminal act, and *being* in the United States without legal permission is a civil, not criminal, offense. Thus, the illegality of the *actions* these individuals have committed (not the illegality of the people themselves) is in the same class of violations as speeding and public intoxication. (This changes, however, if an individual is detained more than once while trying to enter the United States without proper documentation. A second offense is a felony, not a misdemeanor, under federal immigration law.) Other offenders in those misdemeanor categories, they argue, are not referred to as illegal drivers or illegal drinkers.

Critics of the term also assert that calling someone an "illegal immigrant" fails to distinguish or recognize the many gray areas into which individuals without legal status can fall—such as people who have been brought to the United States as victims of human trafficking, people who were brought into the country as children and had no voice in the decision, people who came legally but have fallen out of legal status, or those whose legal status is tied directly to an abusive sponsor who threatened to take the legal status away (Haque-Hausrath, 2009). Additionally, they point out that this terminology fails to recognize the many refugees, asylum seekers, and applicants for citizenship or legal standing who are awaiting court hearings or judges' rulings, and whose present status is therefore fluid (Vargas, 2012).

In 2013, the Associated Press dropped use of the phrase "illegal immigrant" from its style guide, clarifying that the term "illegal" should only be used with a verb such as immigration and not with a noun describing a person. Several major news organizations followed suit (Guskin, 2013). In April 2016 the Colorado House of Representatives passed a bill that would change the language used in state laws from "illegal alien" to "undocumented worker" or "foreign national" (Colorado Bill Tracker, 2016). That same month, citing the decision of the Associated Press to drop its usage and noting the phrase's "pejorative tone in recent years," the Library of Congress announced it would retire use of the phrase "illegal aliens" from its international subject headings and replace it with "noncitizens" and "unauthorized immigration" (Dartmouth Senior Staff, 2016; Padilla & Rivera, 2016). Congressional Republicans fought back, including a provision in a House spending bill that would require the Library of Congress to use the terms "alien" and "illegal alien" in their subject headings (Congressional Record, 2016).

Making the dialogue about how to describe unauthorized persons more complex is the fact that many of those individuals live in mixed-status families, in which some family members are U.S. citizens or have legal status, and others lack official permission to be present. Politicians who threaten to deport "undocumented immigrants" or "illegal aliens" may not take into account mixed-status families and their sometimes varied levels of legal status. This can be particularly troubling for those in the process of trying to resolve their immigration status through the courts, which face enormous backlogs due to case overloads and a shortage of judges. For example, at the end of FY 2011, there were 298,171 pending immigration cases. By the end of FY 2015, the number had soared to 457,106 cases pending (U.S. Department of Justice, 2016). Thousands in the U.S. immigration court system have received word of hearings being canceled or pushed out as far as 2019, leaving their status in legal limbo until then (Robbins, 2015).

While additional questions related to children and immigration are discussed in Chapter 6, it is noteworthy that from 2009 to 2013, 5.1 million U.S.-citizen children under the age of 18 (7 percent of the

U.S. child population) were living with at least one unauthorized immigrant parent (Zong & Batalova, 2016). In Nevada, the state with the largest percentage of unauthorized immigrant parents in the nation, nearly one in five children in 2012 lived with an adult who lacked legal status (Krogstad & Passel, 2015). Although these children themselves enjoy full benefits of U.S. citizenship, they often live in fear that one or both of their parents may be arrested and deported at any time. The threat or reality of such deportations and detentions creates significant emotional trauma and places undue responsibility, fear, and stress on these minors (Zayas et al., 2015). Additionally, children in mixed-status families that have experienced a deportation or detention often face housing instability and/or food insecurity (Chaudry et al., 2010). In both instances, the legal status of those living in the United States without authorization can have a profound impact on immigrants legally present as well as on U.S. citizens.

FURTHER READING

Chaudry, A., Capps, R., Pedroza, J. M., Castañeda, R. M., Santos, R., & Scott, M. M. (2010, February). *Facing our future: Children in the aftermath of immigration enforcement.* Washington, DC: The Urban Institute. Retrieved from http://www.urban.org/sites/default/files/alfresco/publication-pdfs/412020-Facing-Our-Future.PDF

Colorado Bill Tracker. (2016, April 8). Replace alien with undocumented immigrant CRS—HB 16—1396. Retrieved from Denver Post Legislature section http://extras.denverpost.com/app/bill-tracker/bills/2016a/hb_16-1396/

Congressional Record. (2016, June 9). Legislative Branch Appropriations Act, 2017 (House of Representatives—June 9, 2016). *Congressional Record*, 162(91). Retrieved from https://www.congress.gov/congressional-record/2016/06/09/house-section/article/H3635-5

Dartmouth Senior Staff. (2016, March 26). Library of Congress approves CoFIRED petition. *The Dartmouth.* Retrieved from http://thedartmouth.com/2016/03/26/library-of-congress-approves-cofired-petition/

Guskin, E. (2013, June 17). *"Illegal," "undocumented," "unauthorized": News media shift language on immigration.* Pew Research Center's Journalism Project. Washington, DC: Pew Research Center. Retrieved from http://www.pewresearch.org/fact-tank/2013/06/17/illegal-undocumented-unauthorized-news-media-shift-language-on-immigration/

Haque-Hausrath, S. (2009, Feb. 5). *No human being is illegal: Why use of the term "illegal alien" is inaccurate, offensive, and should be eliminated from our public discourse*. Helena, MT: Border Crossing Law Firm P.C. Retrieved from http://bordercrossinglaw.com/why-use-of-the-term-illegal-alien-is-inaccurate-offensive-and-should-be-eliminated-from-our-public-discourse/

Hudson, J. (2012, September 28). Looking for the first use of the term "illegal immigrant." Thewire.com. Retrieved from http://www.thewire.com/national/2012/09/looking-first-use-term-illegal-immigrant/57424/

Internal Revenue Service (IRS). (2016, March 3). Immigration terms and definitions involving aliens. Retrieved from https://www.irs.gov/individuals/international-taxpayers/immigration-terms-and-definitions-involving-aliens

Krogstad, J. M., & Passel, J. S. (2015, November 19). *5 facts about illegal immigration in the U.S.* Washington, DC: Pew Research Center. Retrieved from http://www.pewresearch.org/fact-tank/2015/11/19/5-facts-about-illegal-immigration-in-the-u-s/

Liberty Ellis Foundation. (n.d.). Immigration timeline [Web site]. The Statue of Liberty—Ellis Island Foundation, Inc. Retrieved from http://libertyellisfoundation.org/immigration-timeline

Padilla, S., & Rivera, S. (2016, April 3). Library of Congress to stop using term "illegal alien." *Los Angeles Times*. Retrieved from http://www.latimes.com/nation/la-na-library-congress-alien-20160403-story.html

Passel, J. S., & Cohn, D. (2015, July 22). *Unauthorized immigrant population stable for half a decade*. Washington, DC: Pew Research Center. Retrieved from http://www.pewresearch.org/fact-tank/2015/07/22/unauthorized-immigrant-population-stable-for-half-a-decade/

Robbins, S. (The Associated Press). (2015, February 1). Immigrants could wait until 2019 to have cases resolved. abc13.com. Retrieved from http://abc13.com/news/immigrants-could-wait-until-2019-to-have-cases-resolved/499889/

U.S. Citizenship and Immigration Services. (n.d.). Glossary. USCIS.gov. Washington, DC: Department of Homeland Security. Retrieved from https://www.uscis.gov/tools/glossary?topic_id=a#alpha-listing

U.S. Department of Justice. (2016, April). *FY 2015 statistics yearbook*. Washington, DC: USDOJ, Executive Office for Immigration Review. Retrieved from https://www.justice.gov/sites/default/files/pages/attachments/2016/04/08/fy15syb.pdf

Vargas, J. A. (2012, September 21). Immigration debate: The problem with the word *illegal*. TIME. Retrieved from http://ideas.time.com/2012/09/21/immigration-debate-the-problem-with-the-word-illegal/

Zayas, L. H., Aguilar-Gaxiola, S., Yoon, H., & Natera Rey, G. (2015, November). The distress of citizen-children with detained and deported parents. *Journal of Child and Family Studies*, 24(11), 3213–3223.

Zong, J., & Batalova, J. (2016, April 16). *Frequently requested statistics on immigrants and immigration in the United States.* Washington, DC: Migration Policy Institute. Retrieved from http://www.migrationpolicy .org/article/frequently-requested-statistics-immigrants-and-immigra tion-united-states/

Q14. IS ILLEGAL IMMIGRATION INTO THE UNITED STATES GETTING WORSE?

Answer: No. Contrary to popular belief, apprehensions of individuals crossing illegally into the United States are at their lowest levels since the 1970s (U.S. Immigration and Customs Enforcement, 2015). Additionally, multiple factors have combined to drop the country's undocumented population over the past nine years, from roughly 12.2 million in 2007 to between 10.9 and 11.3 million in 2014 (Krogstad & Passel, 2015; Warren, 2016).

The Facts: When it comes to the issues considered most important by the U.S. public, illegal immigration has become one of the country's leading concerns. In a July 2014 Gallup public opinion poll, for example, respondents named immigration/illegal aliens as the country's top concern (Saad, 2014). Likewise, "gaining control of the border" was the top priority of immigration reform among likely U.S. voters in a Rasmussen Reports 2016 telephone survey (Rasmussen Reports, 2016).

These results indicate that Republican congressman Steven Stockman of Texas spoke for many fellow countrymen when he said, "The crush of illegals have bankrupted local governments, shut down hospitals, overwhelmed schools and crashed local economies, hurting largely Hispanic citizens. That failure has fueled the growth of violent gangs, like MS-13, that prey upon illegals and target the children of Hispanic citizens" (Gibson, 2013). Numerous others, especially whites with conservative political orientations, have echoed these sentiments. Republican presidential candidate Donald Trump stated that "illegal immigration is beyond belief" (*CBS News*, 2016), and a coalition of five sheriffs' organizations in the Southwest stated the immigration crisis is "spiraling out of control" (Nikolewski, 2014). Newspapers, magazines, airwaves, and Web sites are filled with stories and statements about the threat of illegal aliens to U.S. security and the merit of proposed solutions to the problem of illegal immigration. Stories of "illegals" pouring across the southern U.S. border, the defeat of bipartisan immigration reform legislation, calls by state and national politicians for a wall to be built between the United States and

Mexico, and demands by top Republicans that all unauthorized immigrants in the United States be deported have further added to the sense of crisis.

Based on the content and number of political speeches and news stories about the nature and extent of "illegal immigration," impressions that it is more widespread than ever before are understandable. But while conservative politicians and pundits have called the current state of illegal immigration a "crisis" and implied that the numbers of unauthorized entrants are greater than ever, illegal immigration has actually been on an overall decline since 2007, which the population of unauthorized persons in the United States hit a peak of roughly 12.2 million (Krogstad & Passel, 2015). By 2014 that number had dropped to an estimated 10.9 million according to one study (Warren, 2016) or 11.3 million according to another (Krogstad & Passel, 2015) depending on the study referenced. The estimate of 10.9 million reflects the smallest number of unauthorized persons in the United States since 2003 (Warren, 2016).

These recent trends among unauthorized populations have evolved as the result of policies and changes over the past three decades. In spite of contemporary political rhetoric that seems to indicate otherwise, the largest increases in the unauthorized population in the United States actually took place prior to 2007. Between 1986 and 2000 estimates indicate that the unauthorized population increased by just over 5 million, from roughly 3.2 million to roughly 8.5 million (Wasem, 2012). From 2000 to 2007 the numbers increased again, with illegal immigration peaking at 12.2 million in 2007, or 4 percent of the U.S. population (Krogstad & Passel, 2015).

The number of unauthorized persons in the United States then declined during the Great Recession of 2007–2009. The decline is attributed primarily to fewer Mexicans entering the country due to a decline in employment opportunities north of the border; however, a variety of other factors also likely contributed, including large numbers of Mexicans leaving the United States, increased border enforcement efforts, lower birth rates in Mexico, and an improved Mexican economy. During the five years after the Great Recession, the estimated population of unauthorized persons in the United States remained relatively stable. Only minor fluctuations occurred during this time, resulting in a 2014 estimate that unauthorized persons made up roughly 3.5 percent of the total population of the United States (Krogstad & Passel, 2015).

Given that exact numbers of unauthorized immigrants in the country are difficult to determine, however, why do officials believe that this population is declining?

One major factor indicating a downturn in the number of unauthorized persons in the United States is a drop in the number of their arrests.

Apprehensions by Border Patrol and arrests by Immigration and Customs Enforcement (ICE) peaked in FY 2000 at 1.8 million, with Border Patrol alone accounting for 1.6 million of these (U.S. Department of Homeland Security, 2014). (Border Patrol typically apprehends people at the border, while ICE typically makes arrests of unauthorized individuals in the interior of the country.) Over the next 15 years those numbers dropped significantly. Border Patrol and ICE apprehensions in FY 2015 totaled just 486,651 (U.S. Immigration and Customs Enforcement, 2015). Secretary of Homeland Security Jeh Johnson pointed out that the 337,117 individuals apprehended at the border in FY 2015 made up the "second lowest apprehension number since 1972, reflecting a lower level of attempted illegal migration at our borders" (U.S. Immigration and Customs Enforcement, 2015).

It is important to note that the number of apprehensions does not correspond directly to the number of individuals attempting to cross the border. The Department of Homeland Security points out that some individuals make numerous crossing attempts and are apprehended more than once (Sapp, 2011). Thus, the number of apprehensions may be higher than the number of actual persons who have been detained by officials at the border. On the other hand, many unauthorized border-crossers are successful at evading apprehension. Because those individuals have not been caught, their numbers are unknown. Thus, the number of apprehensions is likely far lower than the total number of people crossing the border because many are never caught.

Select officials have disputed the notion that there has been a decline in attempted entries. Arizona's Pinal County Sherriff Paul Babeau asserted that the reduction in apprehensions is a result of "lack of enforcement" and claimed that the Obama administration had ordered Border Patrol agents out of "high-traffic" areas of drug and human smuggling so fewer apprehensions would indicate a more secure border (Wright, 2016). United States Border Patrol statistics indicate, however, that there were nearly five times as many U.S. Border Patrol agents in 2015 as there were in the early 1990s. In fact, the number of Border Patrol agents quintupled between 1993 and 2011. From 2011 to 2015 the number of agents was reduced by 1,171—less than one-half of 1 percent of the peak of 21,444 agents in 2011 (U.S. Border Patrol, 2015c). In spite of that, the number of apprehensions per Border Patrol agent in 2013 was one-fifteenth the levels seen in the early 1990s (Isacson, 2014).

During those same years, the number of aliens *apprehended* dropped by nearly half between 1992 and 2013 (U.S. Department of Homeland Security, 2014). Similarly, the number of aliens *removed (legally) or returned* (*informally*) dropped even more dramatically, from 1,105,829 in 1992 to 178,371 in 2013 (the most recent year for which data was available) (ibid.). Thus, long before Obama was elected, apprehensions had begun falling, even as the number of Border Patrol agents was rising.

One additional gauge of change in the unauthorized population can be found in departure statistics. Not only are fewer people trying to enter the United States without authorization, but greater numbers of those already in the country are leaving and returning to their native countries. Increasing numbers of Mexicans in particular have opted to return home. The number of Mexicans without documentation in the USA has declined by more than 600,000 since 2010 (Warren, 2016). This major drop in the unauthorized Mexican population, which has historically been the largest unauthorized population in the United States, offers another strong indicator that the overall unauthorized population has declined (Warren & Kerwin, 2015). Additionally, statistics from Mexico show that the emigration rate to other countries (including the United States) dropped from 144 emigrants per 10,000 Mexican residents in 2006 to 39 per 10,000 in 2015 (Instituto Nacional de Estadística y Geografía, 2016).

Finally, the percentage of unauthorized adults who have lived in the United States for a decade or more nearly doubled from 2000 to 2012 (Passel & Cohn, 2015), indicating fewer new arrivals. Additionally, says Mexican Migration Project codirector Douglas Massey, it has resulted in an unauthorized population that, because the risks and costs of circular migration have become too great, has chosen to "age in place" rather than return home (Markon, 2015).

FURTHER READING

Baker, B., & Rytina, N. (2013). *Estimates of the unauthorized immigrant population residing in the United States: January 2012.* Washington, DC: Department of Homeland Security, Office of Immigration Statistics.

Brown, A., & Stepler, R. (2016, April 19). *Statistical portrait of the foreign-born population in the United States.* Washington, DC: Pew Research Center. Retrieved from http://www.pewhispanic.org/2016/04/19/statistical-portrait-of-the-foreign-born-population-in-the-united-states-key-charts/

Bruno, A. (2014, May 8). *Unauthorized aliens in the United States: Policy discussion* (CRS R41207). Washington, DC: Congressional Research Service.

CBS News. (2016, January 15). Transcript: Sixth republican top-tier debate 2016. *CBS News.* Retrieved from http://www.cbsnews.com/news/transcript-sixth-republican-top-tier-debate-2016/

Gibson, G. (2013, January 28). Stockman unhappy with immigration plan. *Politico: On Congress blog.* Retrieved from http://www.politico.com/blogs/on-congress/2013/01/stockman-unhappy-with-immigration-plan-155454

Instituto Nacional de Estadística y Geografía (INEGI) [National Institute of Statistics and Geography]. (2016, January 28). Boletín de prensa número 29/16 [Press release 29/16]. Información de migración internacional con datos de la ENOE al tercer trimestre de 2015 [International migration information with data from the third trimester 2015 National Occupation and Employment Survey]. INEGI: Aguascalientes, MX. Retrieved from http://www.inegi.org.mx/saladeprensa/boletines/2016/especiales/especiales2016_01_10.pdf

Isacson, A. (2014, January 30). *What new border patrol statistics reveal about changing migration to the United States.* Washington, DC: Washington Office on Latin America. Retrieved from https://www.wola.org/analysis/what-new-border-patrol-statistics-reveal-about-changing-migration-to-the-united-states/

Krogstad, J. M., & Passel, J. S. (2015, November 19). *5 facts about illegal immigration in the U.S.* Washington, DC: Pew Research Center. Retrieved from http://www.pewresearch.org/fact-tank/2015/11/19/5-facts-about-illegal-immigration-in-the-u-s/

Markon, J. (2015, May 27). Fewer immigrants are entering the U.S. illegally, and that's changed the border security debate. *The Washington Post.* Retrieved from https://www.washingtonpost.com/politics/flow-of-illegal-immigration-slows-as-us-mexico-border-dynamics-evolve/2015/05/27/c5caf02c-006b-11e5-833c-a2de05b6b2a4_story.html

Nikolewski, R. (2014, September 17). Sheriffs in Southwest: The border is "spiraling out of control." Newsmax.com. Retrieved from http://www.newsmax.com/US/illegal-immigration-border-crisis-amnesty-sheriffs/2014/09/17/id/595340/

Nowrasteh, A. (2015, June 11). *What explains the flow of unlawful immigration?* CATO at Liberty. Washington, DC: CATO Institute. Retrieved from http://www.cato.org/blog/what-explains-flow-unlawful-immigration

Passel, J. S., & Cohn, D. (2015, July 22). *Unauthorized immigrant population stable for half a decade.* Washington, DC: Pew Research Center. Retrieved from http://www.pewresearch.org/fact-tank/2015/07/22/unauthorized-immigrant-population-stable-for-half-a-decade/

Passel, J. S., Cohn, D., & Gonzalez-Barrera, A. (2013, September 23). *Population decline of unauthorized immigrants stalls, may have reversed.* Pew Research Center. Retrieved from http://www.pewhispanic.org/2013/09/23/population-decline-of-unauthorized-immigrants-stalls-may-have-reversed/

Rasmussen Reports. (2016, February 23). *Immigration update: Border control still top immigration priority for most voters.* Rasmussenreports.com. Retrieved from http://www.rasmussenreports.com/public_content/poli tics/current_events/immigration/immigration_update

Saad, L. (2014, July 16). One in six say immigration most important U.S. problem. Gallup.com. Retrieved from http://www.gallup.com/poll/173 306/one-six-say-immigration-important-problem.aspx

Sapp, L. (2011, July). *Apprehensions by the U.S. Border Patrol—2005–2010.* Washington, DC: Department of Homeland Security, Office of Immigration Statistics.

U.S. Border Patrol. (2015a). *Total illegal alien apprehensions by fiscal year.* Washington, DC: U.S. Customs and Border Protection. Retrieved from http://www.cbp.gov/sites/default/files/documents/BP%20Total%20 Apps%2C%20Mexico%2C%20OTM%20FY2000-FY2015.pdf

U.S. Border Patrol. (2015b). *United States Border Patrol: Sector profile— Fiscal year 2015.* Washington, DC: U.S. Customs and Border Protection. Retrieved from http://www.cbp.gov/sites/default/files/documents/US BP%20Stats%20FY2015%20sector%20profile.pdf

U.S. Border Patrol. (2015c). *U.S. Border Patrol fiscal year staffing statistics (FY 1992–FY 2015).* Washington, DC: U.S. Customs and Border Protection. Retrieved from http://www.cbp.gov/sites/default/files/docu ments/BP%20Staffing%20FY1992-FY2015.pdf

U.S. Census Bureau. (2016, February 28). *American fact finder: Selected characteristics of the native and foreign-born populations. 2010–2014 American Community Survey 5-year estimates.* Washington, DC: Author.

U.S. Department of Homeland Security. (2014, August). *Yearbook of immigration statistics: 2013.* Washington, DC: U.S. Department of Homeland Security, Office of Immigration Statistics. Retrieved from https:// www.dhs.gov/sites/default/files/publications/ois_yb_2013_0.pdf

U.S. Immigration and Customs Enforcement (ICE). (2015, December 22). *DHS releases end of fiscal year 2015 statistics.* Washington, DC: Department of Homeland Security. Retrieved from https://www.ice.gov/news/ releases/dhs-releases-end-fiscal-year-2015-statistics

Warren, R. (2016). U.S. undocumented population drops below 11 million in 2014, with continued declines in the Mexican undocumented population. *Journal on Migration and Human Society,* 4(1), 1–15. New York: Center for Migration Studies. Retrieved from http://jmhs.cmsny .org/index.php/jmhs/article/view/58

Warren, R., & Kerwin, D. (2015). Beyond DAPA and DACA: Revisiting legislative reform in light of long-term trends in unauthorized immigration to the United States. *Journal on Migration and Human Society,*

3(1), 80–108. New York: Center for Migration Studies. Retrieved from http://jmhs.cmsny.org/index.php/jmhs/article/view/45

Wasem, R. E. (2012, December 13). *Unauthorized aliens residing in the United States: Estimates since 1986* (CRS RL33874). Washington, DC: Congressional Research Service.

Wright, B. (2016, March 9). Border security—Babeau: Obama is misleading Americans. *Casa Grande Dispatch*. Retrieved from http://www.trivalleycentral.com/casa_grande_dispatch/area_news/border-security---babeu-obama-is-misleading-americans/article_519da9b8-e609-11e5-afa9-7f53f0462823.html

Q15. ARE MOST UNAUTHORIZED IMMIGRANTS IN THE UNITED STATES FROM MEXICO? AND DOES THE MEXICAN GOVERNMENT MAINTAIN A POLICY OF PUSHING THE "WORST" OF ITS CITIZENS INTO THE UNITED STATES?

Answer: The largest percentage of unauthorized immigrants in the United States originates from the country's southern neighbor, Mexico. That number (roughly 49–55 percent of the total number of unauthorized immigrants), however, has decreased since 2009, as fewer Mexicans have tried to enter the United States and increasing numbers of Mexicans have returned to their home country. However, there is no evidence to indicate that Mexican authorities are pushing their citizens into the United States to reduce crime or poverty within their own borders.

The Facts: There exists a widespread assumption that the great majority of people who enter the United States illegally come from Mexico. Republican presidential candidate Donald Trump, for example, whose focus on illegal immigration thrust him into the spotlight at the beginning of his campaign, has repeatedly pointed to Mexico when discussing problems associated with the issue. Trump has suggested on numerous occasions that unauthorized Mexican migrants are the biggest threat to border security and that their illegal entry necessitates the construction of a full border wall, which, he says, he will force Mexico to fund. Trump sent out a statement in July 2015 condemning illegal immigration in which he stated, "The worst elements in Mexico are being pushed into the United States by the Mexican Government" (Walker, 2015). Trump has further implied that the Mexican government purposely sends criminal nationals northward into the United States. During a Republican presidential debate hosted by Fox News, he said, "Because our leaders are stupid, our politicians are stupid, and the Mexican government is much smarter, much sharper, much more cunning, and they send the bad ones over because they don't want to pay for them, they don't want to take care of them. Why should they when the stupid leaders of the United States will do it for them? And that's what's happening whether you like it or not" (TIME, 2015).

Trump's comments earned a "pants on fire" rating from politifact.com. (Jacobson, 2015). Researchers from this Pulitzer Prize–winning fact-check Web site consulted a number of immigration experts regarding Trump's allegation, who all agreed there was no truth to the claim. Trump, when asked, also could not provide any evidence, relying instead on conversations with "border patrol people" (ibid.).

Instead of being pushed northward by the government, researchers from the Mexican Migration Project (MMP), a study based on over three decades of fieldwork, found that Mexican migration was driven primarily by both labor demands and well-developed migrant networks in the United States (Massey & Gentsch, 2014). MMP director Douglas Massey said that social and economic circumstances in both countries drive migration and that "Mexico has never had a policy of pushing migrants toward the United States, much less 'forcing many bad people into our country'" (Jacobson, 2015). Center for Immigration Studies director Mark Krikorian who advocates for lower levels of immigration, agreed, saying "No, the Mexican government doesn't force anyone to move here illegally, though it certainly doesn't object" (Jacobson, 2015). Additional scholars have reiterated that Mexico does not force anyone to come to the United States and add that family reunification has also been an increasingly important factor in Mexican migration to the United States as well as increasing returns to Mexico from the United States (Gonzalez-Barrera, 2015; Instituto Nacional de Estadística y Geografía, 2016; Mexicans and Americans Thinking Together, 2014). In fact, a Mexican government survey revealed 6 in 10 migrants who left the United States for Mexico between 2009 and 2014 listed family reunification as the primary reason for their return. In comparison, only 14 percent said the reason for their return was deportation (Gonzalez-Barrera, 2015).

HISTORY

With roughly 16.2 million immigrants (legal and unauthorized) having come to the United States from Mexico since 1965, Mexico is the source of the largest immigration wave in U.S. history and "one of the largest mass migrations in modern history" (Gonzalez-Barrera, 2015). For as long as people have lived in the areas of what are now Mexico and the Southwestern United States, in fact, migrants have traveled back and forth across these lands seeking new opportunities. Even after Congress officially formed the United States Border Patrol in 1924 to monitor the crossings of citizens versus noncitizens, generations of Mexicans (primarily men) continued a circular cycle of working in *el norte* (the north) and then returning to their birthplaces where families awaited. Some came legally, under Bracero (guest worker) programs, while others made the journey without formal permission, thus violating U.S. laws. For its part, the U.S. government and U.S. employers actively encouraged Mexican workers to make the journey north at various points in the 20th century, such as to replenish labor pools reduced in the early 1900s by anti-Asian and anti-Eastern European legislation and to address worker shortfalls occasioned by America's entrance into World War I and World War II (Hernandez, 2009; Massey, 2009). In spite of their important economic and cultural contributions, however, Mexicans were generally viewed as undesirable in terms of citizenry or assimilation. In 1912 a leading economist wrote, "Although the Mexicans have proved to be efficient laborers in certain industries, and have afforded a cheap and elastic labor supply for the southwestern United States, the evils to the community at large which their presence in large numbers almost invariably brings may more than overbalance their desirable qualities" (Bryan, 1912).

Throughout the majority of the 20th century, however, Mexican laborers continued to enter the United States and fill jobs in industries that relied on their low-cost labor. Most returned to Mexico once they had earned their target wages in the United States (where salaries were many times higher than those in Mexico), and nearly all considered Mexico home (Massey, Durand, & Malone, 2003).

In 1964, however, the U.S. government ended the Bracero Program and the following year passed the Immigration and Nationality Act, which placed the first numerical caps on the number of immigrant visas issued on a per-country basis. A provision was also included that prohibited unskilled temporary workers from applying for an employment-based legal permanent resident status, affecting the ability of Mexican workers to enter the United States legally. Labor demands that had been fed for the previous 22 years with Bracero workers, however, did not change. Additionally, high birth rates and dislocation of agricultural workers in Mexico served as additional push factors that prompted low-skilled workers to find jobs elsewhere. As a result, Mexicans continued to cross the northern border into the United States to find employment. The number of apprehensions of Mexicans crossing onto U.S. soil without authorization tripled between 1965 and 1970 (Rosenblum et al., 2014).

Then, beginning in the mid-1970s and continuing into the mid-1990s, negative characterizations of Mexicans in the media, changes in immigration policy, and a drastic increase in border security created an even more restrictive and threatening environment in which circular migration cycles were nearly impossible to sustain (Chavez, 2001, 2008; Massey, 2009; Massey & Pren, 2012; Santa Ana, 2002; Treviño, 1985). Repeat border crossings for unauthorized individuals became too risky and too expensive, resulting in a rising population of Mexicans who chose to stay in the United States where work and wages were generally more plentiful. These individuals then sent for relatives to join them when funds allowed. For over a decade this trend continued, inflating the population of unauthorized Mexicans living in the United States and reducing the feasibility of circular migration cycles (Massey, Durand, & Pren, 2016; Massey & Riosmena, 2010).

It was not until after 2007 that this settlement trend began to reverse. The estimated number of unauthorized Mexican individuals living in the United States peaked in 2007 at 6.9 million, but then dropped by 1.3 million people over the next seven years to 5.6 million in 2014 (Gonzalez-Barrera, 2015; Krogstad & Passel, 2015). A combination of factors discouraged migration into the United States and encouraged outmigration from the United States among Mexican nationals. These included reduced employment opportunities in the U.S.A. during the Great Recession of 2007–2009, and its aftermath, improvements in the Mexican economy, stepped up border enforcement and increased funding for border walls and technology, declining birth rates in Mexico, and a desire for family reunification on the southern side of the border (Camarota & Zeigler, 2009; Markon, 2015; Mexicans and Americans Thinking Together, 2014).

According to estimates published in November 2015, Mexicans made up nearly half of all unauthorized immigrants at 49 percent (Krogstad & Passel, 2015). This number is substantially lower than it has been for the past quarter century; in 1990 Mexicans were estimated to comprise 58 percent of the unauthorized population in the United States, in 2000 the number was 69 percent, and in 2010 it was again 58 percent (Immigration and Naturalization Service, 2003; Passel & Cohn, 2011; Zong & Batalova, 2015). Between 2009 and 2014, fewer Mexican migrants (both authorized and unauthorized) entered the country, and increasing numbers of Mexicans in the United States departed, resulting in *negative* net migration to the United States from Mexico (Gonzalez-Barrera, 2015).

This negative net migration from Mexico is reflected in border apprehension statistics that indicate a drop in unauthorized individuals from Mexico attempting to enter the United States (Krogstad & Passel, 2014). The number of unauthorized Mexican nationals apprehended in the United States in FY 2014 was a historic low of 229,178—at that time, the lowest number since 1971. Apprehensions dropped even further during FY 2015 to 188,122 (United States Border Patrol, 2015). The last time numbers that low were recorded was nearly 50 years ago, when just over 159,000 Mexicans were apprehended in 1969 (Gonzalez-Barrera, 2016).

Mexican populations in the United States are also often overestimated as a result of improper assumptions that unauthorized Spanish-speaking immigrants are primarily from Mexico. In reality, unauthorized populations from Central America doubled between 2000 and 2013, and overall diversity has increased among the population of those crossing the border illegally (Rosenblum & Soto, 2015). Among unauthorized individuals in the United States between 2009 and 2013, roughly 56 percent were from Mexico, but an additional 15 percent came from Central America and 29 percent came from other parts of the world (14 percent from Asia; 6 percent from South America; 4 percent from Europe, Canada, or Oceania; 3 percent from Africa; and 2 percent from the Caribbean) (Zong & Batalova, 2016). In fact, 2014 was notable because it marked the first time on record that more non-Mexicans than Mexicans were apprehended at U.S. borders (Krogstad & Passel, 2014).

This shift in border-crossing populations has been partially attributed to an influx of asylum seekers and migrants from Guatemala, El Salvador, and Honduras. Most of these individuals are entering the United States through southern Texas. When examining the numbers of unauthorized border-crossers by year (and not by total population, which includes arrivals over a number of years), scholars estimate that Mexican nationals make up less than one-third of the average 350,000 unauthorized persons entering the United States annually (Passel & Cohn, 2015).

Statistics continue to reflect a decline in the northward flows of unauthorized Mexicans even after the U.S. economy regained strength during post-Recession years. This pattern reverses earlier trends that correlated the strength of the U.S. economy with the number of unauthorized immigrants in the United States, including Mexican nationals (Johnson & Hills, 2011). Further evidence of a decline in arrivals is found in the fact that Mexicans in the United States in 2015 were more likely to be well-established individuals living with U.S.-born children, not recent arrivals (Passel & Cohn, 2015). Data from the past 15 years reveals this trend toward longer residence in the U.S.A. In 2012, 62 percent of unauthorized immigrants had lived in the United States for 10 years or more (compared with 35 percent in 2000), and 85 percent had lived in the country five years or more (compared with 62 percent in 2000) (Passel, Cohn, Krogstad, & Gonzalez-Barrera, 2014).

Additionally, while family reunification, jobs, and an improved Mexican economy have all contributed to increased numbers of Mexican nationals returning to their home country, unprecedented deportations have also contributed to a reduced Mexican population in the United States. In 2013, a record 314,904 Mexican immigrants were deported from the United States, largely because of a 2005 policy shift emphasizing formal deportations instead of voluntary returns (Gonzalez-Barrera & Krogstad, 2015). Whether or not those factors continue to produce negative net migration from Mexico to the United States remains to be seen. What is certain is that the economies and changing demographics of both the United States and Mexico have at least for the time being produced a significant new migratory flow of people of Mexican heritage—to the south.

FURTHER READING

Bryan, S. (1912). Mexican immigrants in the United States. *The Survey*. Retrieved from http://www.digitalhistory.uh.edu/disp_textbook .cfm?smtID=3&psid=597

Camarota, S. A., & Zeigler, K. (2009, July). *A shifting tide: Recent trends in the illegal immigrant population*. Center for Immigration Studies. Washington, DC: CIS. Retrieved from http://cis.org/IllegalImmigration-ShiftingTide

Chavez, L. R. (2001). *Covering immigration: Population images and the politics of the nation*. Berkeley and Los Angeles: University of California Press.

Chavez, L. R. (2008). *The Latino threat: Constructing immigrants, citizens, and the nation*. Stanford, CA: Stanford University Press.

Gonzalez-Barrera, A. (2015, November 19). *More Mexicans leaving than coming to the U.S.* Washington, DC: Pew Research Center. Retrieved from http://www.pewhispanic.org/2015/11/19/more-mexicans-leaving-than-coming-to-the-u-s/

Gonzalez-Barrera, A. (2016, April 14). *Apprehensions of Mexican migrants at U.S. borders reach near-historic low*. Washington, DC: Pew Research Center. Retrieved from http://www.pewresearch.org/fact-tank/2016/04/14/mexico-us-border-apprehensions/

Gonzalez-Barrera, A., & Krogstad, J. M. (2015, July 15). *What we know about illegal immigration from Mexico.* Washington, DC: Pew Research Center. Retrieved from http://www.pewresearch.org/fact-tank/2015/07/15/what-we-know-about-illegal-immigration-from-mexico/

Hernandez, K. L. (2009). Mexican immigration to the United States. *Organization of American Historians Magazine of History, 23*(4), 25–29 (doi:10.1093/maghis/23.4.25).

Immigration and Naturalization Service (INS). (2003, January 31). *Estimates of the unauthorized immigrant population residing in the United States: 1990 to 2000.* Washington, DC: U.S. Immigration and Naturalization Service. Retrieved from https://www.dhs.gov/xlibrary/assets/statistics/publications/Ill_Report_1211.pdf

Instituto Nacional de Estadística y Geografía (INEGI) [National Institute of Statistics and Geography]. (2016, January 28). Boletín de prensa número 29/16 [Press release 29/16]. Información de migración internacional con datos de la ENOE al tercer trimestre de 2015 [International migration information with data from the third trimester 2015 National Occupation and Employment Survey]. INEGI: Aguascalientes, MX. Retrieved from http://www.inegi.org.mx/saladeprensa/boletines/2016/especiales/especiales2016_01_10.pdf

Jacobson, L. (2015, August 6). *Donald Trump: "The Mexican government . . . they send the bad ones over."* Politifact.com. Retrieved from http://www.politifact.com/truth-o-meter/statements/2015/aug/06/donald-trump/trump-mexican-government-they-send-bad-ones-over/#

Johnson, H., & Hills, L. (2011). *At issue: Illegal immigration.* San Francisco: Public Policy Institute of California. Retrieved from http://www.ppic.org/content/pubs/atissue/AI_711HJAI.pdf

Krogstad, J. M., & Passel, J. S. (2014, December 30). *U.S. border apprehensions of Mexicans fall to historic lows.* Washington, DC: Pew Research Center. Retrieved from http://www.pewresearch.org/fact-tank/2014/12/30/u-s-border-apprehensions-of-mexicans-fall-to-historic-lows/

Krogstad, J. M., & Passel, J. S. (2015, November 19). *5 facts about illegal immigration in the U.S.* Washington, DC: Pew Research Center. Retrieved from http://www.pewresearch.org/fact-tank/2015/11/19/5-facts-about-illegal-immigration-in-the-u-s/

Markon, J. (2015, May 27). Fewer immigrants are entering the U.S. illegally, and that's changed the border security debate. *The Washington Post.* Retrieved from https://www.washingtonpost.com/politics/flow-of-illegal-immigration-slows-as-us-mexico-border-dynamics-evolve/2015/05/27/c5caf02c-006b-11e5-833c-a2de05b6b2a4_story.html

Massey, D. S. (2009). Racial formation in theory and practice: The case of Mexicans in the United States. *Race and Social Problems*, 1(1), 12–26. Retrieved from http://doi.org/10.1007/s12552-009-9005-3

Massey, D. S., Durand, J., & Malone, N. J. (2003). *Beyond smoke and mirrors: Mexican immigration in an era of economic integration*. New York: Russell Sage Foundation Publications.

Massey, D. S., Durand, J., & Pren, K. A. (2016, March). Why border enforcement backfired. *American Journal of Sociology*, 121(5), 1557–1600 (doi:10.1086/684200).

Massey, D.S., & Gentsch, K. (2014), Undocumented migration to the United States and the wages of Mexican immigrants. *International Migration Review*, 48(2), 482–499.

Massey, D. S., & Pren, K. A. (2012). Origins of the new Latino underclass. *Race and Social Problems*, 4(1), 5–17.

Massey, D. S., & Riosmena, F. (2010, July 1). Undocumented migration from Latin America in an era of rising U.S. enforcement. *The Annals of the American Academy of Political and Social Science*, 630(1), 294–321. Retrieved from http://doi.org/10.1177/0002716210368114

Mexicans and Americans Thinking Together (MATT). (2014, January). *The U.S./Mexico cycle: The end of an era*. Austin, TX: MATT. Retrieved from http://www.matt.org/uploads/2/4/9/3/24932918/dc_launch_pre sentation_012014_final.pdf

Passel, J. S., & Cohn, D. (2011, February 1). *Unauthorized immigrant population: National and state trends, 2010*. Washington, DC: Pew Research Center. Retrieved from http://www.pewhispanic.org/2011/02/01/unau thorized-immigrant-population-brnational-and-state-trends-2010/

Passel, J. S., & Cohn, D. (2015, July 22). *Unauthorized immigrant population stable for half a decade*. Washington, DC: Pew Research Center. Retrieved from http://www.pewresearch.org/fact-tank/2015/07/22/un authorized-immigrant-population-stable-for-half-a-decade/

Passel, J.S., Cohn, D., Krogstad, J.M., & Gonzalez-Barrera, A. (2014, September 3). *As growth stalls, unauthorized immigrant population becomes more settled*. Pew Research Center. Washington, DC: Pew. Retrieved from http://www.pewhispanic.org/files/2014/09/2014-09-03_Unautho rized-Final.pdf

Rosenblum, M. R., Kandel, W. A., Seelke, C. R., & Wasem, R. E. (2012, June 7). *Mexican Migration to the United States: Policy and Trends* (CRS-R42560). Washington, DC: Congressional Research Service. Retrieved from http://www.fas.org/sgp/crs/row/R42560.pdf

Rosenblum, M. R., & Soto, A. G.R. (2015, August). *An analysis of unauthorized immigrants in the United States by country and region of birth.*

Washington, DC: Migration Policy Institute. Retrieved from http://www.migrationpolicy.org/research/analysis-unauthorized-immigrants-united-states-country-and-region-birth

Santa Ana, O. (2002). *Brown tide rising: Metaphors of Latinos in contemporary American public discourse*. Austin: University of Texas Press.

TIME. (2015, August 11). Transcript: Read the full text of the primetime Republican debate [Transcript]. TIME.com. Retrieved from http://time.com/3988276/republican-debate-primetime-transcript-full-text/

Treviño, J. S. (1985, March). Latino portrayals in film and television. *Jump Cut: A Review of Contemporary Media*, 30, 14–16. Retrieved from https://blogs.uprm.edu/film/files/2012/12/Latino-portrayals-in-film-and-television_Trevino.pdf

United States Border Patrol. (2015). *Illegal alien apprehensions from Mexico by fiscal year*. Washington, DC: Customs and Border Protection Agency. Retrieved from http://www.cbp.gov/sites/default/files/documents/BP%20Total%20Apps%2C%20Mexico%2C%20OTM%20FY2000-FY2015.pdf

Walker, H. (2015, July 6). Donald Trump just released an epic statement raging against Mexican immigrants and 'disease.' *Business Insider*. Retrieved from http://www.businessinsider.com/donald-trumps-epic-statement-on-mexico-2015-7

Zong, J., & Batalova, J. (2015, February 26). *Frequently requested statistics on immigrants and immigration in the United States*. Washington, DC: Migration Policy Institute. Retrieved from http://www.migrationpolicy.org/article/frequently-requested-statistics-immigrants-and-immigration-united-states/

Zong, J. & Batalova, J. (2016, April 14). *Frequently requested statistics on immigrants and immigration in the United States*. Washington, DC: Migration Policy Institute. Retrieved from http://www.migrationpolicy.org/article/frequently-requested-statistics-immigrants-and-immigration-united-states/

Q16. HOW EXPENSIVE AND FEASIBLE WOULD IT BE TO DEPORT ALL "ILLEGAL IMMIGRANTS" LIVING IN THE UNITED STATES?

Answer: The effort that would be required to locate, arrest, and deport all of the roughly 11 million unauthorized individuals in the United States would be enormous. Even if it were possible to carry out this strategy, researchers estimate the financial cost of such a policy to be in the billions of dollars for the arrests and deportations alone. Those figures do not include the financial costs of losing workers and contributors to local economies. Finally, such mass deportations would have a tremendous social and emotional impact on mixed-status families and on communities in which many long-term unauthorized migrants have settled.

The Facts: Republican presidential candidate Donald Trump has stated on numerous occasions that if elected, he would deport all unauthorized immigrants in the country. His plan calls for removing all of the estimated 11 million people living illegally in the United States and then allowing the "really good people" to return (Colvin & Caldwell, 2015). Later, he explained, "We're going to keep the families together, but they have to go" (Jaffe, 2015). Other public figures have expressed similar sentiments. Former Republican Senator Rick Santorum, for example, stated that the United States should give 6 million illegal immigrants "the gift" of being sent back to their home countries. Santorum added that to stop the flow of immigrants, "Let's send 6 million Mexicans, Hondurans, Guatemalans . . . back into their country so they can start a renaissance in their country so they won't be coming over here anymore" (Swan, 2016).

Analysts caution, however, that the costs of deporting nearly 11 million unauthorized persons would be very high. At a 2007 Senate Committee hearing for the nomination of Julie Myers as assistant secretary of Immigration and Customs Enforcement (ICE), Myers was asked how much it would cost to locate, detain, and deport all persons living in the United States without authorization (which at the time was roughly 12 million). Myers estimated the cost would be roughly $94 billion (U.S. Congress, Senate Committee on Homeland Security and Governmental Affairs, 2007). A 2012 estimate that took into consideration costs for apprehension, detention, legal proceedings, and transportation concluded that a deportation campaign over five years would cost $285 billion (Kasperkevic, 2012). The American Action Forum (AAF), a conservative nonprofit issue advocacy group, estimated in 2015 that deporting all unauthorized immigrants from the United States would take roughly 20 years and cost between $400 billion and $600 billion (Collins, 2015). The next year, AAF revised its estimates to consider the resources necessary to deport all undocumented immigrants in *two* years, as advocated by Trump. The conclusion was that such an effort would both strain federal resources and drastically reduce the labor force by 10.3 million workers, thus shrinking the U.S. economy by $1 trillion over the course of those two years (Gitis, 2016). An ICE official testified in 2011 that 400,000 deportations were possible annually based on the agency's budget that year ($5.8 billion), resulting in a cost of $12,500 per deportation (Kibble, 2011). Considering the current estimate of roughly 11 million undocumented individuals in the United States, the total cost to deport all these individuals would be $137 billion. One final estimate comes from the liberal Center for American Progress, which estimated in 2014 that mass deportation and continued efforts to secure both the border and interior of the United States would cost $285 billion over five years (Center for American Progress, 2014).

Even if mass deportations were economically feasible, they would be next to impossible to complete under Trump's proposed two-year plan. First of all, deporting the estimated 11 million unauthorized persons in the United States in two years would require removal of over 15,000 people per day. Deporting that many individuals through formal removal proceedings in such a short amount of time would be very difficult, even under the best of circumstances. Under current immigration law, formal removal is most often both a costly and lengthy legal process. However, adherence to the legal process is necessary to avoid mistakes of the past, such as mass deportations of the 1930s and mid-1950s when U.S. citizens of Mexican descent were inadvertently deported along with unauthorized populations (Carrasco, 1998). Current backlogs in U.S. federal immigration courts have slowed the rate of deportations and increased the wait times of those required to appear before an immigration judge to have their cases decided (Dominguez Villegas & Rieti, 2015). As of April 2015 there was a backlog of over 445,000 cases, resulting in delays of many years between apprehension and adjudication for immigration-related offenses (ibid.).

Communities also suffer ill effects of deportations, as evidenced in accounts of raids on communities like Lowell, Massachusetts, and Postville, Iowa (Juby & Kaplan, 2011; Sládková et al., 2012). Federal raids and subsequent arrests and/or deportations breed mistrust and fear of interaction with law enforcement in immigrant families due to fears of arrest or deportation. These raids have a dramatic psychological and economic effect not only on the foreign populations living within them but also on the communities as a whole, where migrants have developed deep relationships, contributed to the economy, and helped form the cultural identity of the local populace. This was evident in Postville, Iowa, where a single raid cut the adult population of the Iowa town by one-third, and numerous businesses subsequently went bankrupt (Adams, 2009; Olivo, 2009).

Detention and deportation practices themselves have been challenged by civil groups and researchers who have documented systematic practices of Customs and Border Protection officials, such as permanently seizing migrants' personal belongings while they are in detention (Martínez & Slack, 2013; No More Deaths, 2014). These belongings include forms of identification, money, medications, and telephone numbers in addition to wedding rings, family photos, and other personal effects. The studies published highlight that dispossessing and subsequently deporting these migrants places them at great risk of exploitation and abuse on the other side of the border. Without money, the deported (who most often end up in unfamiliar towns) have no means of paying for transportation home, buying food, or paying for shelter or a change of clothing; without identification they cannot apply for jobs, receive a money transfer, or even buy a phone card. Their risk of extortion, kidnapping, and sexual assault increases dramatically with no way to prove their identity or provide for their basic needs. Deportees without money or identity cards also face harassment by local police and exploitation by cartels or gangs who recognize their vulnerable status. The result is that some deportees are either forcibly or out of necessity pushed into criminal networks. Finally, confiscation of medicine can prove disastrous for detainees who rely on those medications (ibid.).

Economically, mass deportations would have a negative effect on local and state economies. A study by the Institute on Taxation and Economic Policy (ITEP) concluded that unauthorized immigrants living in the United States collectively pay $11.64 billion a year in state and local taxes (Gee, Gardner, & Wiehe, 2016). In addition to sales tax on purchases, unauthorized persons pay property taxes through rent or homeownership. In fact, over 30 percent of all unauthorized immigrant households own their homes (Migration Policy Institute, 2014). Unauthorized workers and their families also consume goods and services, thus helping to create jobs by contributing to economic activity in their communities (Costa, Cooper, & Shierholz, 2014).

Nationally, the U.S. economy and job growth overall would suffer if mass deportations were to occur. Although it is difficult to calculate the percentage of income taxes paid by unauthorized workers because many are paid under the table for their labor, ITEP estimates that at least half of unauthorized immigrants pay income taxes (Gee, Gardner, & Wiehe, 2016). Social Security and Medicare are two programs that greatly benefit from taxes paid to the government by workers who are unlikely to ever reclaim those contributions because they have used fraudulent numbers or numbers of the deceased. The chief actuary of the Social Security Administration believes that such individuals working illegally in the United States pay an *annual* net contribution of $12 billion (or more than $100 billion contribution over a decade) into the Social Security trust fund (Germano, 2014). The Social Security Administration also notes the importance of contributions from unauthorized workers to its "earnings suspense file," where W-2 names and Social Security numbers that don't match are recorded. Unauthorized workers are thought to make up the vast majority of contributors to this fund. It is estimated that between 2001 and 2010 around $21 billion was directed to Medicare through money from the suspense file (Solana, 2013).

FURTHER READING

Adams, P. (2009, November 4). Immigrants in the American heartland. *BBC News*. Retrieved from http://ensign.ftlcomm.com/ensign2/mcin tyre/pickofday/2009/011november09/november004/Immigrants.pdf

Carrasco, G. P. (1998). Latinos in the United States: Invitation and exile. In R. Delgado & J. Stefancic (Eds.), *The Latino/a condition: A critical reader* (pp. 77–85). New York: New York University Press.

Center for American Progress. (2014, October). *The facts on immigration today*. Washington, DC: Center for American Progress. Retrieved from https://cdn.americanprogress.org/wp-content/uploads/2013/04/Immi grationFacts-brief-10.23.pdf

Collins, L. (2015, August 18). *A costly immigration policy*. Washington, DC: American Action Forum. Retrieved from http://www.americanac tionforum.org/insight/a-costly-immigration-policy/

Colvin, J., & Caldwell, A. A. (2015, July 30). Trump's call for mass deportations runs into messy realities. *The Associated Press*. Retrieved from http://finance.yahoo.com/news/trumps-call-mass-deportations-runs-220828951.html

Costa, D., Cooper, D., & Shierholz, H. (2014, August 12). *Facts about immigration and the U.S. economy*. Washington, DC: The Economic Policy Institute. Retrieved from http://www.epi.org/publication/immi gration-facts/

Dominguez Villegas, R., & Rietig, V. (2015, September). *Migrants deported from the United States and Mexico to the Northern Triangle: A statistical and socioeconomic profile*. Washington, DC: Migration Policy Institute. Retrieved from http://www.migrationpolicy.org/research/ migrants-deported-united-states-and-mexico-northern-triangle-statis tical-and-socioeconomic

Gee, L. C., Gardner, M., & Wiehe, M. (2016, February). *Undocumented immigrants' state and local tax contributions*. Washington, DC: The Institute

on Taxation & Economic Policy. Retrieved from http://www.itep
.org/pdf/immigration2016.pdf

Germano, R. (2014, August 4). Unauthorized immigrants paid $100 bil-
lion into Social Security over last decade. *Vice News*. Retrieved from
https://news.vice.com/article/unauthorized-immigrants-paid-100-
billion-into-social-security-over-last-decade

Gitis, B. (2016, February 28). *The personnel and infrastructure needed to
remove all undocumented migrants in two years*. Washington, DC: American Action Forum. Retrieved from http://finance.yahoo.com/news/
trumps-call-mass-deportations-runs-220828951.html

Jaffe, A. (2015, August 16). Donald Trump: Undocumented immigrants
"Have to go." nbcnews.com. Retrieved from http://www.nbcnews.com/
meet-the-press/donald-trump-undocumented-immigrants-have-go-
n410501

Juby, C., & Kaplan, L. (2011). Postville: The effects of an immigration
raid. *Families in Society: The Journal of Contemporary Social Services*,
92(2), 147–153.

Kasperkevic, J. (2012, January 30). Deporting all of America's illegal immigrants would cost a whopping $285 billion. *Business Insider*.
Retrieved from http://www.businessinsider.com/deporting-all-of-amer
icas-illegal-immigrants-would-cost-a-whopping-285-billion-2012-1

Kibble, K. C. (2011, March 10). Testimony of Deputy Director Kumar C.
Kibble, Immigration and Customs Enforcement, Before the United
States House Committee on the Judiciary, Subcommittee on Immigration and Policy Enforcement, "Immigration and Customs Enforcement
Worksite Enforcement—Up to the Job?" [House testimony]. Washington, DC: Department of Homeland Security. Retrieved from https://
www.dhs.gov/news/2011/03/10/written-testimony-ice-house-judiciary-
subcommittee-immigration-and-policy#

Martínez, D. E., & Slack, J. (2013, December). *Bordering on criminal: The
routine abuse of migrants in the removal system—Part II: Possessions taken
and not returned*. Washington, DC: The Immigration Policy Center.
Retrieved from http://www.immigrationpolicy.org/sites/default/files/
docs/ipc/Border%20-%20Possessions%20FINAL.pdf

Migration Policy Institute (MPI). (2014). *Profile of the unauthorized population: United States*. Washington, DC: MPI. Retrieved from http://
www.epi.org/publication/immigration-facts/

No More Deaths. (2014). *Shakedown: How deportation robs immigrants
of their money and belongings* [Report]. Tucson, AZ: No More Deaths.
Retrieved from http://forms.nomoredeaths.org/abuse-documentation/
shakedown/

Olivo, A. (2009, May 12). Immigration raid leaves damaging mark on Postville, Iowa. *Los Angeles Times.* Retrieved from http://articles.latimes .com/2009/may/12/nation/na-postville-iowa12

Sládková, J., García Mangado, S. M., & Reyes Quinteros, J. (2012, December). Lowell immigrant communities in the climate of deportations. *Analyses of Social Issues and Public Policy,* 12(1), 78–95.

Solana, K. (2013, January 7). *Illegal immigrants give billions to Medicare, Social Security with no hope of benefit.* Los Angeles: USC Annenberg Center for Health Journalism [Member blog]. Retrieved from http://www .centerforhealthjournalism.org/2013/01/07/illegal-immigrants-give-billions-medicare-social-security-no-hope-benefit

Swan, J. (2016, January 14). Santorum calls mass deportation a "gift." *The Hill.* Retrieved from http://thehill.com/blogs/ballot-box/presidential-races/265981-santorum-calls-mass-deportation-a-gift

U.S. Congress, Senate Committee on Homeland Security and Governmental Affairs. (2007, September 12). *Nomination of Hon. Julie L. Myers to be assistant secretary, U.S. Immigration and Customs Enforcement, U.S. Department of Homeland Security* (GPO, 2008, p. 11). Washington, DC; 110th Congress.

Q17. ARE MOST PEOPLE ILLEGALLY CROSSING THE BORDER INTO THE UNITED STATES DOING SO IN ORDER TO FIND WORK?

Answer: Not anymore. While this was once the case, the demographics have shifted from laborers seeking employment (although such people still account for a large number of unauthorized immigrants) to those seeking asylum from violence, instability, and poverty in their home countries. Countries of origin have also shifted, with a larger percentage of unauthorized border-crossers now coming from Central America than ever before. In addition, family reunification has become an increasingly important motive for unauthorized individuals to enter the United States.

The Facts: When illegal immigration once again became part of the national discourse around the turn of the 21st century, public discussion focused primarily on Mexican workers crossing the border into the United States to find jobs. At that time, the U.S. government was engaged in multiple efforts to militarize the border by placing thousands more Customs and Border Protection officers along the boundary and constructing border walls in the most heavily trafficked crossing areas (Massey,

Durand, & Pren, 2016). These stepped-up enforcement efforts pushed the majority of border-crossers to the remote desert landscape of northern Sonora, Mexico, and southern Arizona. Thousands died as they attempted the journey through the harsh, unforgiving terrain (International Organization for Migration, 2014).

Ten years later, however, a new trend began to emerge as the epicenter of border crossing once again shifted. This time, the flow moved eastward to Texas, with most individuals entering the United States through the Border Patrol's Río Grande Valley (U.S. Border Patrol, 2015). In addition to the change in location, the new border-crossing trends marked a demographic transformation. The majority of these Texas border-crossers were not young men from Mexico looking for work; they were tens of thousands of women, children, and families from Central America seeking refuge from intense violence and poverty in their home countries (ibid.).

The Central Americans who crossed into Texas in such large numbers from roughly 2010 to 2014 are commonly referred to as illegal, undocumented, or unauthorized immigrants. In some cases, they are called unauthorized migrants. However, these classifications are not entirely accurate. Instead of journeying north with the intention of permanently settling or finding jobs in the United States, the majority of women, children, and families that arrived on U.S. soil during those years sought asylum. Asylees, as opposed to migratory workers or settlers, are individuals who flee persecution in their home countries "on account of race, religion, nationality, and/or membership in a particular social group or political opinion" (U.S. Citizenship and Immigration Services, 2015). In order to be granted asylum, petitioners must first pass a "credible fear" interview with an immigration officer. After that, those from countries other than Mexico and Canada must await court proceedings where it is ultimately up to an immigration judge to determine whether they meet the qualifications for asylum status. (Under current immigration law, Mexicans and Canadians can be sent home through "expedited removal" without formal hearings.)

What is particularly notable about the border-crossers in Texas's Río Grande Valley is that so many were unaccompanied children who had made the dangerous journey to the United States without parents. Their numbers quintupled in just five years, from 4,977 in 2010 to 49,959 in 2014 in the Río Grande Valley sector alone (U.S. Border Patrol, 2016). The United Nations High Commissioner for Refugees conducted a study which found that 72 percent of the children they interviewed from El Salvador, and 58 percent of the children overall from Mexico, Guatemala, El Salvador, and Honduras, qualified for international protection (possible asylum) (United Nations High Commissioner for Refugees, 2014). However, because immigration law does not provide for legal representation, individuals seeking asylum—including children as young as three years old—are left to defend themselves in immigration court. A national study of children's immigration cases found that when children had legal representation in court, nearly three-fourths were granted permission to remain in the United States. However, among those without a lawyer, only 15 percent were allowed to stay, and the remaining 85 percent were deported (Transactional Records Access Clearinghouse, 2014). Another study of deportation proceedings nationally found that individuals with attorneys were 15 times more likely to seek relief from removal and 5½ times more likely to obtain that relief than those without representation (Eagly & Shafer, 2015).

Further evidence that those entering the Río Grande Valley are asylum seekers and not laborers is found in accounts describing these border-crossers running *to* Border Patrol officers and asking for help rather than hiding or running away (Avila, 2014; Miroff & Partlow, 2014). Many gave personal testimony of gang-related violence against themselves and their families, and told authorities they would be killed if they returned. Their stories are supported by reports of widespread crime and political violence in Central America's so-called Northern Triangle—Guatemala, El Salvador, and Honduras (Gonzalez-Barrera, Krogstad, & Lopez, 2014). El Salvador's homicide rate was high enough in the first half of 2016 to make it the murder capital of the Western Hemisphere, displacing long-standing title holder Honduras, where the homicide rate in 2015 was 10 times higher than the world average (Partlow, 2016). As violence has risen in the Northern Triangle, so have the number of applicants for asylum—not just in the United States but also throughout Central America. Since 2009 the number of asylum applications from Northern Triangle countries to Mexico, Panama, Nicaragua, Costa Rica, and Belize increased by 712 percent (Washington Office on Latin America, 2014).

Another of the most notable changes in immigration over the past 30 years has been the transformation from circular labor flows to permanent settlement patterns among unauthorized border-crossers. Immigration policy changes of the mid-1960s and mid-1980s restricted access to legal channels of migration to the United States, and massive border securitization campaigns in the mid-1990s made repeated border crossings too costly and too risky for unauthorized migrants to continue circular migration patterns. Thus, most unauthorized crossers who reached the United States decided to stay and send for loved ones, in essence compounding the numbers of unauthorized family members within the country's borders whose purpose in coming was not work but to reunite with family (Massey, Durand, & Pren, 2016).

Thus, while many who enter the country without inspection still seek employment, asylum and family reunification have become increasingly important motivations for individuals making the unauthorized journey into the United States.

FURTHER READING

Avila, J. (2014, July 6). U.S. border protection head: Central American immigrants not dangerous. Abcnews.com. Retrieved from http://abcnews.go.com/blogs/politics/2014/07/u-s-border-protection-head-central-american-immigrants-not-dangerous/

Eagly, I. V., & Shafer, S. (2015). A national study of access to counsel in immigration court. *University of Pennsylvania Law Review*, 164(1), 1–91. Retrieved from http://papers.ssrn.com/sol3/papers.cfm?abstract_id=2581161

Gonzalez-Barrera, A., Krogstad, J. M., & Lopez, M. H. (2014, July 1). *DHS: Violence, poverty is driving children to flee Central America to U.S.* Washington, DC: Pew Research Center. Retrieved from http://www.pewresearch.org/fact-tank/2014/07/01/dhs-violence-poverty-is-driving-children-to-flee-central-america-to-u-s/

International Organization for Migration. (2014). *Fatal journeys: Tracking lives lost during migration.* Geneva, Switzerland: IOM. Retrieved from http://www.iom.int/files/live/sites/iom/files/pbn/docs/Fatal-Journeys-Tracking-Lives-Lost-during-Migration-2014.pdf

Massey, D. S., Durand, J., & Pren, K. A. (2016, March). Why border enforcement backfired. *American Journal of Sociology*, 121(5), 1557–1600.

Miroff, N. & Partlow, J. (2014, June 12). Central American migrants overwhelm Border Patrol station in Texas. *The Washington Post*. Retrieved from https://www.washingtonpost.com/world/the_americas/central-american-migrants-overwhelm-border-patrol-station-in-texas/2014/06/12/7359534e-2e1b-4a6b-b010-f622f1cac3f0_story.html

Partlow, J. (2016, January 5). Why El Salvador became the hemisphere's murder capital. *The Washington Post*. Retrieved from https://www.washingtonpost.com/news/worldviews/wp/2016/01/05/why-el-salvador-became-the-hemispheres-murder-capital/

Transactional Records Access Clearinghouse (TRAC). (2014, November 25). *Representation for unaccompanied children in immigration court.* Syracuse, NY: Syracuse University. Retrieved from http://trac.syr.edu/immigration/reports/371/

United Nations High Commissioner for Refugees (UNHCR). (2014, March). *Children on the run*. Washington, DC: UNHCR Regional Office for the United States and the Caribbean. Retrieved from http://www.unhcrwashington.org/children

U.S. Border Patrol. (2015). *Juvenile (0–17 years old) and adult apprehensions—fiscal year 2015* (October 1–September 30). Washington, DC: Customs and Border Protection. Retrieved from https://www.cbp.gov/sites/default/files/documents/USBP%20Stats%20FY2015%20sector%20profile.pdf

U.S. Border Patrol. (2016). *U.S. Border Patrol total monthly UAC apprehensions by sector* (FY 2010–FY 2016 to date through January). Washington, DC: Customs and Border Protection. Retrieved from http://www.cbp.gov/sites/default/files/documents/BP%20Total%20Monthly%20UACs%20by%20Sector%2C%20FY10-FY16TD-Jan.pdf

U.S. Citizenship and Immigration Services (USCIS). (2015, November 12). *Refugees & asylum*. USCIS. Retrieved from https://www.uscis.gov/humanitarian/refugees-asylum

Washington Office on Latin America (WOLA). (2014, June 10). *Three myths about Central American migration to the United States*. Washington, DC: WOLA. Retrieved from http://www.wola.org/commentary/3_myths_about_central_american_migration_to_the_us

Zong, J., & Batalova, J. (2016, April 14). *Frequently requested statistics on immigrants and immigration in the United States*. Washington, DC: Migration Policy Institute. Retrieved from http://www.migrationpolicy.org/print/15611#.Vx5rvY-cFMs

4

❖

Assimilation, Education, and Social Programs

Q18. DO IMMIGRANTS TO THE UNITED STATES GENERALLY MAKE AN EFFORT TO ASSIMILATE AND LEARN ENGLISH?

Answer: Yes. Contrary to the statements of many politicians, immigrants throughout U.S. history have as a whole assimilated thoroughly into U.S. culture, particularly by the second and third generations.

The Facts: Contemporary political immigration debate is rife with references to the lack of assimilation of newcomers.

While discussing the process of vetting of Muslim immigrants to the United States, presidential candidate Donald Trump asserted, "Assimilation has been very hard. It's almost—I won't say nonexistent, but it gets to be pretty close . . . for some reason, there's no real assimilation" (Farley, 2016).

Louisiana Governor Bobby Jindal went even further in implying that immigrants do not fully assimilate, stating "Immigration without assimilation is invasion. We need to insist people that want to come to our country should come legally, should learn English and adopt our values, roll up their sleeves, and get to work" (Kaplan, 2015).

And former vice presidential candidate Sarah Palin voiced her opinion about immigrants' need to assimilate during a CNN interview when she stated: "I think we can send a message and say, 'You want to be in America, A, you'd better be here legally or you're out of here. B, when you're here, let's speak American'" (Palin, 2015).

Sentiments negating the willingness of newcomers to adapt to the language and cultural norms of the United States are not limited to conservative politicians and pundits, however. Even before nationhood, prominent leaders were pointing to specific racial or ethnic groups as dangers to the civilized society established on the new continent. Consider the following sentiments, written in 1753 by Benjamin Franklin as he decried the undesirable characteristics of German migrants to the United States:

> Those who come hither are generally of the most ignorant Stupid Sort of their own Nation . . . now they come in droves, and carry all before them, except in one or two Counties; Few of their children in the Country learn English; they import many Books from Germany . . . the Signs in our Streets have inscriptions in both languages, and in some places only German . . . they will soon so out number us, that all the advantages we have will not in My Opinion be able to preserve our language, and even our Government will become precarious. (Franklin, 1753)

American author Kenneth Roberts also wrote harshly in the early 20th century about a perceived lack of assimilation among immigrants. "The United States Immigration Commission proved conclusively that the bulk of the more recent immigrants from Central and Southeastern Europe hived up in settlements of their own, where they retained the customs and the languages and the ideals of the countries from which they came, and failed utterly to become Americans," he wrote. "In the cant phrase of the day, the majority of the more recent immigrants didn't assimilate. An ostrich could assimilate a croquet ball or a cobble-stone with about the same ease that America assimilated her newcomers from Central and Southeastern Europe" (1922, p. 4).

But for all the negative comments addressing immigrants and their inability to adapt to American culture or become somehow fully American, studies indicate that today's newcomers are actually quite well adjusted. Numerous studies have examined English-language acquisition, naturalization rates, homeownership, incomes, and various other demographics of immigrants to measure their success after a number of years in the

United States. By nearly all measures, they had not only done well for themselves but had exceeded expectations in contributing to American life and culture.

Demographer Dowell Myers spent two decades analyzing the progress of immigrants who arrived in the United States between 1985 and 1989. He first looked at census data in 1990 and then again in 2008 to determine how much those immigrants had progressed in cultural and socioeconomic terms. He found that during those 18 years homeownership jumped from 16 to 62 percent (among Latinos it jumped from 9.3 to 58 percent), the number of foreign-born men above the "low-income" income level rose from 35 to 66 percent, and the number of immigrants who chose to become U.S. citizens rose from 7 to 56 percent (Myers & Pitkin, 2010).

The Myers study also found that first-generation immigrants (the parents) do not always gain English-language skills as rapidly as their offspring because of less access to education and learning centers and lack of opportunity (they work long hours to provide for their families), or because classes are not readily available where they live. However, the children of these immigrants bridge the gap, picking up English-language skills quickly (ibid.).

A National Academies of Sciences, Engineering, and Medicine report issued in 2015 also found that "across all measurable outcomes, immigrants and their descendants are integrating into U.S. society" (Waters & Pineau, 2015). The well-being of immigrants in the areas of education, income, English-speaking ability and occupational distribution improved over time, and was generally on par with or exceeding the levels of natives by the third generation. In fact, the only major area in which assimilation lagged was that of earnings among Hispanic immigrants. However, their progress was still positive over time, just not as fast as among other immigrant groups. Authors suggest the slower growth may have to do with the fact that immigrant men with little education are more likely to be employed than comparable native-born men, perhaps implying that the jobs they take are more undesirable, lower-paying jobs that natives do not want (ibid.).

Assimilation, however, is not always a good thing. The Waters and Pineau study also found that immigrant assimilation over time in the areas of crime, health, and divorce rates produced a negative effect for immigrants who, until they fully assimilated, had enjoyed more positive standards of living in these areas. For example, crime rates among young immigrant men start out lower than those of similarly aged native men. By the third generation, however, incarceration rates equal those of natives. Quality of health also declines over generations, and divorce rates and out-of-wedlock birth rates rise.

The Census Bureau reports that in 2012, 44 percent of the foreign-born population over the age of five who had been in the country less than 12 years reported high English-language speaking ability. Among those who had been in the United States for more than 30 years, 63 percent of immigrants had high English-speaking ability (U.S. Census Bureau, 2014). Latino immigrant children show particularly high gains in language acquisition. In 1980, just 43 percent of foreign-born Latino children spoke English at home or spoke it "very well," but by 2013, 70 percent spoke it "very well" (Krogstad, Stepler, & Lopez, 2015). In addition, a different 2013 survey showed that 50 percent of Latino adults who are children of immigrant parents were bilingual, and 35 percent of Hispanic immigrants overall were bilingual (Krogstad & Gonzalez-Barrera, 2015).

Homeownership is another mark of assimilation. Studies have shown that the probability of owning a home increases with immigrants' length of time in the United States, as do other aspects of assimilation. Rates of homeownership among the foreign-born increased from 49.8 percent in 2000 to 52.4 percent in 2010; during that same time period homeownership among native populations decreased (Fannie, 2014).

Finally, some have argued that assimilation does not mean totally abandoning all past cultural practices and adopting 'all things American.' A vibrant political culture in this multicultural society, they say, does not require individuals to abandon their histories but rather to build on them as they learn from and respect their neighbors' building processes as well. Political scientist Robert Putnam once commented that political institutions could help immigrant societies "bridge" with one another, and by doing so "we shall see that the challenge is best met not by making 'them' like 'us,' but rather by creating a new, more capacious sense of 'we'" (2007).

In spite of the language, cultural, and economic barriers immigrants often face upon arriving in the United States, their assimilation rates overall are high. The newcomers' determination to successfully establish a good life for themselves in a new place reflects the sentiments of President Ronald Reagan, who once commented on a letter he had received:

> I received a letter just before I left office from a man. I don't know why he chose to write it, but I'm glad he did. He wrote that you can go to live in France, but you can't become a Frenchman. You can go to live in Germany or Italy, but you can't become a German, an Italian. He went through Turkey, Greece, Japan and other countries. But he said anyone, from any corner of the world, can come to live in the United States and become an American (Reagan, 1990)

FURTHER READING

Fannie Mae (2014, August 25). Homeownership rate gap between immigrants and the native-born population narrowed faster during the last decade. *Fannie Mae Housing Insights*, 4(5). Retrieved from http://www1.fanniemae.com/resources/file/research/datanotes/pdf/housing-insights-082514.pdf

Farley, R. (2016, June 17). Fact check: Trump's baseless assimilation claim. *USA Today*. Retrieved from http://www.usatoday.com/story/news/politics/elections/2016/06/17/fact-check-trump-baseless-assimilation-claim-muslim-immigrants/86051900/

Franklin, B. (1753, May 9). The support of the poor [Letter to Peter Collinson]. Retrieved from http://teachingamericanhistory.org/library/document/letter-to-peter-collinson/

Kaplan, R. (2015, August 30). Bobby Jindal: "Immigration without assimilation is invasion." cbsnews.com. Retrieved from http://www.cbsnews.com/news/bobby-jindal-immigration-without-assimilation-is-invasion/

Krogstad, J. M., & Gonzalez-Barrera, A. (2015, March 24). A majority of English-speaking Hispanics in the U.S. are bilingual. Pew Research Center, Fact Tank. Retrieved from http://www.pewresearch.org/fact-tank/2015/03/24/a-majority-of-english-speaking-hispanics-in-the-u-s-are-bilingual/

Krogstad, J. M., Stepler, R., & Lopez, M. H. (2015, May 12). *English proficiency on the rise among Latinos*. Washington, DC: Pew Research Center, Hispanic Trends. Retrieved from http://www.pewhispanic.org/2015/05/12/english-proficiency-on-the-rise-among-latinos/

Margolin, E., & Sakuma, A. (2015, September 17). Hours before Constitution Day, GOP candidates demonstrate constitutional confusion. MSNBC.com. Retrieved from http://www.msnbc.com/msnbc/hours-constitution-day-gop-candidates-demonstrate-constitutional-confusion

Myers, D., & Pitkin, J. (2010, September). *Assimilation today: New evidence shows the latest immigrants to America are following in our history's footsteps*. Washington, DC: Center for American Progress. Retrieved from https://www.americanprogress.org/wp-content/uploads/issues/2010/09/pdf/immigrant_assimilation.pdf

Palin, S. (2015, September 6). Sarah Palin on state of the Union: Full interview. State of the Union with Jake Tapper. CNN.com. Retrieved from http://www.bing.com/videos/search?q=sarah+palin+cnn+jake+tapper+immigration&view=detail&mid=9E66749BF0F7A1B869BC9E66749BF0F7A1B869BC&FORM=VIRE

Putnam, R. (2007). E Pluribus Unum: Diversity and community in the twenty-first century. The 2006 Johan Skytte Prize lecture. *Scandinavian Political Studies*, 30(2), 137–174.

Reagan, R. (1990, November 19). The brotherhood of man [Speech]. Retrieved from http://www.pbs.org/wgbh/americanexperience/features/primary-resources/reagan-brotherhood/

Roberts, K. L. (1922). *Why Europe leaves home: A true account of the reasons which cause central Europeans to overrun America*. Indianapolis, IN: Bobbs-Merrill Publishers.

U.S. Census Bureau. (2014, June 10). Close to half of new immigrants report high English-language speaking ability, Census Bureau reports (Release Number: CB14-105). Washington, DC: U.S. Census Bureau.

Waters, M. C., & Pineau, M. G. (Eds.). (2015). *The integration of immigrants into American society*. Washington, DC: National Academies of Sciences, Engineering, and Medicine Press.

Q19. DO IMMIGRANTS COMPRISE THE LEAST EDUCATED GROUP OF PEOPLE LIVING IN THE UNITED STATES?

Answer: Actually, the most educated *and* least educated groups of people in the United States are immigrants.

The Facts: According to researchers at the Center for Immigration Studies, an organization that advocates for lower levels of legal immigration, the United States is attracting poor, uneducated immigrants (Camarota, 2015). "Low levels of education—not legal status—are the main reason immigrant welfare use is high," said a preview of the center's 2015 report on immigrant welfare use (Bedard, 2015).

However, that same year, a report from the Pew Research Center stated that recent immigrants are more likely than U.S.-born adults to hold a college degree. In fact, the immigrants coming to the United States today are the most educated in the country's history. The Pew research report found that 41 percent of those who arrived between 2008 and 2013 held a bachelor's degree or higher. In comparison, in 2013 the share of U.S.-born adults with a bachelor's degree was 30 percent (Fry, 2015).

WHAT EXPLAINS THE DISCREPANCY?

Actually, there is not necessarily a discrepancy between the two reports. While it is true that more educated immigrants than ever before are coming to the United States, it is also a fact that nearly a quarter of new arrivals (23 percent) do not have a high school diploma (Fry, 2015). This is actually an improvement since 1970, when the number who had not finished high school was 50 percent (ibid.). And in specified areas, the numbers are even higher. In 2011 in California, 72 percent of all high school dropouts in the state were foreign-born residents (Mejia & Johnson, 2013). Such a variation in numbers illustrates the wide diversity of socio-economic backgrounds among recent immigrants.

Both the high and low educational attainments of today's newcomers are, at least in part, a by-product of immigration policies and legislation since 1965 that have emphasized family reunification and specialized employment.

Historically, a large slice of the immigrant labor pool came from Mexico, where laborers would come north for seasonal work and later return to Mexico when that season of employment was finished. Many of these unauthorized laborers began to settle permanently in the United States in the 1980s and 1990s as militarization of the border made circular migration more difficult (Massey, 2015). Then in 1986, with passage of the Immigration Reform and Control Act (IRCA), 2.7 million unauthorized immigrants were granted legal status (Rytina, 2002). By 2001, one-third had become U.S. citizens, making it possible for them to petition legally for their families to come join them. This development, in combination with legal Mexican migration, led to a large increase in the population from south of the border. In 2013, Mexico was the largest country of origin for U.S. immigrants, with 11.4 million Mexican immigrants in the United States (Gonzalez-Barrera & Lopez, 2013). These immigrants from Mexico, however, tend to have lower educational attainment than the native population. Fifty-nine percent of Mexican immigrants in the United States in 2012 had *not* earned a high school diploma (ibid.).

Since the Great Recession ended in 2009, more Mexicans have actually left the United States than entered it (Gonzalez-Barrera, 2015). In their place are Central American families and children, fleeing violence and poverty in their home countries. While not all come legally and many are not allowed to stay, those who do stay tend to be less educated (Fry, 2015). The same is true of the Mexican immigrants.

At the same time, since the end of the Great Recession, Asian immigration has increased greatly. During much of the U.S.A.'s first two centuries of existence, Asian immigrants were primarily low-skilled, low-wage laborers. Today, however, "Asian Americans are the highest-income, best-educated and fastest-growing racial group in the United States" (Pew Research Center, 2012). More than 61 percent of Asian immigrants aged

25 to 64 have at least a bachelor's degree, and Asians are three times more likely than immigrants from other parts of the world to receive their green card on the basis of employer sponsorship (ibid.). Many have come to work in the high-tech industry; in 2012 Asians made up half of the Silicon Valley workforce (Hall, 2012).

So while the number of Latino immigrants with lower educational levels was declining, the number of Asian immigrants with high educational levels was rising.

Among all immigrants, the U.S. Department of Education found that similar percentages of foreign-born and native-born students had bachelor's degrees in 2007 but that immigrant students made up a lower proportion of students who had attended college but not completed a bachelor's degree (Staklis & Horn, 2012). Educational attainment, however, had significantly improved among second-generation foreign-born populations (ibid.).

One additional irony of the current immigration system's prioritization of family reunification and skilled labor is that many of those who immigrate to join their families in the United States are overeducated for their jobs. Nearly half of all male immigrants to the United States between 1980 and 2009 could not find a job that matched their educational level (Beckhusen et al., 2013). One reason for this immigrant "brain drain" is that many of these workers come on family visas, not work visas, and therefore have not been recruited by a specific employer.

FURTHER READING

Beckhusen, J., Florax, R. J. G. M., Poot, J., & Waldorf, B. S. (2013). Attracting global talent and then what? Overeducated immigrants in the United States. *Journal of Regional Science*, 53, 834–854 (doi:10.1111/jors.12030).

Bedard, P. (2015, September 10). Report: America attracting poor, uneducated immigrants. *The Washington Examiner*. Retrieved from http://www.washingtonexaminer.com/report-america-attracting-poor-uneducated-immigrants/article/2571730

Camarota, S. A. (2015, September). *Welfare use by legal and illegal immigrant households*. Washington, DC: Center for Immigration Studies. Retrieved from http://cis.org/Welfare-Use-Legal-Illegal-Immigrant-Households

Fry, R. (2015, October 5). *Today's newly arrived immigrants are the best-educated ever*. Washington, DC: Pew Research Center, Fact Tank. Retrieved from http://www.pewresearch.org/fact-tank/2015/10/05/todays-newly-arrived-immigrants-are-the-best-educated-ever/

Gonzalez-Barrera, A. (2015, November 19). *More Mexicans leaving than coming to the U.S.* Washington, DC: Pew Research Center, Hispanic Trends. Retrieved from http://www.pewhispanic.org/2015/11/19/more-mexicans-leaving-than-coming-to-the-u-s/

Gonzalez-Barrera, A., & Lopez, M. H. (2013, May 1). *A demographic portrait of Mexican-origin Hispanics in the United States.* Washington, DC: Pew Research Center, Hispanic Trends. Retrieved from http://www.pewhispanic.org/2013/05/01/a-demographic-portrait-of-mexican-origin-hispanics-in-the-united-states/

Hall, S. (2012, November 30). Asians now half of Silicon Valley work force. Itbusinessedge.com. Retrieved from http://www.itbusinessedge.com/blogs/charting-your-it-career/asians-now-half-of-silicon-valley-work-force.html

Massey, D. S. (2015). A missing element in migration theories. *Migration letters*, 12(3). Retrieved from http://tplondon.com/journal/index.php/ml/article/viewFile/568/411

Mejia, M. C., & Johnson, H. (2013, May). Immigrants in California. Public Policy Institute of California, Just the Facts. Retrieved from http://www.ppic.org/main/publication_show.asp?i=258

Pew Research Center. (2012, June 19). *The rise of Asian Americans.* Washington, DC: Pew Research Center, Social & Demographic Trends.

Rumbaut, R. (2015, July 21). Undocumented immigration and rates of crime and imprisonment: Popular myths and empirical realities [The role of local police—appendix D]. *Police Foundation.* Retrieved from http://www.policefoundation.org/publication/the-role-of-local-police-appendix-d/

Rytina, N. (2002, October 25). *IRCA legalization effects: Lawful permanent residence and naturalization through 2001.* Washington, DC: U.S. Immigration and Naturalization Service. Retrieved from https://www.dhs.gov/xlibrary/assets/statistics/publications/irca0114int.pdf

Staklis, S., & Horn, L. (2012, July). *New Americans in postsecondary education: A profile of immigrant and second-generation American undergraduates* [NCES 2012-213]. U.S. Department of Education.

Q20. DO ALL IMMIGRANTS COME TO THE UNITED STATES BECAUSE THEY WANT TO EXPERIENCE THE "AMERICAN DREAM"?

Answer: No. Some immigrants do not choose to come at all; the choice is made for them by their parents or guardians. Others come not for ideological or practical reasons, but because circumstances dictate that they cannot return to their homelands. The unique circumstances and backgrounds of these individuals also merit consideration in discussions about immigrants and their integration into U.S. society.

The Facts: The United States was founded on conflict. The first settlers and first citizens were largely products of discrimination, conflict, stigmatization, or poverty in their home countries. They came seeking new freedoms—opportunities to believe and live in a way that had not been afforded them in Europe. On the other hand, slaves, were brought here by no choice of their own and forced into servitude that offered them little or no opportunity for freedom.

For the men who first settled our nation, coming to this new country meant an opportunity to break free of limiting circumstances and start over in a new place. They sought opportunities to experience religious freedom, to establish trades, and to make a way of life for themselves and their families. Stories of their efforts to forge new paths and create their own success through hard work and determination became synonymous with the notion of shaping the "American dream."

In reality, of course, it was not like that for everyone. Many new arrivals suffered a harsh reality upon reaching 'the land of golden opportunity.' Asians were rejected, as were Italians, Germans, Irish, Mexicans, and people of almost every ethnic and racial background at some point in U.S. history. Catholics experienced discrimination, as did Mormons and Jews (Daniels, 2005). The U.S.A. was a melting pot, but the pot was constantly bubbling with discontent as new groups tried to assimilate to their new homeland.

What most of the country's first citizens had in common, however, was the notion that coming to this new land was better or offered greater opportunity than what they had left behind. There are exceptions, of course, and the story of the slave trade is not to be discounted or overlooked. For most white males, however, America was the land of promise and opportunity.

It is this historical remembrance and ideal that has largely shaped our country's notions of immigration and what it should be. From the time of their first passage, U.S. immigration laws have given preference to newcomers with skills and labor that would strengthen the country's economy. Until 1965, immigration laws also favored Europeans whose cultural backgrounds were similar to those of U.S. citizens. After passage of the Immigration and Nationality Act that year, immigration laws shifted their emphasis from national origin, race, and ancestry to family reunification and skilled labor (Orchowski, 2015).

Current immigration law continues to place a heavy emphasis on family reunification, while still maintaining per-country quotas. Employment preferences and the recruitment of highly skilled workers have also been hallmarks of immigration laws in recent years (U.S. Department of State, n.d.). In many countries immigration visas to the United States are oversubscribed, meaning there are more people applying to come than there are visas available. As of November 2015, there were four and a half million people around the world on waiting lists for family-preference-based visas, and another four and a half million waiting for employment-based visas (U.S. Department of State, 2015). Some countries, like Mexico and the Philippines, have wait times of more than two decades (U.S. Department of State, 2016).

Contemporary discourse about immigration, whether in homes or in the halls of Congress, tends to remain based on the idea that those who come to the United States are eager to arrive—for either work or family purposes or because they wish to experience the same freedom and opportunities that have shaped the country's identity. This is most likely true for the majority of those who arrive, as evidenced in the high immigrant naturalization rates and the ever-lengthening wait lists overseas for immigrant visas.

One aspect of immigration discourse that has been evident in recent years is the notion that poor immigrants or those who enter without legal authorization come because they want to take advantage of welfare or social systems. Politicians and media pundits have argued that too many immigrants drain the funds of U.S. taxpayers because they either don't want to work or find it easier to benefit from government assistance programs, and this line of thinking has found its way into social discourse as well.

Senator Jeff Sessions has also been known for his criticism of immigrant use of welfare programs. He blasted the Obama administration's handling of immigration, saying "Virtually no one is being examined before they enter the country on whether or not they'll . . . immediately begin to depend on government welfare." He continued by stating any immigration reform package "has got to end that" (Foxnews.com, 2013).

In spite of the fact that such generalizations have been proven false, these arguments continue to circulate through the Internet, family discussions, and political circles. This line of thinking is based on the perception that those who come to the United States choose to do so because they see net benefits of doing so. However, by overlooking the unique circumstances that have driven migration from many parts of the globe, such reasoning fails to acknowledge that some immigrants did not make the choice to come to the United States, and others have arrived because they have no other place to go.

One example of such a group is the children who are brought into the United States without authorization by their parents. Thousands such children find themselves in a position of lacking the documents they need to travel, work, and further their educations, and more importantly, live without constant fear of deportation. These children have largely already assimilated into U.S. society. For many, English is the only language they speak and they have never returned to their birth countries. Advocates for these children argue they had no say in whether or not to come to the United States. They have grown up in hiding, or as an underclass in a country that offers them little opportunity to move forward and become productive members of the society. President Obama has tried to offer these children some deportation protection under his Deferred Action for Childhood Arrivals (DACA) program which does not grant legal status, but does allow work permits and temporary relief from immigration enforcement (U.S. Citizenship and Immigration Services, 2016). However, the expansion of this program and a similar program for parents of unauthorized children was blocked by a federal appeals court ruling that declared Obama's actions an overreach of executive power. That court's decision stood after the Supreme Court, in June 2016, deadlocked 4–4 in its ruling on the case.

Additional groups whose unique circumstances prompted their arrival are the Central American families and unaccompanied children who have crossed the border in large numbers since roughly 2011–2012. These individuals are most often referred to as immigrants, but in reality many are asylum seekers who are fleeing horrific violence and extreme poverty in their home countries of Guatemala, El Salvador, and Honduras. (For more information about these groups, see Chapter 7). The differentiation in how they are classified is important, as it is not illegal for an asylum seeker to be in the United States. Also, because they come from non-contiguous countries, even those who do not qualify for asylum cannot be immediately deported. Instead, all who ask for asylum are to be given credible fear interviews or placed in formal court proceedings to determine whether or not they will be allowed to stay.

The general public, however, has tended to classify these families and children as "illegal immigrants," prompted by politicians and media critics who have made references to their arrival in terms such as "immigrant flood" (Unruh, 2014), "endless waves of illegal immigrants" (Winter, 2014), or "an invasion" (Limbaugh, 2015), and have called for their deportation. Many are housed indefinitely in detention centers while they

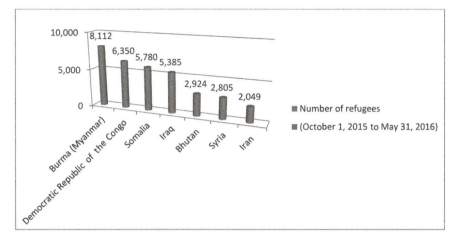

Figure 4.1 Refugees to the United States: seven top countries of origin
Source: Data from Igielnik, R. (2016). *Where refugees to the U.S. come from.* Washington, DC: Pew Research Center, Fact Tank.

await proceedings (see discussion of private prisons and detention centers in Chapter 8). Unaccompanied children are generally released to family members or foster families as they await their court dates. For those who are granted asylum or legal status in the United States, assimilation may be a challenge at first. The unaccompanied children are particularly vulnerable emotionally, as many have experienced trauma that has affected both their emotional and physical health (Fazel et al., 2012). However, mothers and family units who have all witnessed or been subject to such violence face similar challenges. The fact that many have been the targets of anti-immigrant hate speech or have been indefinitely detained while awaiting their court cases exacerbates the trauma they have already experienced and fails to recognize their need for assistance as they try to adapt and move forward.

Likewise, refugees from war-torn nations who arrive in the United States face similar assimilation challenges. Many have been uprooted from their homes by violence and war, and have lived in refugee camps for extended periods of time. The decision to come to the United States is a voluntary one made by the refugee himself or herself, but unlike other immigrant arrivals who control the circumstances of their arrivals, many refugees come because it is unsafe to return to their home countries and they *must* choose a new place to rebuild their lives. In spite of much rhetoric that refugees are not well screened, the application and vetting process is complicated and usually takes 18–24 months or more (U.S. Department of State, 2014). As seen in figure 4.1, the top five countries of origin (in order) for refugees coming to the United States are Burma, the Democratic Republic of the Congo, Somalia, Iraq, and Bhutan (Igielnik, 2016). Many do not speak English and hail from countries and cultures drastically different than the United States. These individuals, because of the trauma they have likely experienced, cultural differences, and lack of control over the circumstances of their situation, will undergo a different process of assimilation than immigrants who come on regular family or employment-based visas.

FURTHER READING

Daniels, R. (2005). *Guarding the golden door*. New York: Hill and Wang Publishers.

Fazel, M., Reed, R. V., Panter-Brick, C., & Stein, A. (2012, January). Mental health of displaced and refugee children resettled in high-income countries: Risk and protective factors. *The Lancet*, 379(9812), 266–282.

FoxNews.com. (2013, February 18). Land of the free? Senator says immigration stats show welfare rules not enforced. FoxNews.com. Retrieved from http://www.foxnews.com/politics/2013/02/18/come-to-us-live-on-dole-senator-says-immigration-stats-show-welfare-rules-not.html

Igielnik, R. (2016, June 17). *Where refugees to the U.S. come from*. Washington, DC: Pew Research Center, Fact Tank. Retrieved from http://www.pewresearch.org/fact-tank/2016/06/17/where-refugees-to-the-u-s-come-from/

Limbaugh, R. (2015, August 19). It's an invasion, not immigration. Rush limbaugh.com. Retrieved from http://www.rushlimbaugh.com/daily/2015/08/19/it_s_an_invasion_not_immigration

Orchowski, M. S. (2015). *The law that changed the face of America: The Immigration and Nationality Act of 1965*. Lanham, MD: Rowan & Littlefield Publishers.

Unruh, B. (2014, June 11). Ex-Border agents: Immigrant flood "orchestrated." *WorldNetDaily*. Retrieved from http://www.wnd.com/2014/06/ex-border-agents-immigrant-flood-orchestrated/#!

U.S. Citizenship and Immigration Services. (2016, January 4). *Consideration of deferred action for childhood arrivals (DACA)*. Washington, DC: Department of Homeland Security. Retrieved from https://www.uscis.gov/humanitarian/consideration-deferred-action-childhood-arrivals-daca

U.S. Department of State. (2014, May 23). *Refugee resettlement in the United States.* Washington, DC: U.S. Department of State. Retrieved from http://www.state.gov/j/prm/releases/factsheets/2014/228681.htm

U.S. Department of State. (2015, November 1). *Immigrant visa statistics: Annual immigrant visa waiting list report as of November 1, 2015.* Washington, DC: U.S. Department of State, Bureau of Consular Affairs. Retrieved from https://travel.state.gov/content/dam/visas/Statistics/Immigrant-Statistics/WaitingListItem.pdf

U.S. Department of State. (2016, June). *Visa bulletin for June 2016.* Washington, DC: U.S. Department of State, Bureau of Consular Affairs. Retrieved from https://travel.state.gov/content/visas/en/law-and-policy/bulletin/2016/visa-bulletin-for-june-2016.html

U.S. Department of State. (n.d.). *The immigrant visa process.* Washington, DC: U.S. Department of State, Bureau of Consular Affairs. Retrieved from https://travel.state.gov/content/visas/en/immigrate/immigrant-process.html

Winter, J. (2014, July 14). Endless wave of illegal immigrants floods Río Grande valley. FoxNews.com. Retrieved from http://www.foxnews.com/us/2014/07/14/night-time-on-border-endless-wave-illegal-immigrants-floods-rio-grande-valley.html

5

Immigration and Crime/Public Safety

Q21. ARE IMMIGRANTS MORE LIKELY TO COMMIT CRIMES THAN NATIVE-BORN U.S. CITIZENS?

Answer: No.

The Facts: Although notions of immigrants being linked to criminality have become commonplace in political discourse, media coverage, and even national policy, such accusations are largely unfounded. Scholarship on the topic spanning decades has overwhelmingly found that immigrants actually show less propensity toward crime than native-born citizens and that immigration can even be considered a factor in the decrease of violent crime in the United States.

Discourse linking immigrants to criminality has been present since the late 1800s, when public debates over the potential criminal nature of the foreign-born in the United States prompted the federal government to first become involved in immigration regulation (Moehling & Piehl, 2009). Both the Dillingham Commission in 1911 and the Wickersham Commission in the early 1930s devoted great time and resources to identifying the links between immigration and crime. Although neither commission found satisfactory evidence indicating the foreign-born had greater propensity toward crime or caused more crime, immigrants continued to be blamed for increasing crime rates (ibid.).

Public policy in the early part of the 20th century was influenced to a large degree by preconceived beliefs about immigrants. It was also developed during an era when eugenics played an influential role in scientific research about the supposed inferiority of certain races. The Johnson–Reed Immigration Restriction Act of 1924 was a product of these beliefs. The act, which banned immigration from Asia and severely limited immigration from Southern Europe, Eastern Europe, and Africa, was passed partly upon the recommendation of Eugenics Record Office director Harry Laughlin, who had testified before the House Committee on Immigration and Naturalization (University of Missouri Libraries, 2012).

Not surprisingly, public perceptions of immigrants as criminals continued throughout the 20th century, often informed by stereotypes and data that have since been dismissed by most of the scientific community. However, the association between immigration and criminality became notably more widespread after the terrorist attacks of September 11, 2001 (Chebel, 2012; Tirman, 2006). In the words of two prominent researchers, the immigrant–crime link "has flourished in a post-9/11 climate of fear and ignorance where terrorism and undocumented immigration often are mentioned in the same breath" (Rumbaut & Ewing, 2007). National security discussions dominated immigration policy after 9/11, leading to the removal of thousands of noncitizens who posed no demonstrated security risk (Chacón, 2007). Immediate government responses to the terrorist attacks included the arrest and detention of over 1,200 Muslim and Arab immigrants, none of which was found to be directly linked to the terrorist attacks (Johnson, 2005). Many detainees were held for weeks without charges; others were charged with minor crimes or held for immigration-related offenses. Public fear of additional terrorist threats also resulted in a surge of violence against persons perceived to be Arab, Muslim, Sikh, and South Asian. Such incidents included the murder of a Pakistani convenience store owner in Texas, the firebombing of a Pakistani restaurant in Salt Lake City, and an attack on a Mosque in Seattle. In fact, the Federal Bureau of Investigation (FBI) reported that in 2001 there was a 1,600 percent increase in anti-Muslim hate crime incidents (Department of Justice, 2011).

Statements made by prominent politicians in the years following the 9/11 attacks also created verbal linkages between immigrants and terrorism. Former Colorado Governor Richard Lamm warned, "One of the most important but most neglected subjects of the new national agenda is the relationship between immigration and terrorism" (2002). Well-known actor and former U.S. Senator Fred Thompson stated in 2007, "Twelve million illegal immigrants later, we are now living in a nation that is beset by people who are suicidal maniacs and want to kill countless innocent men, women and children around the world. . . . We're sitting here now with essentially open borders" (Associated Press, 2007). Fox News channel's Sean Hannity, addressing what he felt was inadequate scrutiny of those entering the United States, stated, "And that is as big a problem as the southern border where somebody wants a job and ISIS has the ability to walk across at will" (Poor, 2015).

Thompson's comments in particular reflect a tendency in political discourse to place unauthorized or "illegal" immigrants squarely at the center of intense debate and distrust. The opening lines of California's Proposition 187 (passed in 1984 and later overturned by a federal court) state, "The people of California . . . have suffered and are suffering personal injury and damage caused by the criminal conduct of illegal aliens in this state" (Proposition 187, 1994). In his 2006 special address to the nation, President George W. Bush stated that illegal immigration, among other things, "brings crime to our communities" (Bush, 2006). This idea that unauthorized immigrants pose a threat to the American public has been reinforced through massive federal expenditures for militarization of the southern U.S. border and increased governmental emphasis on border security since the mid-1990s (Andreas, 2012; Dunn & Palafox, 2007; Payan, 2006; Staudt, Payan, & Kruszewski, 2009).

Media have become podiums for politicians and media personalities who believe immigrants are responsible for rising crime rates and violence in the United States. In 2008 Maricopa County sheriff Joe Arpaio became star of his own reality show based on his aggressive and highly disputed immigration enforcement tactics. Arpaio, known for his hardline opposition to people in the United States without authorization, said "Illegal immigration breeds crime, disease" (Finnegan, 2009). In 2011 a federal judge ordered Arpaio to halt his immigration patrols, citing violation of constitutional rights through racial profiling and illegal detentions of Latinos (Santos, 2013). News anchors have also perpetuated the notion that immigrants are linked with higher rates of crime; in 2007 Lou Dobbs cited immigration and crime links on 94 episodes of *Lou Dobbs Tonight*, and that same year Bill O'Reilly discussed the connection on 66 episodes of *The O'Reilly Factor* (Media Matters, 2008).

Tragedies such as the random fatal shooting of 32-year-old Kathryn Steinle by suspect Juan Francisco López-Sanchez on a San Francisco pier in July 2015 have been used as examples to reinforce these assertions. López-Sanchez, who was in the United States illegally, held seven prior felony convictions and had been previously deported five times to his native Mexico (Melendez, 2015). Other serious crimes committed by immigrants in recent years have received similar widespread attention and have fueled debates and at times outrage over sanctuary city policies, border enforcement, national security, and similar immigrant-related topics.

It is hardly surprising, then, that public perceptions of immigrants seem to mirror widespread political discourse and media coverage linking immigrants to crime. In a 2015 survey, half of U.S. adults responded that when it comes to crime immigrants make American life worse (Pew Research Center, 2015, September 28). Little seems to have changed since 1993 when a *Time* magazine poll showed 59 percent of respondents believed recent immigrants added to the crime problem (Nelan, 1993).

One possible reason for the public's skeptical attitudes toward foreigners is that many citizens have erroneous beliefs about the number of immigrants in the United States. In a study conducted by criminologist Xia Wang of Arizona State University, immigrants (and undocumented immigrants in particular) were consistently perceived as criminal (Wang, 2012). The perception of criminal threat rose in tandem with people's perception of the size of the immigrant community, particularly undocumented immigrant populations. The larger the "illegal immigrant" population was believed to be, the larger the perceived criminal threat. Many study respondents also significantly overestimated the size of undocumented population as over half the overall foreign-born population, when in actuality the number is somewhere around 28 percent (ibid.).

In spite of this long-standing public perception that immigration is connected to increased crime, scientific evidence does not support those claims. In fact, scores of studies over time indicate precisely the opposite—that immigrants are less likely to commit crimes than their native-born counterparts (Bersani, Loughran, & Piquero, 2014; Butcher & Piehl, 2007; Ewing, Martínez, & Rumbaut, 2015). Scholars attribute these results to several factors. First, the process by which immigrants legally apply to come to the United States requires screening for criminal backgrounds. Those with clean records are the most likely to be granted entrance into the United States. Second, immigrants who come to the United States to make a better life for themselves have incentive to be self-disciplined and to avoid wrongdoing in order to succeed in their new environment. Third, immigrants in the United States without authorization have incentives to not commit crimes because doing so increases their likelihood of encountering law enforcement and potentially being deported (Butcher & Piehl, 2008).

However, numbers provide the strongest evidence that immigrants are not more likely than natives to commit crimes. Data indicating lower crime and incarceration rates among immigrants comes from contemporary and historical studies, official crime statistics and victimization surveys since the early 1990s, three decennial (10-year) censuses, national and regional surveys in areas where immigrants are highly concentrated, and investigations by major government commissions during the past century (Rumbaut, 2008). One exception is a study by Jorg Spenkuch that finds a correlation between immigration and higher property crime rates. This study found that a 10 percent increase in the immigrant population led to a property crime rate increase of roughly 1.2 percent. Violent crime rates, however, remained unchanged (2011). Even Spenkuch notes that with the exception of this finding, no other academic research has found a positive link between immigration and higher crime rates. He states, "Almost three quarters of Americans believe immigration increases crime, yet existing academic research has shown no such effect" (2011, p. 1).

Indeed, nearly all of the literature on immigration and crime finds no correlation between the foreign-born and increased crime rates. "The major finding of a century of research on immigration and crime is that . . . immigrants nearly always exhibit lower crime rates than native groups" (Martinez & Lee, 2000, p. 496). Following are examples of some of these findings.

STUDIES USING NEIGHBORHOOD-LEVEL ANALYSIS

- Living in neighborhoods with immigrant concentrated populations was directly associated with lower rates of violence (Sampson, 2008). The study indicates that immigration diversity, whether the immigrants were authorized or unauthorized, is protective against violence. In the words of Harvard sociologist Robert Sampson who conducted the research, "Cities of concentrated immigration are some of the safest places around" (p. 30).
- Crime rates of first- and second-generation immigrants have been found to be lower than those of their native-born peers (Hagan, Levi, & Dinovitzer, 2008). More specifically, in a study involving 3,000 individuals in Chicago who had committed violent crimes, it was found that first-generation immigrants (born outside the United States) were 45 percent less likely to commit violence than third-generation Americans (who are, by place of birth, citizens).

Second-generation immigrants (who are citizens) were 22 percent less likely than third-generation Americans (also citizens) to commit violence (Sampson, 2008).

- In a similar 2014 study, the crime rate among first-generation immigrants aged 12–24 was found to be significantly lower than the overall crime rate. However, by the second generation (American citizens by birth) the crime rate soars, almost catching up to native-born levels (Bersani, 2014). Researchers theorize that through the process of assimilation, second-generation immigrants become as susceptible to temptation and harmful influences as their native peers, resulting in more criminal acts (ibid.).

- A study of Miami, El Paso, and San Diego neighborhoods indicates that immigration does not generally increase homicide levels among Latinos and African Americans (Lee, Martinez, & Rosenfeld, 2001).

STUDIES USING METROPOLITAN-LEVEL AND NATIONAL ANALYSIS

- In a study examining the relationship between immigration and homicide rates in large cities across the United States, it was found that cities with greater concentrations of immigrant populations had lower homicide rates. The study did find, however, that in regard to gang-related homicides, there was a positive correlation with immigration (Kubrin & Ousey, 2009).

- Broad reductions in violent crime between 1994 and 2004 were partially attributed to increases in immigration (Stowell et al., 2009). This conclusion was reached based on multivariate analyses indicating a decrease in violent crime as metropolitan areas experienced gains in their immigrant populations.

- In California between 2000 and 2005, crime rates fell further in cities with a higher percentage of recent immigrants than they did in cities with a lower share of immigrants. This was especially true of the rate of violent crimes (Butcher & Piehl, 2008).

- Violent crime in the United States *decreased* between 2002 and 2013, according to FBI statistics, and 2013 data shows a 4.4 percent overall decrease from 2012 crime rates (Federal Bureau of Investigation, 2014). During roughly the same time period, the immigrant population in the United States increased by roughly 10 million people (Zong & Batalova, 2015). If immigrants are more likely to commit crimes, it would be expected that the crime rate would rise in correspondence with immigrant populations.

- A study examining how Mexican weather patterns and rainfall affected migration patterns to U.S. cities found that "Mexican immigration is associated with no appreciable change in the rates of either violent or property crimes in U.S. cities" (Chalfin, 2014, p. 1).

INCARCERATIONS AND CRIMINALITY

- According to analysis of 2010 data, approximately 1.6 percent of immigrant males aged 18–39 are incarcerated compared to 3.3 percent of the native-born. Census data demonstrates that this has been true for decades, with native-born incarceration rates being anywhere from two to five times higher than that of immigrants (Ewing, Martínez, & Raumbaut, 2015).

- For every ethnic group without exception, incarceration rates among young men were found to be lowest for immigrants, even those who are the least educated. Researchers found this to be especially true for those who make up the majority of the undocumented population—Mexicans, Salvadorans, and Guatemalans. In 2000, the incarceration rate among men aged 18–39 was five times higher for the native-born than for the foreign-born (Rumbaut & Ewing, 2007).

- Foreign-born persons make up roughly 35 percent of the adult population in California, but only about 17 percent of the adult prison population in the state. In fact, in California native-born adult men have an incarceration rate over two-and-a-half times that of foreign-born men (Butcher & Piehl, 2008). This same study found that when the focus was broadened from prisons to multiple forms of institutionalization (e.g., jails and halfway houses), U.S.-born men aged 18–40 have an institutionalization rate 10 times higher than that of foreign-born men (ibid.).

- Despite the pledge by Jeh Johnson, secretary of Department of Homeland Security, to focus the department's efforts and resources on individuals convicted of serious crimes, two-thirds or more of the persons issued detainers (immigration holds) in April 2015 by local or state police departments on behalf of the Immigration and Customs Enforcement (ICE) agency did not have any type of criminal conviction (Transactional Records Access Clearinghouse, 2015b). In 2012, that number was 50 percent, reflecting an increase in the issuance of detainers to individuals without criminal backgrounds (ibid.).

With so much evidence to the contrary, why, then, do so many politicians and public figures continue to point the finger at immigrants as a source of increased crime? Reasons are varied and complex, but often making such claims focuses attention on a tangible source of blame and away from discussion of failed policies or complex social issues. For example, Barbara Coe who drafted Proposition 187 in California claimed, "You get illegal alien children, Third World children, out of our schools, and you will reduce the violence. That is a fact . . . You're not dealing with a lot of shiny face, little kiddies . . . You're dealing with Third World cultures who come in, they shoot, they beat, they stab and they spread their drugs around in our school system. And we're paying them to do it" (Johnson, 1995). Coe garnered a great deal of support statewide, even though no data was offered in support of her statements.

More recent political rhetoric invoking national security has been based on similarly unsupported claims that draw on the public's post-9/11 fears. Texas Governor Rick Perry, for example, said, "The number of illegal activities up to and including homicides—I think over 3,000 homicides by illegal aliens over the course of the last years; that's unacceptable and that's the reason that we have to secure that border" (Beck, 2014). However, no factual evidence could be found to back up Perry's statement. According to PolitiFact Texas, for this statistic to be true, "one would have to assume illegal immigrants committed nearly half of the state's homicides since 2008; we found no such data" (Selby, 2014).

Misunderstandings based on changing definitions of criminality also add confusion to the statistical pool. Researchers point out that in contemporary discussions about immigration, there are no clear distinctions made between "undocumented migrants, 'criminal aliens,' and individuals who pose threats to national security" (Chacón, 2007, p. 1834). Furthermore, as U.S. immigration policy has evolved, resulting in prosecution of greater numbers of unauthorized immigrants for lesser offenses, the image of the immigrant as a criminal threat has become more pronounced. ICE's definition of a convicted criminal or "criminal alien" has expanded in recent years to include even those immigrants who commit offenses as small as a misdemeanor. Thus, those who commit immigration violations such as illegal entry, defined as a petty offense under the law, now fall under the definition of "criminal alien" (Transactional Records Access Clearinghouse, 2010). Any slight brush with authorities can result in detention, removal, and a ban from returning. Some scholars have called this a "double standard when it comes to consequences for criminal behavior" as the government uses "increasingly stringent definitions and standards of 'criminality' that do not apply to U.S. citizens" (Ewing, Martínez, & Rumbaut, 2015, p. 2).

Broader interpretation of immigrant criminality can create confusion in the interpretation of official reports and documents. For instance, a FY 2013 ICE immigration removal report states that 59 percent of all ICE removals, or 82 percent of all *interior* removals, that year involved individuals previously convicted of a crime (Immigration and Customs Enforcement, 2013). However, a case-by-case analysis of these convictions showed that only 12 percent of deportees had committed a serious (Level 1) offense based on ICE's own definitions of who poses a serious threat to public safety (Transactional Records Access Clearinghouse, 2014). The largest percentage of deportees had no criminal history, followed by those who had committed immigration and traffic violations (ibid.). Those figures are not an anomaly. As figure 5.1 shows, in 2016, over 83 percent of noncitizen deportations were for immigration-related charges or entry without inspection. A mere 2.5 percent of deportations were for aggravated felonies, 0.02 percent for national security charges, and 5.5 percent for other criminal charges (Transactional Records Access Clearinghouse, 2016). Likewise, a *New York Times* analysis of internal government records revealed that between 2009 and 2014 two-thirds of the nearly 2 million deportees had committed only minor infractions, such as traffic violations, or had no criminal record at all (Thompson & Cohen, 2014).

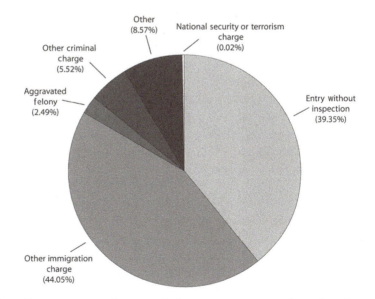

Figure 5.1 Composition of national deportation proceedings by charge, FY2016

Source: Adapted from TRAC Reports, Inc.

Based on a large body of evidence and decades of research, the overwhelming consensus is that immigrants are not more likely to engage in crime than native-born citizens and therefore do not pose a greater threat to public safety than their native counterparts. Current policy approaches targeting immigrants under the guise of public safety are thus based on a false premise of higher-than-average immigrant criminality. On the contrary, evidence of greater propensity toward crime among native-born individuals than among immigrants led one journalist to reflect, "Maybe they should be afraid of us" (Bailey, 2014).

Therefore, while anecdotal stories of heinous crimes committed by individuals who are immigrants are successful in capturing public attention and evoking emotional responses, they are not representative of immigrants as a whole. A century of research concludes that the immigrant presence, if anything, may make communities safer.

FURTHER READING

Andreas, P. (2012). *Border games: Policing the U.S.-Mexico divide*. Ithaca, NY: Cornell University Press.

Associated Press. (2007, May 26). Ex-senator faults '86 law on immigrants. *The New York Times*. Retrieved from http://www.nytimes.com/2007/05/26/us/politics/26thompson.html?_r=0

Bailey, R. (2014, July 11). *Immigrants are less criminal than native-born Americans: Maybe they should be afraid of us*. Reason Foundation: Reason.com. Retrieved from https://reason.com/archives/2014/07/11/immigrants-are-less-criminal-than-native

Beck, G. (2014, July 17). Gov. Rick Perry says Texas may soon take steps to secure the border—with or without the federal government's help. *The Glenn Beck Program* [Talk-show program episode]. Retrieved from http://www.theblaze.com/stories/2014/07/17/gov-rick-perry-says-texas-may-soon-take-steps-to-secure-the-border-with-or-without-the-federal-governments-help/

Bersani, B. (2014, February). A game of catch-up? The offending experience of second-generation immigrants. *Crime & Delinquency*, 60(1), 60–84.

Bersani, B., Loughran, T. A., & Piquero, A. R. (2014, November). Comparing patterns and predictors of immigrant offending among a sample of adjudicated youth. *Journal of Youth and Adolescence*, 43(11), 1914–1933.

Bush, G. W. (2006, May 15). *Immigration and American society: Primetime address to the nation*. Washington, DC. Retrieved from http://www.presidentialrhetoric.com/speeches/05.15.06.html

Butcher, K. F., & Piehl, A. M. (1998). Cross-city evidence on the relationship between immigration and crime. *Journal of Policy Analysis and Management*, 17(3), 457–493.

Butcher, K. F., & Piehl, A. M. (2007, July). Why are immigrants' incarceration rates so low? Evidence on selective immigration, deterrence, and deportation. Cambridge, MA: National Bureau of Economic Research. Retrieved from http://www.nber.org/papers/w13229

Butcher, K. F., & Piehl, A. M. (2008, February). Crime, corrections, and California: What does immigration have to do with it? *California Counts: Population Trends and Profiles*. San Francisco: Public Policy Institute of California.

Chacón, J. M. (2007, July). Unsecured borders: Immigration restrictions, crime control and national security. *Connecticut Law Review*, 39(5), 1827–1891.

Chalfin, A. (2014, Spring). What is the contribution of Mexican immigration to U.S. crime rates? Evidence from rainfall shocks in Mexico. *American Law and Economics Review*, 16(1), 220–268.

Chebel, A. A. (2012). *Frontiers of fear: Immigration and insecurity in the United States and Europe*. Ithaca, NY: Cornell University Press.

Department of Justice. (2011, October 19). *Confronting discrimination in the post-9/11 era: Challenges and opportunities ten years later* [A report on the Civil Rights Division's Post-9/11 Civil Rights Summit]. Washington, DC: George Washington University Law School.

Dunn, T. J., & Palafox, J. (2007, May 4). Militarization of the Border. In S. Oboler & D. J. González (Eds.), *The Oxford Encyclopedia of Latinos and Latinas in the United States*, Vol. 3, (pp. 150–155). New York: Oxford University Press.

Ewing, W. A., Martínez, D. E., & Rumbaut, R. G. (2015, July). *The criminalization of immigration in the United States* [Special report]. Washington, DC: American Immigration Council. Retrieved from http://immigrationpolicy.org/special-reports/criminalization-immigration-united-states

Federal Bureau of Investigation. (2014, November 10). FBI releases 2013 crime statistics. Washington, DC: FBI National Press Office. Retrieved from https://www.fbi.gov/news/pressrel/press-releases/fbi-releases-2013-crime-statistics/

Finnegan, W. (2009, July 20). Sheriff Joe. *The New Yorker*. Retrieved from http://www.newyorker.com/magazine/2009/07/20/sheriff-joe

Fox News Sunday. (2015, October 18). Donald Trump talks taxes, trade, 9/11, and why he takes personal shots at political rivals [Transcript]. Fox News.com. Retrieved from http://www.foxnews.com/transcript/2015/10/18/donald-trump-talks-taxes-trade-11-and-why-takes-personal-shots-at-political/

Hagan, J., Levi, R., & Dinovitzer, R. (2008, February 19). The symbolic violence of the crime-immigration nexus: Migrant mythologies in the Americas. *Criminology and Public Policy, 7*(1), 95–112.

Hagan, J., & Palloni, A. (1999, November). Sociological criminology and the mythology of Hispanic immigration and crime. *Social Problems, 46*(4), 617–632.

Harrison, P. M., & Beck, A. J. (2006, May). Prison and jail inmates at midyear 2005. Bureau of Justice Statistics Bulletin, U.S. Department of Justice. Retrieved from http://www.bjs.gov/content/pub/pdf/pjim05.pdf

Immigration and Customs Enforcement (ICE). (2013). *FY 2013 ICE immigration removals.* Washington, DC: Department of Homeland Security. Retrieved from http://www.ice.gov/doclib/about/offices/ero/pdf/2013-ice-immigration-removals.pdf

Johnson, K. R. (1995, July). Symposium on immigration policy: An essay on immigration politics, popular democracy, and California's proposition 187: The political relevance and legal irrelevance of race. *Washington Law Review, 70*, 629.

Johnson, K. R. (2005, September). The forgotten "repatriation" of persons of Mexican ancestry and lessons for the "war on terror." *Pace Law Review, 26*(1), 1–26.

Kiley, E. (2015, July 15). Graham wrong on 9/11 visas, again. FactCheck .org. Retrieved from http://www.factcheck.org/2015/07/graham-wrong-on-911-visas-again/

Kubrin, C. E., & Ousey, G. C. (2009). Immigration and homicide in urban America: What's the connection? In W. F. McDonald (Ed.), *Immigration, Crime and Justice (Sociology of Crime, Law and Deviance),* Vol. 13 (pp. 7–32). Bingley, UK: Emerald Group Publishing.

Lamm, R. (2002, Spring). Terrorism and immigration. *The Social Contract, 12*(3). Retrieved from http://www.thesocialcontract.com/artman2/pub lish/tsc1203/article_1074_printer.shtml

Lee, M. T., & Martinez, R. (2009). Immigration reduces crime: An emerging scholarly consensus. In W. F. McDonald (Ed.), *Immigration, Crime and Justice (Sociology of Crime, Law and Deviance),* Vol. 13 (pp. 3–16). Bingley, UK: Emerald Group Publishing.

Lee, M. T., Martinez, R., & Rosenfeld, R. (2001). Does immigration increase homicide? *The Sociological Quarterly, 42*(4), 559–580.

Martinez, R., & Lee, M. T. (2000). On immigration and crime. *Criminal Justice 2000.* Retrieved from https://www.ncjrs.gov/criminal_justice2000/vol_1/02j.pdf

Media Matters. (2008, May 21). Fear and loathing in prime time: Immigration myths and cable news. Media Matters Action Network Report.

Retrieved from http://immigrationpolicy.org/sites/default/files/docs/fear-and-loathing.pdf

Melendez, L. (2015, September 4). Undocumented immigrant to face San Francisco murder trial. Abc7news.com. Retrieved from http://abc7news .com/news/undocumented-immigrant-to-face-san-francisco-murder-trial/970116/

Moehling, C., & Piehl, A. M. (2009, November). Immigration, crime, and incarceration in early twentieth-century America. *Demography,* 46(4), 739–763.

Nelan, B. W. (1993, December 2). Not quite so welcome anymore. TIME. Retrieved from http://content.time.com/time/magazine/article/0,9171,9 79734,00.html

Payan, T. (2006). The three U.S.-Mexico border wars: Drugs, immigration, and homeland security. Westport, CT: Praeger Security International.

Pew Research Center. (2015, September 28). Modern immigration wave brings 59 million to U.S., driving population growth and change through 2065. Retrieved from http://www.pewhispanic.org/2015/09/28/ modern-immigration-wave-brings-59-million-to-u-s-driving-popula tion-growth-and-change-through-2065/

Poor, J. (2015, June 2). Coulter on U.S. immigration policy: "Never has a country been transformed like this, never in world history" [Transcript of "Hannity" show]. *Fox News.* Retrieved from http://www.breitbart .com/video/2015/06/02/coulter-on-us-immigration-policy-never-has-a-country-been-transformed-like-this-never-in-world-history/

Proposition 187. (1994). Proposition 187: Text of proposed law. Retrieved from http://kpbs.media.clients.ellingtoncms.com/news/documents/2014/ 10/24/Proposition_187_.pdf

Rumbaut, R. G. (2008, August). Undocumented immigration and rates of crime and imprisonment: Popular myths and empirical realities. Invited address to the "Immigration Enforcement and Civil Liberties: The Role of Local Police" National Conference, August 21–22, 2008. Washington, DC: Police Foundation. Retrieved from http://ssrn.com/ abstract=1877365

Rumbaut, R. G., & Ewing, W. A. (2007). *The myth of immigrant criminality and the paradox of assimilation: Incarceration rates among native and foreign-born men.* Immigration Policy Center Special Report. Washington, DC: American Immigration Law Foundation.

Sabol, W. J., & Couture, H. (2008, June). Prison inmates at midyear 2007. Bureau of Justice Statistics Bulletin, U.S. Department of Justice. Retrieved from http://www.bjs.gov/content/pub/pdf/pim07.pdf

Sabol, W. J., Minton, T. D., & Harrison, P. M. (2007, June). Prison and jail inmates at midyear 2006. Bureau of Justice Statistics Bulletin, U.S. Department of Justice. Retrieved from http://www.bjs.gov/content/pub/pdf/pjim06.pdf

Sampson, R. J. (2008, Winter). Rethinking crime and immigration. *Contexts*, 7(1), 28–33.

Santos, F. (2013, May 24). Judge finds violations of rights by sheriff. *The New York Times*. Retrieved from http://www.nytimes.com/2013/05/25/us/federal-judge-finds-violations-of-rights-by-sheriff-joe-arpaio.html?_r=0

Selby, W. G. (2014, July 23). Rick Perry claim about 3,000 homicides by illegal immigrants not supported by state figures. PolitiFact Texas. Retrieved from http://www.politifact.com/texas/statements/2014/jul/23/rick-perry/rick-perry-claim-about-3000-homicides-illegal-immi/

Spenkuch, J. (2011, June 5). Understanding the impact of immigration on crime. *American Law and Economics Review*, 16(1), 177–219.

Staudt, K. A., Payan, T., & Kruszewski, Z. A. (2009). *Human rights along the U.S.-Mexico border: Gendered violence and insecurity*. Tucson: University of Arizona Press.

Stowell, J. I., Messner, S. F., McGeever, K. F., & Raffalovich, L. E. (2009). Immigration and the recent violent crime drop in the United States: A pooled, cross-sectional time-series analysis of metropolitan areas. *Criminology*, 47(3), 889–928.

Tate, K. (2014, July 21). Dewhurst: One fourth of illegals apprehended at border have criminal records. Breitbart.com. Retrieved from http://www.breitbart.com/Texas/2014/07/21/Dewhurst-One-Fourth-of-Apprehended-Illegals-at-Border-Are-Criminals/

Thompson, G., & Cohen, S. (2014, April 6). More deportations follow minor crimes, records show. *The New York Times*. Retrieved from http://www.nytimes.com/2014/04/07/us/more-deportations-follow-minor-crimes-data-shows.html?_r=0

Tirman, J. (2006, July 28). Immigration and insecurity: Post 9/11 fear in the United States. Social Science Research Council. Retrieved from http://borderbattles.ssrc.org/Tirman/

Transactional Records Access Clearinghouse (TRAC). (2010, February 11). *Detention of criminal aliens: What has Congress bought?* TRAC Immigration. Syracuse, NY: Syracuse University. Retrieved from http://www.trac.syr.edu/immigration/reports/224/index.html

Transactional Records Access Clearinghouse (TRAC). (2014, April 8). *Secure communities and ICE deportation: A failed program?* TRAC Immigration. Syracuse, NY: Syracuse University. Retrieved from http://trac.syr.edu/immigration/reports/349/

Transactional Records Access Clearinghouse (TRAC). (2015a, August). *Nature of charge in new filings seeking removal orders through August 2015.* TRAC Immigration. Syracuse, NY: Syracuse University. Retrieved from http://trac.syr.edu/phptools/immigration/charges/apprep_newfiling_charge.php

Transactional Records Access Clearinghouse (TRAC). (2015b, August 28). *Further decrease in ICE detainer use: Still not targeting serious criminals.* TRAC Immigration. Syracuse, NY: Syracuse University. Retrieved from http://trac.syr.edu/immigration/reports/402/

Transactional Records Access Clearinghouse (TRAC). (2016). Figure 2. *Composition of National Deportation Proceedings by Charge, FY2016.* TRAC Immigration. Syracuse, NY: Syracuse University. Retrieved from http://trac.syr.edu/phptools/immigration/charges/apprep_newfiling_charge.php

University of Missouri Libraries. (2012, March 16). *Controlling heredity: The American eugenics crusade: 1870–1940* [Web site section on eugenics and immigration]. Retrieved from https://library.missouri.edu/exhibits/eugenics/immigration.htm

Wang, X. (2012). Undocumented immigrants as perceived criminal threat: A test of the minority threat perspective. *Criminology,* 50(3), 743–776.

Zong, J., & Batalova, J. (2015, February 26). *Frequently requested statistics on immigrants and immigration in the United States.* Washington, DC: Migration Policy Institute. Retrieved from http://www.migrationpolicy.org/article/frequently-requested-statistics-immigrants-and-immigration-united-states/

Q22. HOW DO CRIME RATES ALONG THE U.S.-MEXICO BORDER COMPARE TO THE REST OF THE UNITED STATES?

Answer: They are generally lower.

The Facts: In spite of media portrayals and public perceptions of border cities and areas as lawless, crime-ridden places, most statistics indicate lower than average crime rates along the southern U.S. border, particularly for violent crimes. From 2004 to 2011, crime declined significantly along the entire southwestern border (Hansen, 2013). More recent statistics indicate that in at least some of these border cities and states, crime rates continue to either remain lower or decrease faster than regional and national crime rates (McGovern, 2015; Woodworth, 2015).

The U.S.-Mexico border has long been depicted as a territory outside the bounds of proper civilization, where crime is commonplace. In movies throughout the past century, this border has been portrayed as a territory of lawlessness, violence, and illegality, as seen in *Río Bravo* (1959), *Alambrista* (1977), and *El Mariachi* (1992). Music and literature have also contributed to the idea of a wild, lawless border; the lyrics of corridos often revolved around stories of violence and intercultural conflict, and historically inspired novels such as Cormac McCarthy's *Blood Meridian* explore border territories as landscapes of ruthlessness and violence (Linares, 2013). In fact, a *USA Today*/Gallup poll in 2011 showed that 83 percent of Americans believed the rate of violence along the southwestern border was higher than national rates (Gomez, Gillum, & Johnson, 2011).

The image of a crime-ridden border has also been shaped by numerous public figures and politicians. Former Arizona Governor Jan Brewer is well known for decrying immigration-associated violence in her state. During an interview with *The New York Times* magazine, Brewer said border violence originating in Mexico was one of her primary concerns. "As the saying goes, there are lies, damned lies and statistics. Fifty thousand people in Mexico have been murdered. Puerto Peñasco, 60 miles south of our border, just had five people and a police officer killed. That is like part of Arizona, and it is spilling over into our state" (Goldman, 2012).

In 2014, Texas Lieutenant Governor David Dewhurst asserted that a huge criminal element exists along the border and "at least a quarter of those apprehended have criminal records" (Tate, 2014). PolitiFact Texas investigated these statements and found that the number of persons apprehended who have prior U.S. convictions is actually under 5 percent. The investigation also found no available public data regarding the number of criminal convictions in immigrants' countries of origin; Dewhurst also could not provide this data (Selby, 2014).

In June 2014, Texas Governor Rick Perry requested a surge of state law enforcement personnel along the border, stating, "Various crimes directly related to cartels—murder, sexual assault, extortion, child prostitution, home invasion—put Texas citizens' lives at risk and strain the resources of state and local law enforcement and criminal justice systems" (Fitzgerald, 2014). A *Houston Chronicle* analysis of FBI Uniform Crime Reports and 911 call logs of individual police departments revealed that the Río Grande Valley (and south Texas in general) had been experiencing a steady crime reduction that was not significantly affected by the presence of extra law enforcement. In fact, when the surge of enforcement was ordered, the Río Grande Valley serious crime rate was at its lowest level in years (Rosenthal & Collette, 2015). Critics dismissed the findings, saying the FBI Uniform Crime Reporting (UCR) data does not include crimes like kidnapping, money laundering, and drug smuggling that are more common in border areas. However, the 911 call log analysis did include some of those categories and revealed declines as well (ibid.).

Research has shown decreases in violence along the border in recent years, including major border cities such as San Diego and El Paso which have, for years, boasted crime rates lower than the national average (Sampson, 2008). In 2013 in El Paso, the number of both violent crimes and property crimes was lower than the national average (Federal Bureau of Investigation, 2015). The city did see an 80 percent increase in murders in 2014—jumping to 20 from 11 the year before (Aguilar, 2014). In spite of that, however, in 2014 El Paso was once again listed as having the lowest crime rate in the nation for cities larger than 500,000 (CQ Press, 2014). The city has proudly held that designation for a number of years. San Diego also made the list, coming in as the fourth safest city (ibid.). No border cities made the list for highest crime rate, although Houston and Dallas did come in at number 9 and number 10, respectively (ibid.).

In 2011 *USA Today* conducted an analysis of crime reports in four border states. It concluded that cities along the border are statistically safer, on average, than other cities in their respective states, and that violent crime rates along the U.S. side of the border have been falling for years (Johnson & Gomez, 2012). The study also found that of the 13 largest cities in Texas, Arizona, and California closest to the Mexico border, 10 experienced reductions in overall violent crime and 11 saw lower numbers of property crimes. The city of Tucson was one of just a few places that showed an increase in violent crime, but the numbers were so small they were "not noticeable" according to one police spokesperson (ibid.).

Another crime rate analysis for 2013 showed lower than national average overall crime rates for the border cities of San Diego, Brownsville, and El Paso (Citi-data, 2013a, b, e). Rates were slightly higher than average for Laredo and well above the national average for Tucson (Citi-data, 2013c, f). However, that is not a new trend. Tucson has been above the national average ever since at least 2001. Another city close to the border, Las Cruces, New Mexico, has higher than national average property crime rates, but data over 13 years show that overall crime has decreased in that city (Citi-data 2013d). In 2012, violent crime rates were lower in Las Cruces than in the rest of New Mexico (CityRating.com, 2012).

Violent crime in particular tends to be lower in immigrant-heavy populations. A federal report found that from 2004 to 2011 violent crime dropped 33 percent in border counties in Arizona and 22 percent in non-border counties (Hansen, 2013). While the violent crime rate dropped, it was still higher in Arizona's border counties than throughout the rest of the state, seeming to support Governor Brewer's concerns about spillover violence (ibid.). In the other three border states, however, violent crime was lower in border counties than in nonborder counties. The Government Accountability Office report does acknowledge limitations to the data collected, including the fact that Uniform Crime Reports used to analyze crime rates do not include crimes associated with Mexican drug-trafficking organizations, certain types of kidnappings, or home invasions (Government Accountability Office, 2013).

In rankings of the major U.S. cities with the highest murder rates, no cities along the U.S.-Mexico border made the list (Abbey-Lambertz, 2014). A study by Kubrin and Ousey found in 2009 that cities with higher immigrant concentrations had lower homicide rates. They did, however, find a positive correlation between immigration and gang-related homicides (Kubrin & Ousey, 2009).

Conservative news outlets have argued that most studies use FBI Uniform Crime Report data that does not include all crime indicators found along the border, but some of the studies have recognized that and conducted independent research to fill in the gaps. That research, too, points to lower than average crime rates along the border. Judicial Watch observed that the five U.S. federal court districts nearest the Mexico border see the most federal crime convictions. However, this makes sense, as persons caught trying to enter the United States by crossing the border without permission are tried, convicted, and deported in an area relatively close to where they were apprehended. Judicial Watch noted that over 38 percent of all federal cases are for immigration crimes (Tate, 2014).

Contrary to political rhetoric and popular belief, most evidence points to lower than average crime rates along the border region. However, because of the nature of record-keeping and omission of certain crimes in the FBI uniform crime reports of these areas, possible exceptions to this trend include drug-related offenses, human smuggling/kidnapping, money laundering, and gang-related homicides in some cities. One major example of this is the fact that FBI uniform crime reports did not compile or include data about human trafficking until 2013 (FBI, 2013). Even after this category was added to crime reports, participation rates were low among many state agencies during the first year, making analysis of offenses difficult. However, border areas have historically been the sites of many human trafficking offenses, as smugglers take advantage of would-be migrants seeking passage into the United States. To illustrate, between 2012 and 2016, human trafficking incidents rose each year in all four states along the U.S.-Mexico border, with the exception of a slight decline in

Texas between 2014 and 2015 (National Human Trafficking Resource Center, 2016). Therefore, while it is still difficult to determine how these rates compare with other states due to incomplete data, there is no doubt that human trafficking is a major issue in border states like Texas that have seen offense rates rise in recent years.

In spite of these exceptions, the mayor of Nogales, Arizona says the border is a safe place to live, pointing out that even when violence in Mexico's border states has increased, reports of crime along the U.S. border have decreased. "There has been a creation of a culture of fear," he said, "from people north of us" (Hansen, 2013).

FURTHER READING

Abbey-Lambertz, K. (2014, November 12). These are the major U.S. cities with the highest murder rates, according to the FBI. *The Huffington Post*. Retrieved from http://www.huffingtonpost.com/2014/11/12/high est-murder-rate-us-cities-2013_n_6145404.html

Aguilar, J. (2014, December 17). Murders up, but El Paso still safe, lawmakers say. *The Texas Tribune*. Retrieved from http://www.texastribune .org/2014/12/17/el-paso-still-safe-despite-murders-lawmakers-say/

Citi-data. (2013a). Crime rate in Brownsville, TX. Citi-data.com. Retrieved from http://www.city-data.com/city/Brownsville-Texas.html#b

Citi-data. (2013b). Crime rate in El Paso, TX. Citi-data.com. Retrieved from http://www.city-data.com/city/El-Paso-Texas.html#b

Citi-data. (2013c). Crime rate in Laredo, TX. Citi-data.com. Retrieved from http://www.city-data.com/city/Laredo-Texas.html#b

Citi-data. (2013d). Crime rate in Las Cruces, NM. Citi-data.com. Retrieved from http://www.city-data.com/city/Las-Cruces-New-Mexico.html#b

Citi-data. (2013e). Crime rate in San Diego, CA. Citi-data.com. Retrieved from http://www.city-data.com/city/San-Diego-California.html#b

Citi-data. (2013f). Crime rate in Tucson, AZ. Citi-data.com. Retrieved from http://www.city-data.com/city/Tucson-Arizona.html#b

CityRating.com. (2012). Las Cruces crime rate report (New Mexico). Retrieved from http://www.cityrating.com/crime-statistics/new-mexico/ las-cruces.html

CQ Press. (2014). City crime rankings 2014. SAGE Publications. Retrieved from http://os.cqpress.com/citycrime/2013/2014_CityCrime RankingsbyPopulation.pdf

Federal Bureau of Investigation (FBI). (2013). Human trafficking in the uniform crime reporting (UCR) program. Retrieved from https://ucr.fbi .gov/human-trafficking

Federal Bureau of Investigation. (2015). Property crime rate (city) *SAGE stats* [Web site]. Washington, DC: Department of Justice. Retrieved from http://data.sagepub.com/sagestats/document.php?id=6353

Fitzgerald, S. (2014, June 19). Gov. Perry says Texas can't wait for feds, orders border "surge." Newsmax.com. Retrieved from http://www.newsmax.com/US/Texas-illegal-immigrants-Rick-Perry/2014/06/19/id/578088/

Goldman, A. (2012, August 24). Jan Brewer on madmen and mowing lawns. *The New York Times*. Retrieved from http://www.nytimes.com/2012/08/26/magazine/jan-brewer.html?_r=0

Gomez, A., Gillum, J., & Johnson, K. (2011, July 18). U.S. border cities prove havens from Mexico's drug violence. *USA Today*. Retrieved from http://usatoday30.usatoday.com/news/washington/2011-07-15-border-violence-main_n.htm

Government Accountability Office (GAO). (2013, February). *Southwest border security: Data are limited and concerns vary about spillover crime along the Southwest border* (GAO-13-175). Washington, DC: GAO. Retrieved from http://www.gao.gov/assets/660/652320.pdf

Hansen, R. J. (2013, February 26). Crime drops along U.S.-Mexico border. *The Arizona Republic*. Retrieved from http://www.azcentral.com/news/articles/20130226us-mexico-border-crime-drops.html

Johnson, K., & Gomez, A. (2012, November 4). Violent crimes drop overall in U.S. border cities. *USA Today*. Retrieved from http://www.usatoday.com/story/news/nation/2012/11/04/violent-crimes-drop-overall-in-us-border-cities/1681821/

Kubrin, C. E., & Ousey, G. C. (2009). Immigration and homicide in urban America: What's the connection? In W. F. McDonald (Ed.), *Immigration, Crime and Justice* (*Sociology of Crime, Law and Deviance*), Vol. 13 (pp. 7–32). Bingley, UK: Emerald Group Publishing.

Lee, M. T., Martinez, R., & Rosenfeld, R. (2001). Does immigration increase homicide? *The Sociological Quarterly*, 42(4), 559–580.

Linares, G. V. (2013). "This world must touch the other": Crossing the U.S.-Mexico border in American novels and television. University of Nebraska—Lincoln, Dissertations and Theses, Department of English. Paper 78. Retrieved from http://digitalcommons.unl.edu/cgi/viewcontent.cgi?article=1086&context=englishdiss

McGovern, M. (2015, October 9). Congressman Cuellar announces FBI crime stats for Texas Border Region. KGNS.tv. Retrieved from http://www.kgns.tv/home/headlines/border-murder-331752061.html

National Human Trafficking Resource Center. (2016). Find stats from your state. Retrieved from https://traffickingresourcecenter.org/

Rosenthal, B. M., & Collette, M. (2015, May 22). Image of violent Texas border is false, statistics show. *Houston Chronicle*. Retrieved from http://www.houstonchronicle.com/news/houston-texas/houston/article/Image-of-violent-Texas-border-is-false-6282006.php

Sampson, R. J. (2008, Winter). Rethinking crime and immigration. *Contexts*, 7(1), 28–33.

Selby, W. G. (2014, August 29). Unsupported claim: 1 in 4 apprehended border crossers have criminal convictions. PolitiFact Texas. Retrieved from http://www.politifact.com/texas/statements/2014/aug/29/david-dewhurst/unsupported-claim-1–4-apprehended-border-crossers-/

Tate, K. (2014, August 6). DOJ: Regions near Mexico border most crime ridden in U.S. Breitbart California. Retrieved from http://www.breitbart.com/texas/2014/08/06/doj-regions-near-mexico-border-most-crime-ridden-in-us/

Violent crime rate (city) (2013). (2015). *SAGE stats* [Web site]. Washington, DC: CQ Press. Retrieved from http://data.sagepub.com/sagestats/document.php?id=6333

Woodworth, W. (2015, September 30). Maricopa County crime rate drops, outpacing national decline. *The Arizona Republic*. Retrieved from http://www.azcentral.com/story/news/local/arizona/breaking/2015/09/30/maricopa-county-crime-rate-drops-outpacing-national-decline/73101092/

Q23. ARE INDIVIDUALS WHO ENTER THE UNITED STATES ILLEGALLY OR THOSE WHO ENTER LEGALLY BUT OVERSTAY THEIR VISAS REGARDED BY THE U.S. JUSTICE SYSTEM AS CRIMINALS?

Answer: Illegal entry is regarded as a criminal act, but some circumstances are regarded as misdemeanors while others are felonies. Immigrants who overstay legally sanctioned visits, meanwhile, are subject to civil rather than criminal law.

The Facts: Individuals who have physically crossed into the United States without inspection or authorization have committed a misdemeanor (and, as such, a criminal act) under 8 United States Code Section 1325, punishable by a fine and up to six months in prison. Illegal reentry after a previous removal, however, is a felony that carries with it fines, up to two years in prison, and possible permanent barring from reentry. Therefore, both instances of entering the United States without proper authorization are criminal acts—one legally viewed as less serious than the other. While border-crossers were once likely to be quickly returned to Mexico, federal officials have placed greater emphasis in recent years on criminal prosecution of such violators, ensuring that a second attempt to reenter will result in a felony conviction. This also means that more "criminals" are entering the United States, but for many their only prior criminal act was trying to cross the border without legal papers.

In contrast, those who are already present in the United States but have overstayed their authorized periods of admission are in violation of civil, not criminal, laws. Experts largely agree that somewhere around 40 percent of all those unlawfully present in the United States were people who entered lawfully but overstayed visas (Selby, 2013). In 2005 Congress did consider making unlawful presence a felony through passage of the Sensenbrenner Bill (H.R. 4437), but the legislation was rejected by the Senate. Therefore, unlawful presence in the United States, in and of itself, is a civil violation, punishable by deportation and possible bars from reentry (depending on the length of stay in the United States). Overstaying by 180 to 365 days results in a three-year bar from reentry. Overstaying by more than 365 days results in a 10-year bar from reentry (Temple University, n.d.).

Another way to interpret the aforementioned questions is to ask whether the people entering (or remaining in) the United States have criminal backgrounds or propensities toward criminal behavior. Statements made by a number of media personalities and politicians would indicate this is the case. For example, Donald Trump generated both controversy and popularity during a speech announcing his 2016 presidential bid by stating, "When Mexico sends its people, they're not sending their best. . . . They're bringing drugs, they're bringing crime, they're rapists. And some, I assume, are good people" (Trump, 2015, June 16).

While discussing the "Gang of 8" bill during an interview with Newsmax, Iowa Representative Steve King said not all children of illegal immigrants are deserving of a chance at amnesty. "For every one who's a valedictorian there's another 100 out there who, they weigh 130 pounds and they've got calves the size of cantaloupes because they're hauling 75 pounds of marijuana across the desert" (Beamon & Bachman, 2013).

Those statements are not supported by empirical evidence. While there are individuals in the United States unlawfully who have engaged in criminal behavior (or who continue to engage in criminal behavior once in the United States), blanket statements portraying all such immigrants as criminals are erroneous. Research has continuously indicated lower crime rates among all immigrants—both legal and unauthorized.

In addition to the literature examining crime rates, detention and deportation statistics point to lower criminal activity among the foreign-born. Consider the following:

- The majority of immigrants (both legal and unauthorized) detained by ICE between 2005 and 2009 had no prior criminal conviction (Transactional Records Access Clearinghouse, 2010).
- During fiscal year 2014, ICE removed 177,960 undocumented immigrants who had previously been convicted of a crime. This made up 56 percent of all ICE removals that year (U.S. Immigration and Customs Enforcement, 2014). Of those, 85 percent of the interior removals (or 86,923 persons) were removals of persons previously convicted of a crime (ibid.). It is important to note, however, that while the variety of crimes committed by these immigrants ranges widely, not all are violent crimes. In recent years, a broadening of ICE's interpretation of criminality has also had a major impact on criminal immigrant data, greatly inflating the numbers of reported "criminals" inside the United States. According to the 2014 ICE Enforcement and Removal Operations Report, "These individuals include recent border crossers, immigration fugitives, and repeat immigration violators" (U.S. Immigration and Customs Enforcement, 2014). This definition of criminality lumps together violent crimes, traffic violations, and unauthorized border-crossers. Thus, while 85 percent of 2014 interior removals were persons with a criminal record, their only crime may have been an immigration violation. A Transactional Records Access Clearinghouse (TRAC) analysis of the charges filed in deportation proceedings in 2014 supports this. That year, 86 percent of the charges were for entry without inspection or other immigration matters, while the remaining 14 percent pertained to other criminal charges (Transactional Records Access Clearinghouse, 2014).
- A September 2015 report by the Migration Policy Institute shows that the majority of immigrants who are deported do not have a criminal background. According to the report, "Ninety-five percent of child deportees and 61 percent of adult deportees had never been convicted of a crime" (Dominguez Villegas & Rietig, 2015).
- A study of migrants deported to the Northern Triangle (the Central American countries of El Salvador, Guatemala, and Honduras) found that most deportees with criminal records had been convicted of exclusively nonviolent crimes, particularly entry without inspection or other immigration-related offenses (Dominguez Villegas &

Rietig, 2015). Of those with criminal convictions who were deported from the United States to the Northern Triangle, well over half (63 percent) had been convicted of immigration or traffic offenses or other nonviolent crimes. This is in contrast to 29 percent of deportees with criminal convictions found guilty of committing violent offenses (or 11 percent of *all* deportees when considering that 61 percent of deportees to the Northern Triangle had no prior criminal conviction) and 9 percent of deportees with criminal convictions (or 3 percent of all deportees) found guilty of drug offenses. (ibid.)

One final interpretation of the question involves the controversy that has arisen from use of linguistic terms linking immigrants to criminality. Words like "illegal immigrant," "illegal alien," "criminal alien," and "illegal" as a stand-alone noun have become customary in national immigration discourse, but those designations have been criticized in recent years by numerous media agencies and politicians who view them as dehumanizing and inaccurate. For example, a child brought to the United States by a parent without authorization has himself or herself not committed a conscious act of immigration (Costantini, 2013). Although many of these terms originally came from legal immigration documents and continue to be widely circulated, some politicians and news agencies have chosen to drop their use because of the negative connotations that imply all immigrants are criminals. Supreme Court justice Sonia Sotomayor commented that labeling immigrants criminals seemed insulting because "people then paint those individuals as something less than worthy human beings and it changes the conversation" (Associated Press, 2014).

In 2013 the Associated Press (AP) dropped use of the phrase "illegal immigrant" from its stylebook, emphasizing the desire for accuracy in describing the vast number of circumstances that might result in unauthorized status as well as a broad shift toward labeling behavior instead of people (Associated Press, 2013). The AP stylebook is the most widely used in the United States; consequently, a number of other news agencies, including *The New York Times*, also revised its policies regarding usage of these terms (Sullivan, 2013).

FURTHER READING

Associated Press. (2013, April 2). Reviewing the use of "illegal immigrant." AP. Retrieved from http://www.ap.org/Content/Press-Release/2012/Reviewing-the-use-of-illegal-immigrant

Associated Press. (2014, February 4). Sotomayor: Labeling illegal immigrants criminals is insulting. CBSDC. Retrieved from http://washington.cbslocal.com/2014/02/04/sotomayor-labeling-illegal-immigrants-criminals-is-insulting/

Beamon, T., & Bachman, J. (2013, July 23). Rep. Steve King slams Norquist over attacks on immigration [Video podcast]. Retrieved from http://www.newsmax.com/Newsfront/king-norquist-attacks-immigration/2013/07/18/id/515882/

Costantini, C. (2013, April 2). Associated Press drops "illegal immigrant" from stylebook. Abcnews.com. Retrieved from http://abcnews.go.com/ABC_Univision/press-drops-illegal-immigrant-standards-book/story?id=18862824

Dominguez Villegas, R., & Rietig, V. (2015, September). *Migrants deported from the United States and Mexico to the Northern Triangle: A statistical and socioeconomic profile.* Washington, DC: Migration Policy Institute. Retrieved from http://www.migrationpolicy.org/research/migrants-deported-united-states-and-mexico-northern-triangle-statistical-and-socioeconomic

FindLaw. (2015). Illegal reentry into the U.S. after removal: Crime and punishment. Retrieved from http://immigration.findlaw.com/deportation-removal/illegal-reentry-into-the-u-s-after-removal-crime-and-punishment.html

Selby, W. G. (2013, September 6). John Carter claim that 40 percent of nation's illegal residents came by plane and overstayed visas draws on 2006 estimate. PolitiFact Texas. Retrieved from http://www.politifact.com/texas/statements/2013/sep/06/john-carter/john-carter-claim-40-percent-nations-illegal-resid/

Sullivan, M. (2013, April 2). The Times, too, is reconsidering the term "Illegal immigrant." *The New York Times.* Retrieved from http://publiceditor.blogs.nytimes.com/2013/04/02/the-times-too-is-reconsidering-the-term-illegal-immigrant/?smid=tw-share&_r=0

Temple University. (n.d.). Visa overstay and illegal presence in the U.S. Temple University International Student and Scholar Services. Retrieved from http://www.temple.edu/isss/immigration/overstay.html

Transactional Records Access Clearinghouse. (2010, February 11). *Detention of criminal aliens: What has Congress bought?* Syracuse, NY: Transactional Records Access Clearinghouse, Syracuse University. Retrieved from http://trac.syr.edu/immigration/reports/224/index.html

Transactional Records Access Clearinghouse (TRAC). (2014). *U.S. deportation proceedings in immigration courts* [2014]. TRAC Immigration.

Syracuse, NY: Syracuse University. Retrieved from http://trac.syr.edu/
phptools/immigration/charges/deport_filing_charge.php

Trump, D. (2015, June 16). Donald Trump FULL SPEECH: 2016 Presi-
dential campaign announcement June 16 at Trump Tower, New York
[Video file]. Retrieved from https://www.youtube.com/watch?v=0XXc
Pl4T55I

U.S. Government Publishing Office. (n.d.). *8 U.S.C. 1325—Improper entry
by alien, 8 U.S.C. 1326—Reentry of removed aliens.* Washington, DC: U.S.
GPO. Retrieved from http://www.gpo.gov/fdsys/granule/USCODE-2011-
title8/USCODE-2011-title8-chap12-subchapII-partVIII-sec1325

U.S. Immigration and Customs Enforcement. (2014, December 19). ICE
enforcement and removal operations report; fiscal year 2014. U.S.
Department of Homeland Security. Retrieved from https://www.ice
.gov/doclib/about/offices/ero/pdf/2014-ice-immigration-removals.pdf

Q24. HAVE IMMIGRANTS BEEN FOUND TO BE THE SOURCE OF RECENT DISEASE OUTBREAKS IN THE UNITED STATES?

Answer: No. While travel can certainly facilitate the spread of disease,
the incidence of infectious disease has not been found to be any greater
among immigrant populations than in the native-born U.S. population.
The majority of the highly publicized measles outbreaks in 2014, for
example, were traced to U.S. citizens who had traveled abroad, become
infected, and then spread the disease within U.S. borders. In many cases,
overall vaccination rates for measles and other communicable diseases in
Latin America (the region from which the majority of immigrants have
traditionally come into the United States) are equal to or higher than
those in the United States.

The Facts: The linking of immigrants to disease and public health
threats is not a new phenomenon. Throughout U.S. history various ethnic
immigrant groups have been falsely accused of importing and/or spreading disease within the United States. For example, cholera was said to
have been brought by the Irish, tuberculosis by the Jews, polio by the Italians, and bubonic plague by the Chinese (Kraut, 2004; Oshinsky, 2006).
Greeks, Syrians, Italians, Mediterraneans, Asians, and East European Jews
were all targeted as carriers of trachoma (Markel, 2000).

It is true that some immigrant hopefuls were in fact denied entry
because of diseases brought from their home countries or contracted en

route on overcrowded, unsanitary immigrant ships. Public health officials were particularly fearful of deadly contagious diseases like tuberculosis, which affected 70 to 90 percent of urban populations in Europe and North America in the late 1800s and early 1900s (Harvard, 2016). Even healthy would-be immigrants were subjected to these devastating diseases as they journeyed in tightly packed passenger quarters to the United States. Overall, however, the number of individuals turned back by Public Health Service officials was relatively small (less than 1 percent of new arrivals in the late 19th century). Those who were denied entry were not always the source of dangerous communicable diseases, but were certified by public health officials to have varicose veins, old age, poor vision, hernias, or other conditions that could potentially limit their labor contributions (Bateman-House & Fairchild, 2008). Stories of these immigrants being turned back, misconceptions about the overall health and well-being of foreigners, and the spread of diseases in unsanitary, overcrowded tenements where many immigrants lived led to rumors and discrimination against new arrivals considered to be a health threat (Bateman-House & Fairchild, 2008; Brackemyre, 2015).

More recently, immigrants—and specifically unauthorized migrants entering through the southern U.S. border—have been the target of disease importation accusations. Like historical examples, accusations since the mid-1990s have centered on the threat of foreigners importing disease to otherwise healthy populations. Well-known media figures and politicians have thrust such arguments into the public discourse, at times providing false information about the origins of disease threats.

Fear over the spread of leprosy in the United States resulted from a 2005 Lou Dobbs CNN program during which a guest commentator refuted a claim of roughly 900 cases of leprosy in the United States over the past 40 years. She then continued by saying, "There have been 7,000 in the past three years. Leprosy in this country" (Dobbs, 2005). Critics immediately called for a retraction. Actual statistics from the Department of Health and Human Services at that time showed there were indeed 7,000 cases—over the past *thirty* years, not three (Health Resources and Services Administration, 2010). When confronted with the data, Dobbs refused to issue a correction, instead stating he stood by the original claim (Dobbs, 2007). The faulty numbers were circulated widely on conservative Web sites and blogs.

Dobbs was not alone in creating a firestorm of discussion over the issue of immigration and disease. When thousands of mothers and unaccompanied children began crossing the southern U.S. border into Texas in 2013–2014, a small group of conservative politicians and media personalities identified them as health threats that put Americans at risk of contracting certain diseases. In July 2014, Georgia Representative Phil Gingrey, a retired obstetrician-gynecologist, wrote a highly publicized letter to the Centers for Disease Control in which he addressed "grave public health threats" posed by families and unaccompanied children crossing the southern U.S. border. Gingrey wrote that "reports of illegal migrants carrying deadly diseases such as swine flu, dengue fever, Ebola virus, and tuberculosis are particularly concerning. Many of the children who are coming across the border also lack basic vaccinations such as those to prevent chicken pox or measles" (Gingrey, 2014).

Radio host Rush Limbaugh also linked unaccompanied minors to measles outbreaks, saying on his radio show, "We conquered that freaking disease, in case anybody's forgotten. We conquered measles. But the kids that Obama has let flood the country via the Southern border were not vaccinated against anything, and Obama's demanding that they be populated in schools and communities, neighborhoods all over the country. They don't have to be vaccinated before coming into the country. They really don't have to be medically checked after getting into the country because they're here as future voters, and anything that gets in the way of that is gonna be shoved aside" (Limbaugh, 2015).

These comments sparked outrage among professionals, who argued that while flows of undocumented persons across the border can present public health challenges, there is no evidence of immigrants causing disease outbreaks in the United States. Gingrey's and Limbaugh's statements linking undocumented children to disease threats or outbreaks earned both a "Pants on Fire" rating from Politifact.com (Jacobson, 2014). Data from government agencies and various health organizations provides evidence that their claims are primarily false.

The Centers for Disease Control has repeatedly stated that "the unaccompanied children arriving from Central America pose little risk of spreading infectious diseases to the general public" (CDC, 2014, August 1). Contrary to Limbaugh's accusations, childhood vaccination programs in Central America are so widespread that many of the children are crossing the border with vaccination records in hand because "most children have received some or all of their recommended childhood vaccines" (Department of Health and Human Services, 2014; Fox, 2014). Those who have not been vaccinated or do not carry documentation are given all necessary childhood vaccinations on a catch-up schedule and are additionally given tuberculosis and mental health screenings (CDC, 2014, August 1; DHS, 2015). In terms of childhood vaccinations, many Latin American countries are ahead of the United States.

Measles vaccination rates in the primary sending countries of unaccompanied migrant children, for example, are nearly equal to or higher than vaccination rates in the United States. As shown in figure 5.2, on average, the coverage among one-year-olds from 2011 to 2015 was 94 percent in El Salvador, 67 percent in Guatemala, 88 percent in Honduras, and 97 percent in Mexico, compared with 91 percent in the United States (in 2012 Mexico's rate was 99 percent) (World Bank, 2016; World Health Organization, 2014).

Regarding the specific accusation that immigrants were to blame for recent measles outbreaks in the United States, quite the opposite was found to be true. In 2013 and 2014, there were zero confirmed cases of measles in El Salvador, Guatemala, and Honduras and only two cases in Mexico compared to 188 (2013) and 644 (2014) in the United States (WHO, 2015c). Worldwide, 113 countries have higher measles vaccination rates than the United States, partly due to resistance to vaccination among particular religious groups in the United States (Noack, 2015; WHO, 2014). CDC Director Tom Frieden stated that "All of our [measles] cases result, ultimately, from individuals who have traveled and brought it back here" (Kaplan, 2015). In the case of the widely publicized 2014 Disneyland outbreak, National Center for Immunization and Respiratory Diseases Director Dr. Anne Schuchat said, "In fact, this outbreak associated with the Disneyland Park? The U.S. exported [the] measles virus to Mexico" (Tani, 2015).

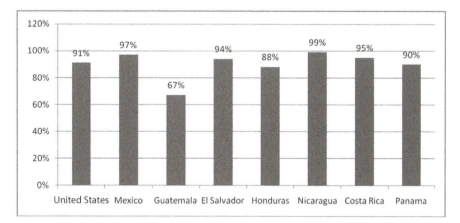

Figure 5.2 Measles immunization rates—percentage of children aged 12–23 months, 2014

Source: Data from World Bank, Immunization, Measles (2016). http://data.world bank.org/indicator/SH.IMM.MEAS/countries

In regard to *Ebola*, infections or deaths from the disease have been limited to Africa or to individuals working or living in Ebola-infected African regions who flew directly to the United States (CDC, 2015). Precautionary measures were taken when the first Ebola death occurred on U.S. soil. On October 8, 2014, just days after arriving to the United States from Liberia, Thomas Eric Duncan died of Ebola in a Dallas hospital. At that point, President Obama and the Centers for Disease Control ordered a series of examinations, questionnaires, and temperature checks for travelers arriving from Sierra Leone, Guinea and Liberia (CDC, 2014, October 8). Also in October of 2014, two health-care workers who provided care for Duncan also tested positive for Ebola, as did a medical aid worker who returned to New York from Guinea (CDC, 2014, December 16). All three health-care workers recovered. As of May 2016 no additional cases of Ebola have been documented in the Western Hemisphere, and specifically none along the U.S. border (WHO, 2015b). Reports of Ebola crossing the southern U.S. border thus far are false.

Dengue is the world's most prevalent mosquito-borne viral disease (Simmons et al., 2012). Although epidemics arose every 10 years in the United States from 1820 to 1940, mosquito eradication programs during World War II essentially wiped out the disease in this country with the exception of the Texas–Mexico border where dengue remains endemic in certain areas (Brunkard et al., 2007; McKenna, 2012). For example, in late 2014 when a dengue outbreak occurred in Sonora, Mexico, 93 travel-associated cases of dengue were documented in Arizona (Jones et al., 2016).

Since 2001 three small dengue outbreaks were reported in Hawaii, Texas, and Florida. Dr. Amesh Adalja, who researches dengue in the United States, attributes these cases largely to (1) less stringent mosquito control in recent decades that has allowed the *Aedes* species of mosquitos to reemerge in the United States, (2) increased numbers of travelers who become infected while visiting dengue-endemic tropic and subtropical regions and then return to the United States, thus holding the potential to start local outbreaks – for example, in Florida in 2012, four residents were diagnosed with "locally acquired" dengue and another 112 were diagnosed with dengue acquired somewhere else that they had brought to the United States (McKenna, 2012) – and (3) greater awareness of and testing for dengue (Pestorius, 2012). The National Institute of Health states that most recent cases in the United States can be attributed to people who recently traveled abroad (NIH, 2011). Two different types of dengue-carrying mosquitos are now found in 26 states—as far north as New York (McKenna, 2012). However, contact between people and dengue-carrying mosquitos in the continental U.S. is infrequent due to a variety of lifestyle and standard of living factors, so secondary transmission of imported dengue infections is rare (CDC, 2014, June 9). Therefore, while it is possible for a mosquito that has bitten an infected individual to transfer the disease to a healthy individual, both history and science point to numerous other factors—including travel by U.S. citizens—as greater risks.

Concern has also been expressed that children and other migrants are spreading *tuberculosis* in the United States. The CDC reports that among unaccompanied children, "a small number of cases of TB have been identified. Given that the children are from countries with higher rates of TB than the United States, public health officials would expect to find TB in some of these children" (CDC, 2014, August 1). Texas health officials confirmed three cases of TB in 2014 among children who crossed into Texas from Mexico (KSAT–abc, 2014). Those found with TB are separated and treated until they are no longer considered to be infectious.

Nationwide, the incidence of tuberculosis among foreign-born persons is higher than that of U.S.-born individuals. The CDC reports that in 2013, 65 percent of all TB cases and 90 percent of multidrug-resistant TB cases in the United States occurred among people born in other countries, and that California, Texas, New York, and Florida accounted for nearly 50 percent of those cases (CDC, 2014, March 20). Those four states not only have large populations of foreign-born persons, but three of the four were among the 15 states with the highest rates of homelessness, a condition that contributes to the spread of TB (CDC, 2015, September). From 2006 to 2010, in fact, the incidence of TB in homeless individuals was 10 times greater than overall national incidence rates (Bamrah et al., 2013).

However, tuberculosis incidence rates overall in the United States have declined each year since 1992, and rates declined among all racial/ethnic groups in 2013 (ibid.). Because the rate of decrease was less among foreign-born populations than that of U.S.-born persons, the incidence rate remains significantly higher among foreign-born individuals (ibid.). Thus, while it is true that tuberculosis rates are higher among foreign-born populations, incidence rates overall in the United States continue to decline.

Finally, a series of studies conducted by researchers at the University of California HIV/AIDS Research Program found that Mexican migrants who come to the United States are at a higher risk of contracting *HIV/AIDS* than Mexicans who do not migrate (Magis-Rodríguez et al., 2009). Their research identified HIV/AIDS among migrants as a significant health threat—not to U.S. citizens, but to families and communities in rural Mexico when the migrants return home.

The spread of HIV in Mexico has been linked to migration to the United States as far back as the early years of the epidemic. In 1983, all of the cases of HIV registered in Mexico were among individuals who had lived in the United States (Magis-Rodríguez et al., 2009). Data up to the year 2000 showed the Mexican states with the highest proportions of AIDS cases were also the states with the highest migration rates to the United States (Magis-Rodríguez et al., 2004). In a 2006 report, the United Nations listed migration as a factor in the worldwide spread of HIV (UNAIDS & WHO, 2006). During that year, the HIV prevalence among individuals aged 15–49 in Mexico was estimated at 0.3 percent—less than half that of the 0.8 percent combined rate in the United States and Canada (ibid.). However, the prevalence of HIV/AIDS in rural Mexico increased once migrants returned from the United States to their home communities. Research showed that for a wide variety of reasons, including isolation from family and exposure to different sexual practices and attitudes, migrants tended to have more sexual partners and/or engage in other high-risk behaviors while in the United States and therefore increased their risk of contracting HIV/AIDS and spreading it upon their return to Mexico (Magis-Rodríguez et al., 2009). The prevalence rate of HIV/AIDS still remains much lower in Mexico than in the United States. According to the United Nations HIV and AIDS estimates, in 2014, the prevalence rate among adults aged 15–49 was 0.2 percent in Mexico, compared to a rate of between 0.4 and 0.9 percent in the United States in 2012 (the latest year for which data was available). Thus, migration and return to Mexico continue to be cited as a potential risk for increased transmission of HIV in Mexico (Sanchez et al., 2012).

Migrants have also been accused of spreading *swine flu* (Savage, 2009) and *enterovirus* (Limbaugh, 2014). No evidence has proven a link between immigrants and the outbreaks of those illnesses. While Mexico was the apparent epicenter for the swine flu outbreak, its spread in the United States was not linked to immigrants. On the contrary, the largest number of confirmed cases was found in a group of school children from New York who had recently visited Mexico (Kang, 2009). As for enterovirus, the EV-D68 virus is not new to the United States. It was first identified in California in 1962, and the CDC has seen small numbers of EV-D68 infections regularly since 1987 (CDC, 2015, March 23). According to the CDC, "There is no evidence that unaccompanied children brought EV-D68 into the United States; we are not aware of any of these children testing positive for the virus" (Corsi, 2014).

What *have* been confirmed are 16 total cases of unaccompanied children hospitalized with *respiratory disease* from July 6 to 19, 2014. As a result, the CDC recommended both influenza and PCV13 vaccines for all children housed in four affected Office of Refugee Resettlement shelters in addition to routinely recommended vaccines. It was thought that crowded conditions likely facilitated the spread of the respiratory diseases and that the circulation of influenza viruses increased the risk for serious pneumococcal disease (CDC, 2014, August 15). Health officials did not find a link between the migrant children, however, and enterovirus. CDC spokesperson Jeanette St. Pierre stated, "Currently, there is no evidence from testing at CDC that EV-D68 infections in the U.S. are a result of unaccompanied minors moving into the country" (Media Matters for America, 2014).

The Department of Homeland Security has also identified *lice and scabies* in children and families who have crossed the southern U.S. border. Both are unpleasant but entirely treatable conditions that do not constitute a public health threat. One Texas pediatrician notes that "head lice are so common and harmless that the American Academy of Pediatrics now recommends that kids not even be kept out of school because of them" (Fox, 2014). Immigrants identified with the conditions are immediately treated (CDC, 2014, August 1).

This is by no means a complete list of potential illnesses. As with native-born populations, diseases of various origins have been detected in immigrants crossing the border as well as those already living in the United States. Some diseases originate in foreign countries and some are contracted here in the United States. However, accusations of migrants causing widespread outbreaks of disease or reintroducing previously eradicated diseases into the United States are, to date, unfounded.

FURTHER READING

American Public Health Association. (2009, November 10). Border crossing deaths: A public health crisis along the U.S.-Mexico border (Policy Number 20092). APHA Policy Statement Database. Retrieved from http://www.apha.org/policies-and-advocacy/public-health-policy-state ments/policy-database/2014/07/24/08/56/border-crossing-deaths-a-public-health-crisis-along-the-us-mexico-border

Bamrah, S., Yelk Woodruff, R. S., Powell, K., Ghosh, S., Kammerer, J. S., & Haddad, M. B. (2013). Tuberculosis among the homeless, United States, 1994–2010. *The International Journal of Tuberculosis and Lung Disease*, 17(11), 1414–1419.

Bateman-House, A., & Fairchild, A. (2008, April). Medical examination of immigrants at Ellis Island. *American Medical Association Journal of*

Ethics, Virtual Mentor, 10(4), 235–241. Retrieved from http://journalof ethics.ama-assn.org/2008/04/mhst1-0804.html

Brackemyre, T. (2015, April 10). Immigrants, cities, and disease. *US History Scene*. Retrieved from http://ushistoryscene.com/article/immigrants-cit ies-disease/

Brunkard, J. M., Robles López, J. L., Ramirez, J., Cifuentes, E., Rothenberg, S. J., Hunsperger, E. A., Moore, C. G., Brussolo, R. M., Villarreal, N. A., & Haddad, B. M. (2007). Dengue fever seroprevalence and risk factors, Texas-Mexico border, 2004. *Emerging Infectious Diseases*, 13(10), 1477–1483.

Bruno, A. (2014, May 8). *Unauthorized aliens in the United States: Policy discussion* (CRS R41207). Washington, DC: Congressional Research Service.

CDC. (2014, March 20). Global tuberculosis (TB). Centers for Disease Control and Prevention. Retrieved from http://www.ksat.com/news/ reports-of-immigrant-children-carrying-tuberculosis-into-u-s-

CDC. (2014, June 9). Dengue homepage. Centers for Disease Control and Prevention. Retrieved from http://www.cdc.gov/dengue/epidemiology/

CDC. (2014, August 1). *Unaccompanied children: Health information for public health partners*. Centers for Disease Control and Prevention PDF document retrieved from http://emergency.cdc.gov/children/pdf/cdc-factsheet-ph-uc-08-01-14-final.pdf

CDC. (2014, August 15). *Notes from the field: Hospitalizations for respiratory disease among unaccompanied children from Central America—Multiple states, June–July, 2014. Centers for Disease Control and Prevention Morbidity and Mortality Weekly Report*, 63(32), 698–699. Retrieved from http://www.cdc.gov/mmwr/preview/mmwrhtml/mm6332a4.htm

CDC. (2014, October 8). Enhanced Ebola screening to start at five U.S. airports and new tracking program for all people entering U.S. from Ebola-affected countries. Centers for Disease Control and Prevention [Archived news release]. Retrieved from http://www.cdc.gov/media/ releases/2014/p1008-ebola-screening.html

CDC. (2014, December 16). Cases of Ebola diagnosed in the United States. Centers for Disease Control and Prevention. Retrieved from http:// www.cdc.gov/vhf/ebola/outbreaks/2014-west-africa/united-states-impor ted-case.html

CDC. (2015, September). Reported tuberculosis in the United States, 2014. Atlanta, GA: U.S. Department of Health and Human Services, CDC. Retrieved from http://www.cdc.gov/tb/statistics/reports/2014/pdfs/ tb-surveillance-2014-report_updated.pdf

CDC. (2015, March 23). Enterovirus D68. Centers for Disease Control and Prevention. Retrieved from http://www.cdc.gov/non-polio-enterovirus/ about/ev-d68.html

CDC (2015, July 22). Ebola (Ebola virus disease): Risk of exposure. Centers for Disease Control and Prevention. Retrieved from http://www.cdc.gov/vhf/ebola/exposure/index.html

Corsi, J. R. (2014, October 15). CDC denies enterovirus link to illegal-alien kids. WND. Retrieved from http://www.wnd.com/2014/10/cdc-speaks-on-enterovirus-link-to-illegal-alien-kids/

Department of Health and Human Services (HHS). (2014, October 13). Unaccompanied children frequently asked questions. Washington, DC: HHS, Administration for Children and Families. Retrieved from https://www.escondido.org/Data/Sites/1/media/agendas/Council/10-15-14_PHG14-0017/sect11/Tab89.pdf

Department of Homeland Security (DHS). (2015, July 17). Unaccompanied children at the southwest border. DHS. Retrieved from http://www.dhs.gov/unaccompanied-children

Dobbs, L. (2005, April 14). Lou Dobbs Tonight: Border insecurity, criminal illegal aliens, deadly imports, illegal alien amnesty [Television program]. CNN.com. Transcript retrieved from http://www.cnn.com/TRANSCRIPTS/0504/14/ldt.01.html

Dobbs, L. (2007, May 16). Lou Dobbs Tonight: GOP Senators threaten to force change in Iraq policy; deadlock on amnesty deal [Television program]. CNN.com. Transcript retrieved from http://www.cnn.com/TRANSCRIPTS/0705/16/ldt.01.html

Fox, M. (2014, July 9). Vectors or victims? Docs slam rumors that migrants carry disease. *NBC News*. Retrieved from http://www.nbcnews.com/storyline/immigration-border-crisis/vectors-or-victims-docs-slam-rumors-migrants-carry-disease-n152216

Gingrey, P. (2014, July 7). Letter to Thomas R. Frieden, Director of Centers for Disease Control and Prevention. Accessed August 13, 2015, from https://drive.google.com/a/colorado.edu/file/d/0B_KEK8-LWmzhLXI2OU0yTFFyRTg/edit

Harvard University Library. (2016). Contagion: Historical views of diseases and epidemics (Tuberculosis in Europe and North America, 1800-1922). Cambridge, MA: Harvard. Retrieved from http://ocp.hul.harvard.edu/contagion/tuberculosis.html

Health Resources and Services Administration. (2010). *Number of U.S. Hansen's disease cases by year*. U.S. Department of Health and Human Services. Retrieved from http://www.hrsa.gov/hansensdisease/casesbyyear.html

Jacobson, L. (2014, July 18). Rep. Phil Gingrey says migrants may be bringing Ebola virus through the U.S.-Mexico border. *Tampa Bay Times*. Politifact.com. Retrieved from http://www.politifact.com/truth-o-meter/

statements/2014/jul/18/phil-gingrey/rep-phil-gingrey-says-migrants-may-be-bringing-ebo/

Jones, J. M., Lopez, B., Adams, L., Gálvez, F. J. N., Nuñez, A. S., Santillán, N. A. H., . . ., Komatsu, K. K. (2016, May 20). *Binational dengue outbreak along the United States–Mexico border—Yuma County, Arizona, and Sonora, Mexico, 2014*. Centers for Disease Control and Prevention, Morbidity and Mortality Weekly Report. Retrieved from http://www.cdc.gov/mmwr/volumes/65/wr/mm6519a3.htm#suggestedcitation

Kang, E. (2009, April 26). Breaking news: Swine flu reaches New York. *Clinical Correlations, The NYU Langone Online Journal of Medicine*. Retrieved from http://www.clinicalcorrelations.org/?p=1302

Kaplan, R. (2015, February 1). CDC "very concerned" about potential for large measles outbreak. CBSNews.com, Face the Nation. Retrieved from http://www.cbsnews.com/news/cdc-very-concerned-about-potential-for-large-measles-outbreak/

Kraut, A. M. (2004). Foreign bodies: The perennial negotiation over health and culture in a nation of immigrants. *Journal of American Ethnic History*, 23(2), 3–22.

KSAT–abc. (2014, July 7). Reports of immigrant children carrying tuberculosis into U.S. *KSAT News*. Retrieved from http://www.ksat.com/news/reports-of-immigrant-children-carrying-tuberculosis-into-u-s-

Limbaugh, R. (2014, September 8). Mysterious virus hits kids in the Midwest; Obama won't tell us where illegal alien kids were sent. Rush Limbaugh show archives. Retrieved from http://www.rushlimbaugh.com/daily/2014/09/08/mysterious_virus_hits_kids_in_midwest_obama_won_t_tell_us_where_illegal_alien_kids_were_sent

Limbaugh, R. (2015, February 3). Vaccine storyline is new war on women. Rush Limbaugh show archives. Retrieved from http://www.rushlimbaugh.com/daily/2015/02/03/vaccine_storyline_is_new_war_on_women

Magis-Rodríguez, C., Gayet, C., Negroni, M., Leyva, R., Bravo-García, E., Uribe, P., & Bronfman, M. (2004, November 1). *Journal of Acquired Immune Deficiency Syndromes*, 37(Supplement 4), S215–S226.

Magis-Rodríguez, C., Lemp, G., Hernandez, M. T., Sanchez, M. A., Estrada, F., & Bravo-García, E. (2009). Going north: Mexican migrants and their vulnerability to HIV. *Journal of Acquired Immune Deficiency Syndromes*, 51(Supplement 1), S21–S25.

Markel, H. (2000, Fall). "The eyes have it": Trachoma, the perception of disease, the United States Public Health Service, and the American Jewish immigration experience, 1897–1924. *Bulletin of the History of Medicine*, 74(3), 525–560.

McKenna, M. (2012, December 21). Dengue, aka "breakbone fever," is back. Slate.com. Retrieved from http://www.slate.com/articles/health_ and_science/pandemics/2012/12/dengue_fever_in_united_states_break bone_fever_outbreaks_florida_texas_and.html

Media Matters for America. (2014, October 8). Conservatives falsely blame undocumented children for deadly enterovirus. Media Matters blog. Retrieved from http://mediamatters.org/blog/2014/10/08/conserva tives-falsely-blame-undocumented-childr/201071

NIH—National Institute of Allergy and Infectious Diseases. (2011, February 8). Overview. *National Institutes of Health*. Retrieved from http:// www.niaid.nih.gov/topics/denguefever/understanding/pages/overview .aspx

Noack, R. (2015, February 3). Map: 113 countries have higher measles immunization rates than the U.S. for 1-year-olds. *The Washington Post*. Retrieved from http://gamapserver.who.int/gho/interactive_charts/imm unization/mcv/atlas.html

Oshinsky, D. M. (2006). *Polio: An American story*. New York: Oxford University Press.

Pestorius, T. (2012, April). Dengue fever in the United States. CDC Podcast. Retrieved from http://www2c.cdc.gov/podcasts/media/pdf/EID_4-12_Dengue.pdf

Poon, L. (2014, July 22). The immigrant kids have health issues—but not the ones you'd think. *National Public Radio: Goats and Soda—Stories of Life in a Changing World*. Retrieved from http://www.npr.org/sections/ goatsandsoda/2014/07/22/332598798/the-immigrant-kids-have-health-issues-but-not-the-ones-youd-think

Sanchez, M. A., Hernández, M. T., Hanson, J. E., Vera, A., Magis-Rodríguez, C., Ruiz, J. D., Garza, A. H., Casteñada, X., Aoki, B. K., & Lemp, G. F. (2012). The effect of migration on HIV high-risk behaviors among Mexican migrants. *Journal of Acquired Immune Deficiency Syndromes*, 61(5), 610–617.

Savage, M. (2009, April 24). Michael Savage—Swine flu virus alert, useless government, precautions. Retrieved from https://www.youtube.com/ watch?v=QZDf1aE0N9I

Simmons, C. P., Farrar, J. J., van Vinh Chau, N., & Willis, B. (2012, April 12). Dengue. *New England Journal of Medicine*, 366, 1423–1432.

Tani, M. (2015, February 23). CDC official dismisses claim that undocumented immigrants bring measles into the U.S. *The Huffington Post*. Retrieved from http://www.huffingtonpost.com/2015/02/23/undocume nted-immigrants-measles-outbreak_n_6737102.html

UNAIDS & WHO. (2006, December). AIDS epidemic update: Special report on HIV/AIDS. Retrieved from http://data.unaids.org/pub/Epi Report/2006/2006_EpiUpdate_en.pdf

UNICEF. (2014, November 20). *The state of the world's children report 2015 statistical tables* (Table 3. Health, 49–52). Retrieved from http://www .data.unicef.org/resources/the-state-of-the-world-s-children-report-2015-statistical-tables

Wiley, E., & Bruno, R. (2014). 2014 APHA policy statement: *Addressing immigrant discrimination and health disparities*. Retrieved from http://eth nomed.org/cross-cultural-health/immigration-naturalization/migrant-children-health/2014-APHA-LB-Migrant-Children-Submission.pdf/ view?searchterm=somalia

World Bank. (2016). Data: Immunization, measles (percent of children ages 12–23 months). Retrieved from http://data.worldbank.org/indica tor/SH.IMM.MEAS/countries

World Health Organization (WHO). (2014). *Immunization surveillance, assessment and monitoring; Measles (MCV) immunization coverage among 1-year olds, 1980–2014 (%): 2014* (Interactive graph). Retrieved from http://gamapserver.who.int/gho/interactive_charts/immunization/mcv/ atlas.html

World Health Organization (WHO). (2015a). HIV/AIDS; Tuberculosis and HIV. Retrieved from http://www.who.int/hiv/topics/tb/en/

World Health Organization (WHO). (2015b). Ebola virus disease: Disease outbreak news. World Health Organization. Retrieved from http://www .who.int/csr/don/archive/disease/ebola/en/

World Health Organization (WHO). (2015, February). Reported measles cases and incidence rates by WHO member states 2013, 2014 as of 11 February 2015. Retrieved from http://www.who.int/immunization/ monitoring_surveillance/burden/vpd/surveillance_type/active/measle sreportedcasesbycountry.pdf

6

❖

Immigration and Children

Q25. IS THE UNAUTHORIZED FLOW OF CHILDREN ACROSS THE MEXICO-U.S. BORDER INTO THE UNITED STATES CREATING A CRISIS?

Answer: Most experts say "yes," but they disagree about the nature of the crisis.

The Facts: During the spring and summer of 2014 the southwestern border of the United States experienced what has widely been described as a "crisis" or "surge" of unauthorized migrants onto U.S. soil. Ebbs and flows in migration patterns have been common throughout U.S. history. What made this influx of migrants so newsworthy, however, was the unprecedented number of children making the dangerous journey across the border. Some came with parents, but most were unaccompanied. (Under U.S. immigration definitions, children are considered unaccompanied if they are not traveling with a parent or guardian. It may be that they have traveled with some other person or relative or that they have made the trip alone.) What's more, whereas prior to 2012 the majority of unaccompanied children crossing the border came primarily from Mexico, the large groups of children entering the United States in 2013 and 2014 were primarily from the Northern Triangle countries of Central America: Guatemala, Honduras, and El Salvador (Government Accountability

Office, 2015; Kandel & Seghetti, 2015). Children from these three countries made up 75 percent of all unaccompanied children apprehended at the border in FY 2014 (Bersin, 2015), with Honduras sending the largest number of "unaccompanied alien children" (UACs) to the United States (Krogstad, Gonzalez-Barrera, & Lopez, 2014).

The numbers of children making their way northward were unprecedented. Apprehensions of children in the United States and Mexico combined grew from around 8,000 in 2010 to more than 72,000 in 2014 (Dominguez Villegas & Rietig, 2015). As illustrated in figure 6.1, in the United States alone, apprehensions of unaccompanied children jumped every year between 2011 and 2014, reaching a peak of 68,541 (United States Border Patrol, 2014). Apprehensions of UACs then dropped by 42 percent in FY 2015 but appear to be on the rise again judging by large numbers during the first four months of FY 2016 (ibid.).

Additionally, the decreases seen in 2015 are somewhat misleading because they do not consider the impact of increased enforcement by Mexican authorities under Mexico's Southern Border Program which began in July 2014. With backing and resources from the U.S. government, Mexico intensified its apprehension and deportation efforts of migrants within its borders (many en route to the United States). From July 2014 to June 2015 apprehensions of Central American migrants in Mexico were 71 percent higher than they were before the program was implemented (Isacson, Meyer, & Smith, 2015). Total apprehensions

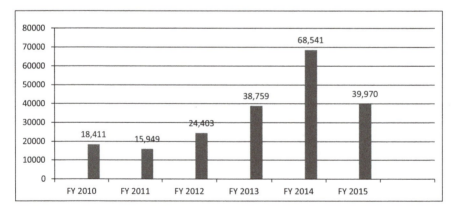

Figure 6.1 Total unaccompanied alien children (ages 0–17) apprehended by U.S. Border Patrol along southwestern U.S. border

Source: United States Customs and Border Protection, 2016a.

of migrants from the Northern Triangle countries by Mexico and the United States together totaled more than 340,000 in 2014 (Dominguez Villegas & Rietig, 2015) and more than 312,000 in 2015 (Isacson, Meyer, & Smith, 2015). President Obama acknowledged the country's enforcement surge in comments to Mexican President Peña Nieto, "I very much appreciate Mexico's efforts in addressing the unaccompanied children who we saw spiking during the summer. In part because of strong efforts by Mexico, including at its southern border, we've seen those numbers reduced back to much more manageable levels" (Hudson, 2015).

However, as statistics indicate, the fact that those migrants have not reached U.S. borders does not mean there are fewer making the journey. An associate from the Washington Office on Latin America commented, "These numbers are striking. They show that the so-called 'surge' of 2014 hasn't really ended. Enormous numbers of Central Americans are still fleeing, but most of them are now getting caught in Mexico instead of the United States" (Washington Office on Latin America, 2015). The violence, poverty, and lack of opportunity plaguing the Northern Triangle persist, as evidenced by continuing flows of individuals leaving those three countries. Asylum applications from Northern Triangle citizens have increased drastically not only in the United States and Mexico but throughout Central America (Sturm & Clayton, 2016); such asylum requests in Mexico, Costa Rica, Belize, and Nicaragua have increased by almost 1,200 percent since 2008 (Washington Office on Latin America, 2016).

The 2012–2014 migrant surges along the southern U.S. border also marked a geographic shift in the primary crossing area, from the Sonora/Arizona border to the Río Grande Valley (RGV) of Texas. As seen in figure 6.2, in FY 2010, nearly 8,000 UACs were apprehended in the Tucson Sector of southern Arizona and just under 5,000 in the RGV. By 2014 the figures remained around 8,000 in the Tucson Sector but jumped to almost 50,000 in the RGV.

In its year-end report for 2014, Customs and Border Protection describes these populations as "unaccompanied children and family units who turned themselves in to Border Patrol agents in South Texas this summer" (Customs and Border Protection, 2014). Unlike other border sectors where border-crossers primarily try to evade Border Patrol, the majority of the RGV crossers *sought out* U.S. officials, asking for help and/or asylum. U.S. House Homeland Security Committee chairman Michael McCaul stated, "When they arrive at the border, the children are simply turning themselves into the nearest Border Patrol agent" (McCaul, 2014).

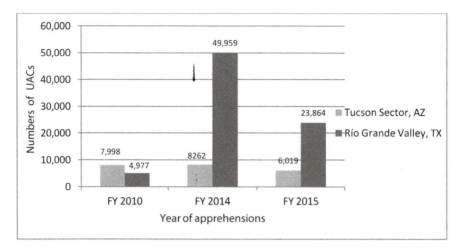

Figure 6.2 Total apprehensions of unaccompanied alien children (UACs) (ages 0–7) in Tucson and Río Grande Valley Border Patrol sectors
Source: United States Customs and Border Protection, 2016a.

The major impetus behind the border "surge" of 2013 and 2014 actually began long before the migrant influxes drew national attention. A worsening climate of crime, violence, and poverty in Central America's Northern Triangle created an environment of fear and desperation that resulted in a rapid increase in unaccompanied children to the United States (Government Accountability Office, 2015). According to a Congressional Research Service (CRS) report, 48 percent of unaccompanied children "said they had experienced serious harm or had been threatened by organized criminal groups or state actors, and more than 20 percent had been subject to domestic abuse" (Kandel et al., 2014). A 2014 Department of Homeland Security (DHS) study concluded that while poverty was a critical factor in the migration of children from Guatemala, extreme violence likely drove the migration of children from El Salvador and Honduras (Department of Homeland Security, 2014). In 2015 Guatemala had the fifth-highest murder rate in the world, El Salvador ranked fourth, and Honduras was first (Shoaib, 2015). However, economic hardships are also a problem in all three countries. Roughly 45 percent of Salvadorans, 55 percent of Guatemalans, and 67 percent of Hondurans live in poverty (Kandel et al., 2014). Additional "push factors" include agricultural job loss and loss of farms due to a coffee rust fungus, educational concerns, a desire to reunite with family in the United States, strong smuggling networks, and misperceptions about the nature of U.S. immigration policy (Bersin, 2015).

For instance, in 2014 the largest sending region by far for unaccompanied children was San Pedro Sula, Honduras (ibid.). Both the country of Honduras and its second-largest city have been named murder capitals of the world; San Pedro Sula alone sees an average of 19 homicides a day (Relph, 2014). Children are frequent victims of this uncontrolled violence, killed because they get caught up in gang disputes, they refuse to join gangs, someone has a vendetta against their parents, or often they were in the wrong place at the wrong time (Robles, 2014). El Salvador also suffers from immense violence. From January 1 to June 14, 2015, the country averaged 26 homicides a day, a 136 percent increase over the same time period in 2014 (López, 2015).

One additional point that bears mentioning is that the United States has seen high rates of migration of unaccompanied children from Mexico for years, but their numbers have sparked little public attention or political discussion (Hernández, 2015). Ever since 2009, when apprehensions of children from Central America hovered around 1,000 per country, apprehensions of Mexican UACs numbered 16,114 (United States Customs and Border Protection, 2015). Figures since then have remained steady, ranging from a high of 17,240 to a low of 11,012 in 2015 (ibid.). The largest share of Mexican UACs come from the eastern state of Tamaulipas (Pew Research Center, 2014), a violent state largely under the control of drug cartels and criminal gangs (Castillo, 2013).

Violence and poverty alone, though, cannot completely predict or explain the large migration of children northward into the United States according to a recent study (Donato & Sisk, 2015). Researchers using data from the Mexican and Latin American Migration Projects found that the migration of children has much to do with the migration history of their parents. Those whose parents have previously migrated to the United States have "migrant human capital" that often informs their decision to travel to the U.S. border; without such a connection, the likelihood of their migration drops dramatically. This is particularly true of migrant children from Mexico (ibid.). The study concludes that child migration from Mexico and Central America is largely the result of long-standing U.S. reliance on immigrant workers and migrant networks they have formed, leaving violence and poverty as structural conditions that may inform migration decisions but cannot predict them without additional consideration of family networks (Donato & Sisk, 2015). It is also noteworthy that although most children who cross into the United States do so because they already have family here, not all UACs are destined for this country. Children from the Northern Triangle of Central America have also sought asylum in Mexico, Costa Rica, Panama, Nicaragua, and Belize (American Immigration Council [AIC], 2014).

By the summer of 2014 President Obama was calling the huge influx of UACs a "humanitarian crisis" (2014, June 30). Likewise, in its year-end report, ICE described the large numbers of unaccompanied children crossing the border as an "urgent humanitarian situation" (ICE, 2014). The government responded aggressively to these flows of children by channeling additional resources to the border, opening emergency detention centers, providing emergency legal counsel to children, implementing public education campaigns in Central America, and supporting repatriation and reintegration programs in Northern Triangle countries (Hernández, 2015; Johnson, 2014; Kandel & Seghetti, 2015). As a result, the number of UACs apprehended in 2015 dropped by 42 percent to 39,970 (United States Customs and Border Protection, 2015). This was the lowest level since January 2013.

Decreased flows of unaccompanied minors into the United States in 2015 were not solely the result of domestic government responses. As mentioned, Mexican authorities also played a major role by initiating a border enforcement crackdown that prevented migrant children from reaching U.S. soil. Researchers explain that "migrants who in the past would have made it to the U.S. border and appeared in U.S. apprehensions data are now intercepted and counted in Mexican statistics" (Dominguez Villegas & Rietig, 2015). Between 2010 and 2014, apprehensions of UACs grew 13-fold in the United States and just 5-fold in Mexico. However, in 2015 U.S. apprehensions dropped by nearly half, while Mexico's were on target to increase nearly 70 percent (ibid.). Children apprehended in Mexico are far more likely to be deported to their home countries than those caught in the United States. Seventy-seven of every 100 children apprehended in Mexico in 2014 were deported, compared to just 3 of every 100 in the United States. Between 2010 and 2014 Mexico was responsible for four out of five child deportations to Northern Triangle countries (ibid.). This high ratio of deportations to apprehensions has created concern about inadequate humanitarian screening and due process protections offered to vulnerable children. In the United States the children are required to go through screening and receive legal representation, but insufficient numbers of judges to adjudicate the large number of UAC cases has created huge backlogs and resulted in both a lengthy judicial process and low deportation rates (ibid.).

WHO ARE THE BORDER-CROSSERS?

The bulk of the UACs apprehended at the border are teenagers, but in 2014 (the peak of the UAC spike), unaccompanied children aged 12 and under made up the fastest-growing group of children apprehended. The largest share of UACs under age 12 comes from Honduras, followed by El Salvador and Guatemala, respectively (Krogstad, Gonzalez-Barrera, & Lopez, 2014). Recent years have also seen a significant increase in the apprehensions of girls and of family units (Dominguez Villegas & Rietig, 2015). This may be linked to reports of Central American gangs "increasingly targeting young children and perpetuating violence against women and girls" (ibid., p. 20).

WHAT HAPPENS TO UACs WHEN THEY ARE APPREHENDED?

When it comes to deciding how U.S. authorities handle cases of UACs, laws differ depending on the country of origin of the children apprehended. According to U.S. immigration law, UACs from contiguous countries can be deported to their home countries without having to go through formal deportation proceedings. Children from noncontiguous countries (countries other than Canada and Mexico), however, must be processed, sheltered, and placed into formal removal proceedings (Pierce, 2015).

Immigration and Customs Enforcement (ICE), by law, does not detain unaccompanied children who are apprehended but instead transfers them to the Department of Health and Human Services (HHS), the agency then responsible for placing them in the "least restrictive setting that is in the best interest of the child, which generally results in placement with a family member" (ICE, 2014, December 19). During FY 2014, ICE helped transfer 56,029 unaccompanied children to HHS (ibid.) where they were sheltered and detained until relatives or sponsors could be found to take responsibility for the children as they awaited deportation proceedings.

Numerous lawsuits and complaints have been filed against CBP, citing abuses of power, mistreatment of migrants, inhumane conditions in detention facilities, among other violations of law and human rights (American Immigration Council, 2013). Many of these cases involved children who suffered severe stress or physical mistreatment or neglect while in the custody of CBP officers.

Given the numbers of UACs seen in recent years, the circumstances from which they are fleeing, and the challenges faced by both the children and the U.S. government once they cross the border, describing these migrant flows as a crisis may not be entirely accurate. "Crises" (plural) may be the more fitting term.

FURTHER READING

American Immigration Council. (2013). CBP abuse of authority: Recently filed cases against CBP. Retrieved from http://www.legalactioncenter .org/cbp-abuse-authority

American Immigration Council (AIC). (2014, July). *Children in danger: A guide to the humanitarian challenge at the border.* Washington, DC: Author. Retrieved from http://www.immigrationpolicy.org/sites/default/ files/docs/children_in_danger_a_guide_to_the_humanitarian_challenge_ at_the_border_final.pdf

Bersin, A. (2015, April 30). Written testimony of PLCY Office of International Affairs Assistant Secretary and Chief Diplomatic Officer Alan Bersin for a House Committee on Foreign Affairs, Subcommittee on Western Hemisphere hearing titled "Migration Crisis: Oversight of the Administration's Proposed $1 billion Request for Central America." Washington, DC: Department of Homeland Security. Retrieved from http://www.dhs.gov/news/2015/04/30/written-testimony-plcy-house- foreign-affairs-subcommittee-western-hemisphere-hearing

Castillo, M. (2013, June 9). Mexico: As dangerous—and safe—as ever. CNN.com. Retrieved from http://www.cnn.com/2013/06/09/world/ americas/mexico-security/index.html

Customs and Border Protection. (2014, December 19). CBP Border Security Report. U.S. Customs and Border Protection: Department of Homeland Security. Retrieved from http://www.cbp.gov/sites/ default/files/documents/FINAL%20Draft%20CBP%20FY14%20 Report_20141218.pdf

Department of Homeland Security. (2014, May 27). *Unaccompanied alien children (UACs) by location of origin for CY 2014: Honduras, El Salvador, and Guatemala.* Washington, DC: Author. Retrieved from http:// adamisacson.com/files/dhsuacmap.pdf

Dominguez Villegas, R., & Rietig, V. (2015, September). *Migrants deported from the United States and Mexico to the Northern Triangle: A statistical and socioeconomic profile.* Washington, DC: Migration Policy Institute. Retrieved from http://www.migrationpolicy.org/research/migrants- deported-united-states-and-mexico-northern-triangle-statistical- and-socioeconomic

Donato, K. M. & Sisk, B. (2015, April 16). Children's migration to the United States from Mexico and Central America: Evidence from the Mexican and Latin American migration projects. *Journal on Migration and Human Society, 3*(1), 58–79.

Government Accountability Office. (2015, February). *Central America: Information on migration of unaccompanied children from El Salvador, Guatemala, and Honduras* (GAO-15-362). Washington, DC: Author.

Hernández, D. M. (2015). Unaccompanied child migrants in "crisis": New surge or case of arrested development? *Harvard Journal of Hispanic Policy, 27,* 11–17.

Hudson, D. (2015, January 6). *President Obama and President Peña Nieto of Mexico meet at the White House.* Washington, DC: The White House Office of the Press Secretary. Retrieved from https://www.whitehouse.gov/the-press-office/2015/01/06/remarks-president-obama-and-president-pe-nieto-after-bilateral-meeting

ICE. (2014, December 19). ICE enforcement and removal operations report. U.S. Immigration and Customs Enforcement: Department of Homeland Security. Retrieved from https://www.ice.gov/doclib/about/offices/ero/pdf/2014-ice-immigration-removals.pdf

Isacson, A., Meyer, M., & Smith, H. (2015, November). *Increased enforcement at Mexico's southern border.* Washington, DC: Washington Office on Latin America. Retrieved from http://www.wola.org/files/WOLA_Increased_Enforcement_at_Mexico's_Southern_Border_Nov2015.pdf

Johnson, J. C. (2014, June 24). *Statement by Secretary Jeh C. Johnson U.S. Department of Homeland Security before the House Committee on Homeland Security.* Washington, DC: U.S. Department of Homeland Security. Retrieved from http://docs.house.gov/meetings/HM/HM00/20140624/102395/HHRG-113-HM00-Wstate-JohnsonJ-20140624.pdf

Kandel, W. A, Bruno, A., Meyer, P. J., Ribando Seelke, C., Taft-Morales, M., & Wasem, R. E. (2014, July 3). *Unaccompanied alien children: Potential factors contributing to recent immigration* (CRS R43628). Congressional Research Service Report. Washington, DC: Congressional Research Service. Retrieved from http://fas.org/sgp/crs/homesec/R43628.pdf

Kandel, W. A., & Seghetti, L. (2015, August 18). *Unaccompanied alien children: An overview* (CRS R43599). Congressional Research Service Report. Washington, DC: Congressional Research Service. Retrieved from http://www.refworld.org/pdfid/55eebcfd4.pdf

Krogstad, J. M., Gonzalez-Barrera, A., & Lopez, M. H. (2014, July 22). *Children 12 and under are fastest growing group of unaccompanied minors at U.S. border.* Washington, DC: Pew Research Center. Retrieved from http://www.pewresearch.org/fact-tank/2014/07/22/children-12-and-under-are-fastest-growing-group-of-unaccompanied-minors-at-u-s-border/

López, J. (2015, June 15). Junio, con 364 asesinatos, podría ser el más violento (June, with 364 killings, could be the most violent). Elsalvador.com. Retrieved from http://www.elsalvador.com/articulo/sucesos/junio-con-364-asesinatos-podria-ser-mas-violento-76529

McCaul, M. (2014, June 24). *McCaul opening statement at hearing on unaccompanied children at border.* Washington, DC: U.S. House of Representatives Committee on Homeland Security. Retrieved from https://homeland.house.gov/press/mccaul-opening-statement-hearing-unaccompanied-children-border/

Obama, B. (2014, June 30). *Remarks by the president on border security and immigration reform.* Washington, DC: Office of the Press Secretary, White House. Retrieved from https://www.whitehouse.gov/the-press-office/2014/06/30/remarks-president-border-security-and-immigration-reform

Pew Research Center. (2014). Where unaccompanied Mexican children apprehended at the border come from [Graphic]. Retrieved from http://www.pewresearch.org/files/2014/08/FT_14.07.29_mexChildMigrants-6401.png

Pierce, S. (2015, October). *Unaccompanied child migrants in U.S. communities, immigration court, and schools* [Issue Brief]. Washington, DC: MPI. Retrieved from https://assets.documentcloud.org/documents/2460908/uac-integration-finalweb.pdf

Relph, J. (2014, October 30). Dispatch from Honduras: What it's like to live in the murder capital of the world. *Business Insider.* Retrieved from http://www.businessinsider.com/murder-capital-san-pedro-sula-2014-10

Robles, F. (2014, July 9). Fleeing gangs, children head to U.S. border. *The New York Times.* Retrieved from http://www.nytimes.com/2014/07/10/world/americas/fleeing-gangs-children-head-to-us-border.html

Shoaib, M. (2015, April 6). Top 10 countries with highest murder rate in the world 2015. *Abc News Point.* Retrieved from http://www.abcnewspoint.com/top-10-countries-with-highest-murder-rate-in-the-world-2015/

Sturm, N., & Clayton, J. (Eds.). (2016, April 5). *UNHCR calls for urgent action as Central America asylum claims soar.* Geneva: United Nations High Commissioner for Refugees. Retrieved from http://www.unhcr.org/news/latest/2016/4/5703ab396/unhcr-calls-urgent-action-central-america-asylum-claims-soar.html

United States Customs and Border Protection. (2015). *Southwest border unaccompanied alien children.* Washington, DC: Department of Homeland Security. Retrieved from http://www.cbp.gov/newsroom/stats/southwest-border-unaccompanied-children

United States Customs and Border Protection. (2016a). *United States Border Patrol: Total unaccompanied alien children (0-17 years old) apprehensions by month [fiscal years 2010-2015].* Retrieved from https://www.cbp.gov/sites/default/files/documents/BP%20Total%20Monthly%20UACs%20by%20Sector%2C%20FY10-FY16TD-Jan.pdf

United States Customs and Border Protection. (2016b, January 12). *U.S. Border Patrol fiscal year Southwest border sector apprehensions (FY 1960–FY 2015).* Washington, DC: Customs and Border Protection Agency. Retrieved from https://www.cbp.gov/sites/default/files/documents/BP%20Southwest%20Border%20Sector%20Apps%20FY1960%20-%20FY2015.pdf

Washington Office on Latin America (WOLA). (2015, June 11). *Mexico now detains more Central American migrants than the United States.* Washington, DC: WOLA. Retrieved from http://www.wola.org/news/mexico_now_detains_more_central_american_migrants_than_the_united_states

Washington Office on Latin America (WOLA). (2016, January 15). *Five facts about migration from Central America's northern triangle.* Washington, DC: WOLA. Retrieved from https://www.wola.org/analysis/five-facts-about-migration-from-central-americas-northern-triangle/

Q26. ARE MOST UNAUTHORIZED ALIEN CHILDREN (UACs) AUTOMATICALLY SENT BACK TO THEIR HOME COUNTRIES UNDER CURRENT U.S. IMMIGRATION LAWS?

Answer: Not necessarily. While most UACs from Mexico are deported within a short period after apprehension, current U.S. law requires that children from noncontiguous countries (any countries other than Canada and Mexico) be processed, sheltered, and placed into removal proceedings. Due to extreme backlogs, they may be in the United States for years as they wait to present their cases in the U.S. immigration court system.

The Facts: In 2002 Congress passed the Homeland Security Act, which divided specific responsibilities for the processing and treatment of Unaccompanied Alien Children (UAC) to the Department of Homeland Security (DHS) and the Department of Health and Human Service's Office of Refugee Resettlement (ORR) (Homeland Security Act, 2002).

Six years later, the William Wilberforce Trafficking Victims Protection Reauthorization Act (TVPRA) of 2008 was passed, establishing concrete policies and procedures for federal agencies to ensure safe repatriation of UACs in the United States back to their home countries. The TVPRA established different guidelines for the handling of children from contiguous countries. Under this legislation UACs from Canada and Mexico can be quickly returned (deported) without further legal penalties. Within 48 hours and before being deported, however, those children are to be screened to determine (1) if the child has been a victim of a severe form of human trafficking or if there is evidence that the minor will be at risk if he or she is returned to the country of origin, (2) whether the unaccompanied child has a possible claim to asylum, and (3) whether the unaccompanied alien child is able to make an independent decision to voluntarily return to the country of nationality (Kandel & Seghetti, 2015). If CBP authorities determine the child is not admissible, that child can withdraw his or her application for admission and voluntarily return home without criminal penalties.

Unaccompanied children from any noncontiguous country, on the other hand, cannot be immediately returned. Under TVPRA, they are required to go through a much lengthier process that ultimately culminates with their case being heard in immigration court. First they are screened, provided medical care including immunizations, and assigned a shelter. ICE then transports them to the shelter and places them in ORR custody "in the least restrictive setting that is in the best interest of the child." There, they are detained until they can be placed with a sponsor who attests that he or she will take financial responsibility for the child and give him or her proper care (DHS, 2014; Kandel & Seghetti, 2015). This process is handled on a case-by-case basis. Ideally, the child's sponsor is a parent or close family member (90 percent are reunified with their families), but in many cases children are turned over to a more distant relative or foster parent. The sponsor is then charged with care of the child until the outcome of his or her removal proceedings are decided in court (ibid.). From the start of FY 2014 through August 31, 2015, ORR released 77,194 unaccompanied minors to communities throughout the United States (Pierce, 2015).

Because the volume of UAC litigation in recent years has resulted in extreme court backlogs, it can take years for a child's case to come before a judge, and even longer to be fully resolved. In late 2014 there were just

228 full-time immigration judges charged with 375,000 cases nationwide (Brown, 2014). In spite of the creation of a "priority docket" for UAC cases in mid-2014, as of August 2015 40 percent of UAC proceedings initiated in 2013 had not yet been resolved (Pierce, 2015).

Legislation has been proposed that would change the law to process all UAC cases the way cases from Mexico and Canada are handled; any child apprehended would have to pass an initial screening test to stay in the country or else be removed (Chaffetz, 2014). Critics charge the rushed process of deportation would send Central American children right back into dangerous environments, as they contend is currently the case for many Mexican children (Lind, 2014). Furthermore, they say Border Patrol officers are not meeting legal screening requirements according to guidelines outlined by TVPRA (Ferriss, 2011). A Government Accountability Office review supported these allegations, finding that Border Patrol officers and Office of Field Operations officers did not consistently apply required screening criteria to UAC cases, were not always fully aware of how to assess screening criteria, and failed to document rationales for decisions resulting from screening (GAO, 2015).

Even though a United Nations High Commissioner for Refugees (UNHCR) report estimates that according to international standards (which differ from U.S. standards) 60 percent of children arriving in the United States from Central America may be eligible for some type of humanitarian protection (2014), federal officials say that only a small number of asylum requests have been filed by children who were apprehended by Customs and Border Protection (CBP) (Wasem, 2014). However, this may not be because they are not eligible or not trying to seek asylum relief. A Human Rights Watch investigation revealed that CBP personnel issued fewer credible fear referrals for Central American migrants (adults and children) than for migrants from other countries, and that migrants were often rushed through interviews and coerced into signing deportation papers in spite of the fact that they stated they feared for their lives in their home countries (Human Rights Watch, 2014). In the case of vulnerable young children who may already be scared, traumatized, and confused about what they are being asked to do, determination and follow-through on "credible fear" claims lie totally in the hands of the CBP officials in charge.

Even among UACs who qualify for and file for asylum, only a tiny percentage are granted formal relief, which results in a grant of immigration status such as asylum or other specific status for victims of crime. Between October 1, 2013, and August 31, 2015, only 313 juveniles were granted formal relief. A larger number, 11,610, were granted informal relief, meaning their cases were closed or terminated so the children no longer had active removal cases pending. Informal relief, however, does not provide immigration status, so those children remain in the country unauthorized. Of the remaining cases during that time period, removal orders were issued to over 17,000 UACs and 55,000 cases remained pending (Pierce, 2015).

One additional option for unaccompanied children in the United States who have been abused, abandoned, or neglected and are unable to be reunited with a parent is Special Immigrant Juveniles (SIJ) status. This status allows the child to receive a green card and live and work permanently in the United States. However, SIJ-status individuals can never petition for a green card for their parents and cannot petition for a green card for siblings until they themselves become U.S. citizens (United States Citizenship and Immigration Services [USCIS], 2015a). In 2010, 1,590 SIJ petitions were approved; by 2014 that number had risen to 4,606 (USCIS, 2015b). The increase most likely reflected the dramatic increase in unaccompanied alien children entering the United States from El Salvador, Guatemala, and Honduras.

The single greatest predictor of a UAC's outcome in court is legal representation. A review of records found that most children do show up for their court hearings, and among those who do most are granted some type of relief (Pierce, 2015). Over 90 percent of unrepresented children, on the other hand, are issued deportation orders, often because they do not understand the system or show up for court (ibid.). Without representation, children as young as three years are left to navigate the system and, in effect, represent themselves before immigration judges (Ortega, 2014). Additionally, UACs are not afforded legal representation by the government; instead, they must pay for a lawyer themselves or find pro bono lawyers willing to take on their cases (Transactional Access Records Clearinghouse, 2014). Eighty percent of pending UAC cases in 2014 involved children with no legal representation (ibid.).

FURTHER READING

Brown, A. (2014, September 26). Backlog of children's immigration cases challenges judges, lawyers and schools. *PBSNewshour*. Retrieved from http://www.pbs.org/newshour/updates/backlog-childrens-immigration-court-cases-challenges-schools/

Chaffetz, J. (2014, July 17). H.R. 5137—Asylum Reform and Border Protection Act of 2014, Summary: H.R.5137–113th Congress (2013–2014).

Washington, DC: U.S. House of Representatives. Retrieved from https://www.congress.gov/bill/113th-congress/house-bill/5137

Department of Homeland Security (DHS). (2014). *Unaccompanied children at the Southwest border*. DHS. Washington, DC: DHS. Retrieved from http://www.dhs.gov/unaccompanied-children

Ferriss, S. (2011, September 2). *Child advocates say more should be done to assist immigrant minors crossing the border*. Washington, DC: The Center for Public Integrity. Retrieved from http://www.publicintegrity.org/2011/09/02/6109/child-advocates-say-more-should-be-done-assist-immigrant-minors-crossing-border

Government Accountability Office (GAO). (2015, July). *Unaccompanied alien children: Actions needed to ensure children receive required care in DHS custody* (GAO-15-521). Washington, DC: Author.

Homeland Security Act. (2002, November). Art. 462 of Homeland Security Act (2002). Retrieved from http://www.legislationline.org/documents/id/7564

Human Rights Watch. (2014, October). "You don't have rights here:" U.S. border screening and returns of Central Americans to risk of serious harm. Retrieved from http://www.hrw.org/sites/default/files/reports/us1014_web_0.pdf

Kandel, W. A., & Seghetti, L. (2015, August 18). *Unaccompanied alien children: An overview* (CRS R43599). Congressional Research Service Report. Washington, DC: Congressional Research Service. Retrieved from http://www.refworld.org/pdfid/55eebcfd4.pdf

Lind, D. (2014, July 29). 14 facts that help explain America's child-migrant crisis. Vox.com. Retrieved from http://www.vox.com/2014/6/16/5813406/explain-child-migrant-crisis-central-america-unaccompanied-children-immigrants-daca

Ortega, B. (2014, November 13). Revisiting the immigration pipeline: Deported into danger. *The Arizona Republic*. Retrieved from http://www.azcentral.com/story/news/politics/immigration/2014/11/13/immigration-pipeline-children-deported/18969561/

Pierce, S. (2015, October). *Unaccompanied child migrants in U.S. communities, immigration court, and schools* [Issue Brief]. Washington, DC: MPI. Retrieved from https://assets.documentcloud.org/documents/2460908/uac-integration-finalweb.pdf

Transactional Access Records Clearinghouse (TRAC). (2014, November 25). *Representation for unaccompanied children in immigration court*. Syracuse, NY: Syracuse University. Retrieved from http://trac.syr.edu/immigration/reports/371/

United Nations High Commissioner for Refugees (UNHCR). (2014, March). *Children on the run: Unaccompanied children leaving Central America and Mexico and the need for international protection.* Washington, DC: UNHCR Regional Office for the United States and the Caribbean.

United States Citizenship and Immigration Services (USCIS). (2015a, June). *Special immigrant juveniles (SIJ) status.* Washington, DC: Author. Retrieved from http://www.uscis.gov/green-card/special-immigrant-juveniles/special-immigrant-juveniles-sij-status

United States Citizenship and Immigration Services (USCIS). (2015b, June). *Number of I-360 petitions for special immigrant with a classification of special immigrant juvenile (SIJ) by fiscal year and case status 2010–2015.* Washington, DC: Author. Retrieved from http://www.uscis.gov/sites/default/files/USCIS/Resources/Reports%20and%20Studies/Immigra tion%20Forms%20Data/Adjustment%20of%20Status/I360-sij_perfor mancedata_fy2015_qtr3.pdf

Wasem, R. E. (2014, July 30). *Asylum policies for unaccompanied children compared with expedited removal policies for unauthorized adults: In brief* (CRS R43664). Washington, DC: Congressional Research Service.

Zong, J., & Batalova, J. (2015, October 28). *Refugees and asylees in the United States.* Washington, DC: Migration Policy Institute. Retrieved from http://www.migrationpolicy.org/article/refugees-and-asylees-united-states

Q27. CAN A CHILD BORN IN THE UNITED STATES TO PARENTS WHO ARE UNAUTHORIZED THEN SPONSOR HIS OR HER PARENTS FOR CITIZENSHIP?

Answer: Yes, but with *major* caveats.

The Facts: The Fourteenth Amendment of the Constitution of the United States states: "All persons born or naturalized in the United States, and subject to the jurisdiction thereof, are citizens of the United States and of the state wherein they reside." That means that under the Fourteenth Amendment of the Constitution, a child born in the United States is a U.S. citizen regardless of the legal status of his or her parents. That child, as a U.S. citizen, can petition for certain family members to receive legal status in the form of a green card, fiancée visa, or K-3/K-4 nonimmigrant visa based on the type of relationship with the family member (U.S. Citizenship and Immigration Services, 2014). Therefore, a

U.S.-citizen child *can* petition for his or her parents to receive green cards which would grant them permanent U.S. residence.

For decades, politicians opposed to the idea of birthright citizenship have argued for an appeal of the Fourteenth Amendment, stating that being born inside the borders of the United States should not guarantee automatic citizenship. Numerous conservative leaders have called for an end to "anchor babies," a pejorative term implying that noncitizens come to the United States with the intention of having children who are, by right of their birthplace, U.S. citizens. They decry the ability of those children to eventually petition for legal status of their parents.

However, what is often missing from political arguments against birthright citizenship is that the possibility of petitioning for legal status on behalf of the parents cannot happen for decades. The U.S. Constitution does not allow a U.S.-citizen child to petition on behalf of a parent until the child has turned 21 years of age. Even at that point, when U.S.-citizen children can petition for legal status of their spouses, children, or parents, these immediate relatives must meet the criteria required of applicants—primarily maintaining their lawful nonimmigrant status prior to application.

For most parents of U.S.-citizen children, this means they must return to their home countries and wait 21 years for the child to become old enough to file a petition on their behalf. Once the child has turned 21, parents must then wait the additional time that it takes for that petition to be filed through a foreign consulate, reviewed, processed, and approved (or denied). Because evidence must be produced to prove the child was born in the United States, it will likely become apparent that the parent(s) resided in the United States illegally for a period of time. If their stay was between 6 and 12 months, they are automatically subject to an automatic three-year ban from reentering the United States (in addition to the 21 years they have already waited). If they were present for over a year, they are automatically subject to a 10-year ban from reentry (in addition to the 21 years). There are waivers to the 3- and 10-year bars on admission, but they are available only to those who can demonstrate that the bar would result in extreme hardship for the applicant's citizen or permanent resident spouse or parent. Hardship for children is not a consideration. These waivers are extremely difficult to obtain and must be lodged from outside the United States. Add to this additional time for application, processing, and review, and most parents of an "anchor baby" face wait times upwards of 24 to 31 years (Immigration and Nationality Act, 2013).

Thus, while there is technically a legal way for U.S.-born children to petition for a visa and green card for their parents, the lengthy wait and strict requirements for eligibility do not make having anchor babies a likely widespread immigration strategy. And even if the parents are granted legal status, they still are not U.S. citizens. Application for citizenship is another long and complicated process.

So how many visas are issued to parents of U.S.-born children each year? There are no numerical limits on the number of visas issued to immediate relatives of U.S. citizens (which includes spouses, unmarried children under age 21, or parents of U.S. citizens), and the numbers of visas issued vary from year to year. During fiscal year 2014, the top four countries from which visas were issued to the parent of a U.S. citizen at least 21 years of age (IR-5 visas) were Mexico (8,570), India (6,139), China (mainland-born) (5,883), and the Philippines (5,331) (Bureau of Consular Affairs, 2015c). Countries with the highest total numbers of immediate relative visas issued (including those for spouses and children) were Mexico (36,300 of which 17,401 were for a spouse of a U.S. citizen), the Philippines (12,605), the Dominican Republic (12,039), China (mainland-born) (11,798), and India (10,467) (ibid.).

While parents (or spouses or children) of U.S. citizens do not face numerical limits for the issuance of visas, siblings and other family members do not fall into this same "immediate relatives" category and are subject to a predetermined number of family preference visas, which are fewer in number and can be much more difficult to obtain.

During fiscal year 2016 family-sponsored preference visas were limited to no more than 226,000 worldwide. Additionally, there was a per-country limit of 7 percent, thus ensuring that no single country monopolized all of the available visas. To put the wait times in perspective, the FY 2016 immigrant waiting list included 1,344,429 registered applicants from Mexico, 417,511 from the Philippines, 344,208 from India, and 282,375 from Vietnam (Bureau of Consular Affairs, 2015b). Thus, the number of applicants from Vietnam alone exceeds the annual worldwide cap for family-sponsored preference visas.

For qualified relatives of a U.S. citizen or permanent resident, there are four preference categories (U.S. Citizenship and Immigration Services, 2011):

1. *First* preference is given to unmarried, adult sons and daughters of U.S. citizens (must be 21 years of age or older).
2. *Second preference (A)* is given to spouses of permanent residents and the unmarried children (under age 21) of permanent residents.
3. *Second preference (B)* is given to unmarried sons and daughters (age 21 or older) of permanent residents.

4. *Third preference* is given to married sons and daughters of U.S. citizens, their spouses, and their minor children.
5. *Fourth preference* is given to brothers and sisters of adult U.S. citizens, their spouses, and their minor children.

Thus, in order for a brother or sister of a U.S. citizen to apply for legal status, the petitioner must be at least 21 years old, the sibling must meet all nonimmigrant requirements at the time of the application, *and* the sibling is relegated to fourth preference, the category with the longest waiting list because the demand for these visas is substantially higher than the number of visas available each year. As of November 1, 2014, there were 2,455,964 applicants for only 65,000 annual available visas (Bureau of Consular Affairs, 2015b). That year, Mexico alone submitted 741,233 applications (ibid.). For countries of the most favorable visa availability, the waiting list was over 12 years. (This means an additional 12-year wait once the U.S.-citizen child has turned 21). For oversubscribed countries, or countries with far more applicants than there are visas available, the wait is even longer. As of October 2015, the wait for a sibling from Mexico was 18 years, and from the Philippines it was 23 years (Bureau of Consular Affairs, 2015a).

Thus, if a child is born in the United States, he or she can eventually decide to petition for legal status for parents, a spouse, and children. However, the waiting periods for these family members, together with the difficulty of obtaining visas for siblings and other relatives, present major obstacles for families of mixed status wishing to remain together. This complexity is not reflected in statements such as that of Roy Beck of NumbersUSA, when he asserted during an interview with *Businessweek*, "Each of these babies becomes an anchor who retards deportation of unlawfully present parents—and who eventually will be an anchor for entire families and villages as chain migration leads to the immigration of grandparents, aunts, uncles, and cousins" (Wooldridge, 2009). Generalizations such as these imply a quick and easy process for entire families (and "villages") to migrate legally because of the citizenship of one child. This is both inaccurate and misleading, and does not adequately explain the complicated, lengthy steps that make up the application process, or the requirements necessary to obtain legal status in the first place.

Additionally, the idea that U.S.-citizen children are anchors who "retard deportation of unlawfully present parents" is incorrect. Parents of U.S.-citizen children, if here without authorization, face the same threat of deportation as anyone else without proper legal authority to be on U.S. soil. Authorizations for relief from deportation or cancellations of removal are available to a limited few, but are extremely difficult to obtain. Only about 4,000 such reliefs are granted each year under the 1952 Immigration and Nationality Act (INA), and for an applicant to even qualify, he or she must establish the following before an immigration judge:

(1) Proof of continuous physical presence in the United States for the past 10 years or more and of the display of good moral character as defined in section 101(f) of the INA during these 10 years; an exception to this 10-year requirement is individuals who have served honorably on active duty in the Armed Forces of the United States for at least 24 months (Executive Office for Immigration Review, 2015)

(2) Proof that he or she has not been convicted of a crime making the alien removable (covered under sections 212(a)(2), 237(a)(2), or 237(a)(3) of the INA)

(3) Evidence that removal would result in exceptional and extremely unusual hardship not just to the individual, but to the individual's U.S.-citizen spouse, parent, or child (Executive Office for Immigration Review, 2015). One additional means of qualifying for a cancellation of removal is reserved for spouses or children of a U.S. citizen who have been battered or suffered extreme cruelty by that person.

This third requirement, proof of exceptional and extremely unusual hardship, is the most difficult to obtain. Hardship on the U.S. citizen or his or her family if a parent were removed is not sufficient to be granted a cancellation of removal. The hardship suffered must be both exceptional and extremely unusual—for example, profoundly ill or disabled children who must be cared for full-time by a parent (Ross, 2015). Even if an applicant meets all of the required criteria, an immigration judge still retains the discretion to decide whether the individual is deserving of the benefits of cancellation of removal. If the individual is not granted a cancellation, that person is then subject to deportation (Executive Office for Immigration Review, 2015).

Opponents of birthright citizenship have also referred to anchor babies as a financial drain and cited the costs of birthright citizenship as a major problem. Conservative Ann Coulter suggested that "anchor babies" should instead be called "'anvil babies' because that's what anchor babies are around the necks of the American taxpayer" (Coulter, 2015). Opponents also decry the tax dollars spent on babies of "illegal immigrants" in hospitals, schools, and prisons (making the assumption that they will be involved in criminal activity) (Risley, 2012).

As U.S. citizens these children qualify for programs like Women, Infants and Children (WIC) and Medicaid, thus providing short-term benefits to their families (Jacobson, 2010). However, their parents and families, without legal status, do not qualify for federal programs. Supporters of birthright citizenship point out that the benefits received by families of U.S.-born babies are minimal compared to the contributions the U.S. citizens will offer the country. Furthermore, they point out that at least 9 million people live in "mixed-status" families made up of at least one unauthorized adult and at least one U.S.-born child (Taylor et al., 2011). The legality of some family members and illegality of others make it difficult to distinguish whether the need for assistance stemmed from immigration status or from the same financial or economic struggles faced by millions of other Americans. Regardless, in this case the economic impact of anchor babies becomes an issue connected to the structure of current immigration policy and discussion of what types of reform need to be made, not a matter of birthright citizenship itself causing undue strain on taxpayers.

In November 2014 President Obama took executive action to address the issue of mixed-status families through a program called Deferred Action for Parents of Americans (DAPA). This program was intended to provide temporary legal status to as many as 3.7 million undocumented immigrant parents of U.S. children or legal permanent residents, allowing those parents to live and work in the United States for three years without fear of deportation (Migration Policy Institute, 2014). Twenty-seven states, almost exclusively Republican-led, challenged the executive actions with a federal lawsuit, alleging executive overreach. Most of those states have small immigrant populations (Brownstein, 2015). In response, in February 2015, just a day before the planned start of the program, a federal judge issued a temporary injunction that blocked implementation of DAPA (as well as an expanded version of the Deferred Action for Childhood Arrivals [DACA] program) (Francis, 2015). This ruling was upheld in June 2016 when the Supreme Court came to an impasse (4–4) on the case.

One additional element of the birthright citizenship debate that merits mention is the argument against birth tourism, described by presidential nominee Carly Fiorina as one of the "festering problems" in the United States (Howard, 2015). This practice is similar to what has been described as entering the United States for purposes of having an anchor baby. However, birth tourism differs from traditional anchor baby arguments because it involves individuals from high-income families who come to the United States on tourist visas, within the confines of the law, with the intention of birthing their babies on American soil and thus obtaining

U.S. citizenship for the children. In most cases, these parents leave the country with the child after giving birth. In recent years, the practice has expanded rapidly among Asians who often spend tens of thousands of dollars to come to "maternity hotels" in Southern California (Fuchs, 2015). According to Chinese state media, the number of Chinese women who gave birth in the United States more than doubled from 4,200 in 2008 to nearly 10,000 in 2012 (Yan, 2015). It is difficult to calculate the total number of birth tourists who have babies in the United States each year, but the highest estimates place the number around 36,000 (Camarota, 2015), which is less than 1 percent of all annual U.S. births (Centers for Disease Control and Prevention, 2013). There are potential downfalls to the practice, however. All U.S. citizens are required to file and pay taxes, regardless of where they live. Therefore, an individual born in the United States who has never lived or worked there would still be required to submit taxes to the U.S. government (Yan, 2014).

FURTHER READING

Brownstein, R. (2015, January 29). Most states suing Obama over immigration have small undocumented populations. *The Atlantic*. Retrieved from http://www.theatlantic.com/politics/archive/2015/01/most-states-suing-obama-over-immigration-have-small-undocumented-populations/431823/

Bureau of Consular Affairs. (2015a, September 25). *Immigrant numbers for October 2015*. Washington, DC: U.S. Department of State. Retrieved from http://travel.state.gov/content/dam/visas/Bulletins/visabulletin_October2015.pdf

Bureau of Consular Affairs. (2015b, September 19). *Annual immigrant visa waiting list report as of November 1, 2014*. Washington, DC: U.S. Department of State. Retrieved from http://travel.state.gov/content/dam/visas/Statistics/Immigrant-Statistics/WaitingListItem.pdf

Bureau of Consular Affairs. (2015c, September 15). *Report of the visa office 2014: Table VIII—Immediate relative immigrant visas issued (by country of birth)—Fiscal year 2014*. Washington, DC: U.S. Department of State. Retrieved from http://travel.state.gov/content/dam/visas/Statistics/AnnualReports/FY2014AnnualReport/FY14AnnualReport-TableVIII.pdf

Camarota, S. (2015, April 28). *There are possibly 36,000 birth tourists annually*. Washington, DC: Center for Immigration Studies. Retrieved from http://www.cis.org/camarota/there-are-possibly-36000-birth-tourists-annually

Centers for Disease Control and Prevention. (2013). Fast stats: Birth and natality. Retrieved from http://www.cdc.gov/nchs/fastats/births.htm

Coulter, A. (2015, August 25). Ann Coulter introduces Donald Trump at Iowa speech, 2016 presidential campaign rally 8/25 [Video file]. Retrieved from https://www.youtube.com/watch?v=wIDjsKw1y8Q

Executive Office for Immigration Review. (2015, July). *Application for cancellation of removal and adjustment of status for certain nonpermanent residents* (Form EOIR-42B). Washington, DC: U.S. Department of Justice.

Francis, L. D. (2015, February 18). Federal judge enjoins DAPA, expanded DACA, says programs aren't an exercise of discretion. *Bloomberg BNA*. Retrieved from http://www.bna.com/federal-judge-enjoins-n17179923133/

Fuchs, C. (2015, March 12). Maternity hotel raids enmesh Chinese tradition in controversy. NBCNews.com. Retrieved from http://www.nbcnews.com/news/asian-america/cultural-practice-feeding-maternity-hotel-growth-n320096

Howard, A. (2015, August 27). Carly Fiorina rails against "industry" of Chinese women having U.S. babies. MSNBC.com Retrieved from http://www.msnbc.com/msnbc/carly-fiorina-rails-against-industry-chinese-women-having-us-babies

Immigration and Nationality Act (INA). (2013, February updated). *Section 212(a)(9)(B) of the Immigration and Nationality Act*. Washington, DC: U.S. Citizenship and Immigration Services. Retrieved from http://www.uscis.gov/iframe/ilink/docView/SLB/HTML/SLB/act.html

Jacobson, L. (2010, August 6). Fact-checking the claims about "anchor babies" and whether illegal immigrants "drop and leave." Politifact.com. Retrieved from http://www.politifact.com/truth-o-meter/statements/2010/aug/06/lindsey-graham/illegal-immigrants-anchor-babies-birthright/

Migration Policy Institute. (2014, November 19). *MPI: As many as 3.7 million unauthorized immigrants could get relief from deportation under anticipated new Deferred Action Program* [Press release]. Washington, DC: Migration Policy Institute. Retrieved from http://www.migrationpolicy.org/news/mpi-many-37-million-unauthorized-immigrants-could-get-relief-deportation-under-anticipated-new

Risley, M. C. (2012, March 15). Are "anchor babies" sinking the American economy? *The Huffington Post*. Retrieved from http://www.huffingtonpost.com/michealene-cristini-risley/the-14th_b_1343158.html

Ross, J. (2015, August 20). The myth of the "anchor baby" deportation defense. *The Washington Post*. Retrieved from https://www.washingtonpost.com/news/the-fix/wp/2015/08/20/the-myth-of-the-anchor-baby-deportation-defense/

Taylor, P., Lopez, M. H., Passel, J. S., & Motel, S. (2011, December 1). *Unauthorized immigrants; Length of residency, patterns of parenthood.* Washington, DC: Pew Research Center. Retrieved from http://www .pewhispanic.org/2011/12/01/unauthorized-immigrants-length-of-residency-patterns-of-parenthood/

U.S. Citizenship and Immigration Services. (2011, March 30). *Green card eligibility.* Washington, DC: Department of Homeland Security. Retrieved from http://www.uscis.gov/green-card/green-card-processes-and-procedures/green-card-eligibility

U.S. Citizenship and Immigration Services. (2014, May 1). *Family of U.S. citizens.* Washington, DC: Department of Homeland Security. Retrieved from http://www.uscis.gov/family/family-us-citizens

Wooldridge, F. (2009, August 10). Anchor babies: No more U.S. citizenship. Newswithviews.com. Retrieved from http://www.newswithviews .com/Wooldridge/frosty490.htm

Yan, S. (2014, December 17). Meet the "accidental American" with a big tax bill. *CNNMoney.* Retrieved from http://money.cnn.com/2014/ 12/15/pf/accidental-american-expat-tax/index.html?iid=EL

Yan, S. (2015, February 9). Why Chinese moms want American babies. *CNNMoney.* Retrieved from http://money.cnn.com/2015/02/08/news/ china-birth-tourism/index.html?section=money_topstories

Q28. IS THE UNITED STATES THE ONLY COUNTRY IN THE WORLD WITH BIRTHRIGHT CITIZENSHIP?

Answer: No. The United States is one of 30 countries in the world that honors birthright citizenship.

The Facts: For years, opponents of birthright citizenship have been calling for the repeal of the Fourteenth Amendment to the Constitution, arguing that it was meant to address the legal status of slaves and their children, not immigrants. Researchers from the Center for Immigration Studies argue that the Citizenship Clause in the Fourteenth Amendment was not intended to benefit either illegal aliens or visitors to the United States whose presence is temporary (Feere, 2010). Former U.S. Representative Tom Tancredo argues that a Supreme Court ruling on the interpretation of the Fourteenth Amendment that considers illegal aliens and foreign visitors is necessary to clearly establish the principles for all types of births because any previous rulings have only considered children of individuals legally in the United States (Tancredo, 2015). Republican presidential candidate Donald Trump went even further, stating, "I don't think they have American citizenship and if you speak to some very, very good lawyers—and I know some will disagree—but many of them agree with me and you're going to find they do not have American citizenship. We have to start a process where we take back our country. Our country is going to hell" (Trump, 2015).

Current interpretation of the Fourteenth Amendment and its application of the concept of jus soli (or, by the right of the soil) stemmed from the 1898 Supreme Court decision in the case *United States v. Wong Kim Ark* (*United States v. Wong Kim Ark*, 1898). This ruling determined that any child born on U.S. soil is a U.S. citizen, with the exception of children born to diplomats or hostile occupying forces or those who are born on public ships belonging to foreign entities (Peralta, 2015). According to sociologist John Skrentny, this civic notion of nationhood based on place or shared ideas (jus soli) applied by the Supreme Court to the Fourteenth Amendment is largely a New World phenomenon, one that is very distinct from citizenship laws of ethnic nations based on the idea of jus sanguinis (or, by right of blood) (National Public Radio, 2010).

Perhaps because of this distinction from European and more ethnocentric nations, certain opponents of birthright citizenship call for the discarding of what they feel is a uniquely American phenomenon. Conservative political commentator Glenn Beck questioned the need for the Fourteenth Amendment during a 2009 *Fox News* program, asking, "Why do we have automatic citizenship upon birth? We're the only country in the world that has it" (Beck, 2009). Tom Tancredo blogged similar sentiments, citing specifically the dangers of awarding citizenship to babies born to Muslim parents from Middle Eastern countries who are studying at U.S. universities. "Those children can later return to the United States as citizens," said Tancredo, "and, moreover, they can bring their parents, who will then become eligible for citizenship as well. No other country in the world allows such insanity, and it is long past time to end it" (Tancredo, 2015).

Both quotes contain inaccuracies. Far from being the only country in the world to bestow citizenship upon any baby born within its borders, the United States is actually one of 30 countries with a policy of birthright citizenship (NumbersUSA, 2015). Opponents point out that the United States and Canada are the only economically advanced countries (as defined by the International Monetary Fund) on the list. However, it is also the case that nearly every country in the Western Hemisphere has a birthright citizenship policy (NumbersUSA, 2015). This evidence seems to support the idea that in the New World, citizenship tended to be based more on ideas and shared sense of space (or place) than on shared ethnic identity.

FURTHER READING

Beck, G. (2009, June 10). Beck decries "the anchor baby thing," asks "Why do we have automatic citizenship upon birth?" [Video file]. Media Matters for America. Retrieved from http://mediamatters.org/video/2009/06/10/beck-decries-the-anchor-baby-thing-asks-why-do/151082

Feere J. (2010, August). *Birthright citizenship in the United States: A global comparison.* Washington, DC: Center for Immigration Studies. Retrieved from http://www.cis.org/birthright-citizenship

National Public Radio (NPR). (2010, August 14). Few nations give guarantees like 14th Amendment [Transcript]. All Things Considered, NPR. Retrieved from http://www.npr.org/templates/story/story.php?storyId=129201845

NumbersUSA. (2015, August 24). Nations granting birthright citizenship. NumbersUSA. Retrieved from https://www.numbersusa.com/content/learn/issues/birthright-citizenship/nations-granting-birthright-citizenship.html

Peralta, E. (2015, August 18). 3 things you should know about birthright citizenship. npr.org. Retrieved from http://www.npr.org/sections/thetwo-way/2015/08/18/432707866/3-things-you-should-know-about-birthright-citizenship

Tancredo, T. (2015, May 1). Time to end ridiculous "birthright citizenship" [Blog]. Retrieved from http://www.wnd.com/2015/05/times-to-end-ridiculous-birthright-citizenship/

Trump, D. (2015). Immigration reform that will make America great again. Positions: From Donald Trump. Retrieved from https://www.donaldjtrump.com/images/uploads/Immigration-Reform-Trump.pdf

United States v. Wong Kim Ark. (1898, March 28). Supreme Court ruling [169 U.S. 649 (1898) No. 132]. Retrieved from https://scholar.google.com/scholar_case?case=3381955771263111765&hl=en&as_sdt=6&as_vis=1&oi=scholarr

Q29. ARE "ANCHOR BABIES" AND BIRTHRIGHT CITIZENSHIP THE PRIMARY MOTIVATIONS BEHIND ILLEGAL IMMIGRATION?

Answer: No.

The Facts: Another string of arguments against birthright citizenship has fueled the notion that having "anchor babies" is the primary motivation for immigrants to enter the United States illegally. This argument asserts that persons purposefully enter the United States illegally to have their babies so that those babies can sponsor their parents' legal status as well.

In 2010 Republican Senator Lindsey Graham told *Fox News* that he was considering introducing legislation that would change the Fourteenth Amendment to prevent birthright citizenship of children born to parents in the United States without authorization. "People come here to have babies," he said. "They come here to drop a child. It's called 'drop and leave.' To have a child in America, they cross the border, they go to the emergency room, have a child, and that child's automatically an American citizen. That shouldn't be the case. That attracts people here for all the wrong reasons" (Graham, 2010).

Graham is not alone in his quest to end birthright citizenship. In mid-2015 Republican presidential candidate Donald Trump stated in his immigration plan that "birthright citizenship" remains the "biggest magnet for illegal immigration" (Trump, 2015). This was one of many harsh immigration-related statements that helped to catapult Trump to the top of the Republican candidate polls during the summer and fall of 2015. Texas Senator and presidential hopeful Ted Cruz said during an interview that birthright citizenship "incentivizes additional illegal immigration" (Cruz, 2015).

Such arguments imply a quick and easy transition to legal resident for the parent of a U.S.-citizen child, providing major motivation for citizen hopefuls to enter the United States illegally. Research indicates otherwise. Not only is obtaining legal status through birthright citizenship an extremely and difficult process, but the very notion of what birthright citizenship means in the context of illegal immigration is often misunderstood.

To begin, as described in question number 27, there is no quick and easy way of petitioning for legal status for a parent. The U.S.-citizen child must be at least 21 years old before any of this process can start, and at that point there are still a number of potential hurdles to overcome in order for legal status to be granted. Most importantly, the parents of the U.S.-citizen baby must maintain their nonimmigrant status and remain out of the country before applying, or they risk additional entry bans and delays.

Comments like those made by Graham and Trump imply that the number of babies born in the United States to unauthorized immigrant parents is rising or is unusually high at this point in time. In fact, the opposite is true. Rather than a boom in the birth of babies to unauthorized parents, there has been a drop. However, outdated statistics about the numbers of so-called anchor babies have been widely circulated to the general public and even to members of Congress. In April 2015 Jon Feere of the conservative Center for Immigration Studies testified during a U.S. House Subcommittee meeting that "every year, 350,000 to 400,000 children are born to illegal immigrants in the United States" (Feere, 2015), and in August 2015 Donald Trump's campaign manager stated during an interview that 400,000 anchor babies are born each year in the United States (Qiu, 2015). These figures were likely accurate when the numbers of babies born to parents without authorization were at their highest—between 2007 and 2010 – but since that time estimates have decreased significantly (McGinty, 2015). The Pew Research Center estimates that in 2013 there were 295,000 babies born to unauthorized immigrant parents (Passel & Cohn, 2015). (Note that only one parent must be in the country illegally in order for a baby to fall into that categorization, not both.) That number represents 8 percent of the 3.9 million births that year, a decline from the peak in 2007 when 9 percent of babies in the United States were born to unauthorized parents (ibid.). Therefore, in fact, the number of "anchor babies" is actually dropping.

Additionally, according to estimates from the Pew Hispanic Center, most of the babies born to unauthorized immigrant parents during 2009 (one of the peak years) were not babies of recent arrivals (Passel & Cohn, 2011). Pew Center analysis indicated that 61 percent of the unauthorized parents of babies born in 2009 entered the United States prior to 2004, 30 percent arrived between 2004 and 2007, and just 9 percent arrived from 2008 to 2010. The numbers seem to indicate that individuals or families have had other motivations for entering the United States illegally and their children were born after they had already lived in the country for a number of years.

Perhaps most importantly, the argument that birthright citizenship is the primary cause for illegal immigration discounts the tremendous impact of economic factors as one of the most important motivations for unauthorized immigration to the United States. Economics has long been considered one of the most important factors affecting the decision to enter the United States illegally (Gans, 2007). A 2013 survey of detainees by the National Center for Border Security and Immigration found that the desire to seek employment was by far the greatest reason given for crossing the border (Grimes et al., 2013). Selecting from a multiple-choice list of possible reasons for entering illegally, 65 percent of detainees indicated that they crossed seeking work, and an additional 51 percent indicated they crossed for an already-established job. In contrast, 24 percent marked that they crossed to reunite with family, and only 9 percent of all those surveyed had children already in the United States. This research contradicts the notion that "anchor babies" are a significant, let alone primary, reason for illegal immigration.

Research by USC Gould School of Law professor Emily Ryo also indicates that birthright citizenship has not been a primary factor in women's decisions to cross the border illegally. In her studies, "None of those female migrants have ever mentioned the desire for birthright citizenship for their children as the reason for their decision to migrate to the U.S. Instead, lack of employment opportunities, violence in their home communities, and family reunification have been the most frequently cited reasons among my research subjects" (Robertson, 2015).

Additional support for this argument can be found in an analysis of the demographics of those crossing the border. If birthright citizenship were the primary motivator for illegal immigration, the number of women should be equal to or higher than the number of men, given the fact that they are the ones who will birth a baby. However, of the 486,651 apprehensions made by U.S. Border Patrol in 2014, only roughly one-fourth (120,629) were of females (U.S. Border Patrol, 2014).

Additionally, if the primary motivation for illegal immigration were to give birth to a child in the United States, it would stand to reason that the majority of border-crossers would be individuals living in close proximity to the Mexico-U.S. border, given that they would have fewer obstacles to confront than those traveling from greater distances during late stages of pregnancy. However, 61 percent of detainees surveyed by the National Center for Border Security and Immigration were born in southern Mexican states, not border states (Grimes et al., 2013). Critics also point out that women in late stages of pregnancy would have a difficult time evading Customs and Border Patrol officials at points of entry or making the more difficult and dangerous crossings through remote areas (Ramakrishnan & Gulasekaram, 2015).

FURTHER READING

Beck, G. (2009, June 10). Beck decries "the anchor baby thing," asks "Why do we have automatic citizenship upon birth?" [Video file]. Media Matters for America. Retrieved from http://mediamatters.org/video/2009/06/10/beck-decries-the-anchor-baby-thing-asks-why-do/151082

Constitution of the United States, Amendment XIV. (1868, July 9). The Charters of Freedom; National Archives. Retrieved from http://www.archives.gov/exhibits/charters/constitution_amendments_11-27.html

Cruz, T. (2015, August 23). Ted Cruz: I support ending birthright citizenship. *Face the Nation* [YouTube video]. New York: CBS News. Retrieved from https://www.youtube.com/watch?v=HYGbPGNTmWw

Diamond, J. (2015, August 19). Donald Trump: Birthright babies not citizens. *CNN Politics*. Retrieved from http://www.cnn.com/2015/08/19/politics/donald-trump-birthright-american-citizenship/index.html

Feere, J. (2015, April 29). Statement of Jon Feere, Center for Immigration Studies. U.S. House of Representatives Committee on the Judiciary: Subcommittee on Immigration and Border Security. Retrieved from http://cis.org/Testimony/Feere-Birthright-Testimony-042915

Gans, J. (2007, February). *Illegal immigration to the United States: Causes and policy solutions.* Tucson, AZ: Udall Center for Studies in Public Policy, the University of Arizona. Retrieved from http://udallcenter .arizona.edu/immigration/publications/fact_sheet_no_3_illegal_immigration.pdf

Graham, L. (2010, July 28). Lindsey Graham on birthright citizenship. On the Record with Greta Van Susteren. *Fox News*. Retrieved from https://www.youtube.com/watch?v=Jctte9Zzu9g

Grimes, M., Golob, E., Durcikova, A., & Nunamaker, J. (2013, May). *Reasons and resolve to cross the line: A post-apprehension survey of unauthorized immigrants along the U.S.-Mexico border.* Tucson, AZ: National Center for Border Security and Immigration, University of Arizona. Retrieved from http://www.borders.arizona.edu/cms/sites/default/files/Post-Apprehension-Survey-REPORT%20may31-2013.pdf

Henderson, T. J. (2011). *Beyond borders: A history of Mexican migration to the United States.* Oxford, UK: Wiley-Blackwell.

McGinty, J. C. (2015, September 11). Fact-checking the figures on "Anchor Babies." *The Wall Street Journal*. Retrieved from http://www.wsj.com/articles/fact-checking-the-figures-on-anchor-babies-1441963800

Passel, J. S., & Cohn, D. (2011, February 1). *Unauthorized immigrant population: National and state trends, 2010.* Washington, DC: Pew Hispanic Center. Retrieved from http://www.pewhispanic.org/files/reports/133.pdf

Passel, J. S., & Cohn, D. (2015, September 11). *Number of babies born in U.S. to unauthorized immigrants declines.* Washington, DC: Pew Research Center. Retrieved from http://www.pewresearch.org/fact-tank/2015/09/11/number-of-babies-born-in-u-s-to-unauthorized-immigrants-declines/

Qiu, L. (2015, August 23). *Donald Trump's campaign manager: 400,000 "anchor babies" born in U.S. every year.* Politifact. Retrieved from http://www.politifact.com/truth-o-meter/statements/2015/aug/23/corey-lewandowski/donald-trumps-campaign-manager-says-there-are-4000/

Ramakrishnan, K., & Gulasekaram, P. (2015, September 23). You've heard the GOP rhetoric on immigration. Here are the facts. *Los Angeles Times*. Retrieved from http://www.latimes.com/opinion/op-ed/la-oe-0923-ramakrishnan-immigration-absurdities-20150923-story.html

Robertson, L. (2015, August 20). Trump's immigration plan. FactCheck .org. Retrieved from http://www.factcheck.org/2015/08/trumps-immigration-plan/

Ryo, E. (2015). Deciding to cross: Norms and economics of unauthorized migration. *American Sociological Review*, 78(4), 574–603.

Trump, D. (2015). Immigration reform that will make America great again. Positions: From Donald Trump. Retrieved from https://www.donaldjtrump.com/images/uploads/Immigration-Reform-Trump.pdf

U.S. Border Patrol. (2014). Sector profile—fiscal year 2014 (Oct. 1st through Sept. 30th). United States Customs and Border Protection. Retrieved from http://www.cbp.gov/sites/default/files/documents/USBP%20Stats%20FY2014%20sector%20profile.pdf

U.S. Citizenship and Immigration Services. (2014, May 1). *Family of U.S. Citizens*. Washington, DC: Department of Homeland Security. Retrieved from http://www.uscis.gov/family/family-us-citizens

7

❖❖❖

Immigration and the U.S.-Mexico Border

Q30. HAS LAX SECURITY AT THE U.S.-MEXICO BORDER RESULTED IN A LARGE INFLUX OF UNAUTHORIZED IMMIGRANTS INTO THE UNITED STATES IN RECENT YEARS?

Answer: The answer to this is highly contested. There has not been a large overall increase in the number of unauthorized immigrants in recent years (numbers have actually dropped), and it is difficult to determine the sufficiency of border security because ideas about what constitutes a sufficiently secure border vary widely. However, in an era of unprecedented funding for border security and enforcement, the number of individuals apprehended along the U.S.-Mexico border has plummeted to levels not seen since the 1970s, and the overall number of unauthorized individuals in the United States has declined by roughly 1 million over the past nine years. Additionally, a significant percentage of those living in the United States without authorization arrived legally and overstayed visa requirements, thus avoiding the border altogether.

The Facts: Immigration reform has repeatedly been touted as a legislative priority since the administration of Republican President George W. Bush, but multiple attempts by Congress to pass comprehensive immigration legislation have failed (Wasem, 2013). One of the most frequent arguments against comprehensive reform has been that the border must be secured before other immigration-related considerations can be made. When asked about proposed immigration reform legislation in 2014, U.S. Representative Paul Ryan responded, "Security first, no amnesty, then we might be able to get somewhere . . . it's a security-first, non-amnesty approach" (FoxNews.com, 2014).

To that end, Republican Representative Michael McCaul of Texas sponsored the *Secure Our Borders First Act* in January 2015. This legislation would have required the Department of Homeland Security to maintain "operational control" of the U.S.-Mexico border within five years, meaning officers would need to arrest 100 percent of the individuals attempting to cross the border (H.R. 399, 2015; Seghetti & Bjelopera, 2015). Department of Homeland Security (DHS) secretary Jeh Johnson called the bill "extreme to the point of being unworkable" and said the proposed legislation "sets mandatory and highly prescriptive standards that the Border Patrol itself regards as impossible to achieve" (2015). Instead, DHS has pointed out various metrics that indicate increasing successes along the border, including lower recidivism rates among unauthorized migrants (U.S. Department of Homeland Security, 2016), increased interdiction effectiveness rates (percentage of known unauthorized entrants who are apprehended or turned back) (U.S. Department of Homeland Security, 2015), and new, more comprehensive border security measurement strategies (Argueta, 2016). Although Representative McCaul's bill ultimately did not make it to the House or Senate floor, the spirit of the legislation prevails among many GOP members who have repeated the "security first" language in their own discussions about immigration reform.

Likewise, 2016 Republican presidential hopefuls repeatedly emphasized the need for a more secure U.S.-Mexico border when asked about their ideas for immigration policy reform during the primaries. During a *Fox News* interview, Donald Trump made the statement, "Without borders we don't have a country, and that [Mexican] border is just like a piece of Swiss cheese; people pour over it" (Van Susteren, 2016). Ben Carson called for the next president of the United States to "seal the border" within a year (Pappas, 2015). And Ted Cruz stated explicitly in his immigration plan that to strengthen national security and stop illegal immigration, we must "first, secure the border, once and for all. No other reform is meaningful if we do not fix our porous southern border" (Cruz, 2016).

Statistics, however, do not support the image of a Swiss cheese-type border with people pouring in through the holes. In fact, never in the history of the United States of America have so many federal resources been directed toward border security and enforcement as they have over the past 15 years (Johnson, 2015, June 8). In 2012 the federal government spent almost $18 billion on immigration enforcement—more than all other federal criminal law enforcement agencies combined (Meissner et al., 2013), and since 1986 the federal government has spent roughly $187 billion on immigration enforcement (ibid.). The Border Patrol, in terms of numbers, has become the biggest law enforcement agency in the country, with the number of BP agents more than quintupling from 4,028 in FY 1993 to 21,444 in FY 2011, then dropping slightly to 20,273 in FY 2015 (U.S. Border Patrol, 2015a). The Border Patrol budget alone increased more than 10-fold in just over a decade, from $363 million in 1993 to nearly $3.8 billion in 2015 (U.S. Border Patrol, 2015c). To date, nearly 700 miles of fence have been completed along the southwestern border, some sections with triple layers (Johnson, 2015). The National Guard has been sent to the southern border on three separate occasions since 2006 (Breisblatt, 2015). And the present U.S. border enforcement strategy includes nearly 12,000 underground sensors, 119 Border Patrol aircraft, 6 drones, 39 mobile surveillance systems, and 179 mobile video surveillance systems—the largest deployment of resources in the Border Patrol's 90-year history (Johnson, 2015, June 8).

Economic conditions and policies since the early 1990s set the tone for the increased emphasis on border security and security-related expenditures over the past 25 years. For example, the early 1990s' anti-immigrant legislation such as California's Proposition 187 grew out of fears that the growing Latino population (including unauthorized immigrants) was to blame for the economic recession and growing social costs to the state. Although most of Proposition 187 was later ruled unconstitutional, it sparked a national dialogue about reducing illegal immigration and defining state and national roles in addressing immigrant populations.

In 1994, as the North American Free Trade Agreement went into effect, the U.S. government simultaneously tightened its borders to laborers who traditionally crossed into the United States to work—the start of the modern campaign to militarize the southwestern border. Two years later, in 1996, the Illegal Immigration Reform and Immigrant Responsibility Act was passed, creating a 3- or 10-year ban on those caught illegally reentering the United States and implementing more stringent security measures to filter those crossing the nation's borders.

The terrorist attacks in the United States on September 11, 2001, raised fears across the country that national security levels were inadequate. Discussion about the threat of terrorists, need for tougher security, and importance of tighter border controls drove much of the subsequent political discussion and has accompanied budget requests ever since.

Finally, a surge in the number of unaccompanied children and families from Central America starting in 2012 produced renewed calls for increased security along the southwestern border (even though many of those entering from Central America sought out Border Patrol and asked for asylum once crossing into the United States) (Rosenblum & Ball, 2016).

Not to be overlooked is the fact that at the same time that unprecedented resources have been directed toward the border, "illegal immigration" has slowed, and the overall population of unauthorized persons in the United States indicates a downward trend. According to Border Patrol data, the numbers of unauthorized individuals apprehended while crossing the southwestern U.S. border dropped significantly over the past decade, and at the end of FY 2015 were at their lowest level in over 40 years (U.S. Border Patrol, 2015b; U.S. Immigration and Customs Enforcement, 2015). Additionally, the total unauthorized immigrant population living in the United States has dropped by nearly a million since its height of 12.2 million in 2007 (Passel & Cohn, 2015). Unauthorized immigration from Mexico in particular dropped by over 1 million between 2007 and 2014 (Gonzalez-Barrera, 2016). Researchers cite a combination of factors that have contributed to the declining unauthorized population, including fewer jobs available in the United States, tougher border enforcement, improved economies south of the border, and a lower birth rate in Mexico (Baker & Rytina, 2013; Gonzalez-Barrera, 2016; Markon, 2015; Nowrasteh, 2015; Passel, Cohn, & Gonzalez-Barrera, 2013; Warren & Kerwin, 2015).

In spite of declining unauthorized populations, some critics have cited the recent surge in children and families crossing the border as evidence of a growing immigration problem. Florida Representative Mario Diaz-Balart said of the women and children entering the United States from Central America, "It's a critical situation and if we don't deal with it urgently but well—done right—then we're facing a crisis of just huge proportions" (Herridge, 2014). Texas Republican Randy Weber introduced the Illegal Entry Accountability Act during the summer of 2014 in an effort to halt foreign aid payments to Guatemala, El Salvador, and Honduras until the flow of children from these countries into the United States was stemmed (U.S. Congress, 2014).

The number of Central American children and families crossing the border without authorization has indeed grown over the past five years, raising slightly the number of overall apprehensions along the southwestern border. However, even with the rise in entries of these populations, apprehension levels (used as indicators of how many people are attempting to cross the border) are still far lower now than they were before the Central American "surge." In 2007, for example, there were 876,704 illegal alien apprehensions nationwide, and in 2014 (the height of the recent Central American influx) there were 486,651 apprehensions (U.S. Border Patrol, 2015b). Additionally, many of these individuals from Central America are *seeking out* Border Patrol agents and asking for asylum, *which is not illegal.* They are a separate category of border-crossers that, while included in Border Patrol apprehension statistics, are actually not all "illegal immigrants" or even "unauthorized border-crossers" because of the nature of their crossing and the fact that many are pleading for asylum once on U.S. soil.

Others who wish to see tougher border enforcement have argued that fewer individuals crossed without permission during previous administrations—and especially the Reagan administration—than under the Obama administration. An analysis of U.S. Border Patrol apprehension figures, however, reveals that the average number of crossing attempts by individuals during the Reagan administration was more than 1 million per year, while the average during the Obama administration (through 2013) was 417,000. Even when taking into consideration that U.S. Border Patrol tactics were different between the two administrations and that data for the Obama administration did not include numbers beyond 2013, a fact-check organization still deemed this allegation false (Greenberg, 2014).

Notably, border security is not the only factor when considering arrival of unauthorized populations in the United States. An estimated 40 percent of unauthorized persons in the United States entered legally, often by air, but overstayed the terms of their visas (PBS.org, 2016; Selby, 2013). Therefore, for over 4 million individuals in the country without permission, border security was not a factor in their arrival.

Former President George W. Bush acknowledged the limitations of a "border security only" approach to immigration reform during his 2008 State of the Union Address to Congress. Bush stated,

> America needs to secure our borders—and with your help, my administration is taking steps to do so. . . . Yet we also need to acknowledge that we will never fully secure our border until we create a lawful way for foreign workers to come here and support our economy. This will take pressure off the border and allow law enforcement to concentrate on those who mean us harm. We must also find a sensible

and humane way to deal with people here illegally. Illegal immigration is complicated, but it can be resolved. And it must be resolved in a way that upholds both our laws and our highest ideals. (2008)

In summary, there is no alarming new influx of border-crossers, and current data indicates that the border is more secure, statistically and functionally, than it has ever been. Although some critics of current immigration policy still demand total operational control of the border with a 100 percent apprehension rate, most officials agree that it is an impossible objective to achieve. Instead, they point to the growing percentage of the border under operational control, indicating advances in the detection, response, and interdiction of illegal activity at or near the border. While opinions may vary about what constitutes "sufficient" border security, the sheer amount of money and resources that the federal government has dedicated to protecting the nation's borders would indicate that security is among the top priorities of U.S. lawmakers. What's more, unauthorized populations have not all arrived via the southern border, so issues related to these populations must be addressed from a broader perspective than just border enforcement alone.

FURTHER READING

Argueta, C. N. (2016, February 16). *Border security metrics between ports of entry* (CRS R44386). Washington, DC: Congressional Research Service. Retrieved from https://www.fas.org/sgp/crs/homesec/R44386.pdf

Baker, B., & Rytina, N. (2013). *Estimates of the unauthorized immigrant population residing in the United States: January 2012.* Washington, DC: Department of Homeland Security, Office of Immigration Statistics.

Breisblatt, J. (2015, January 21). Concerns and costs mount as National Guard watches the border. National Immigration Forum blog. Retrieved from https://immigrationforum.org/blog/keeping-their-eyes-on-the-brush/

Bush, G. W. (2008, January 28). *President Bush delivers State of the Union Address.* The White House. Washington, DC: United States Capitol. Transcript retrieved from http://georgewbush-whitehouse.archives.gov/news/releases/2008/01/20080128-13.html

Cruz, T. (2016). Cruz immigration plan. Cruz for president. Retrieved from https://www.tedcruz.org/cruz-immigration-plan/

FoxNews.com. (2014, February 2). Top Republicans support immigration reform, but stress border security must come first. FoxNews.com Politics. Retrieved from http://www.foxnews.com/politics/2014/02/02/

top-republicans-support-immigration-reform-but-stress-border-security-must-come.html

Gonzalez-Barrera, A. (2016, April 14). *Apprehensions of Mexican migrants at U.S. borders reach near-historic low*. Washington, DC: Pew Research Center. Retrieved from http://www.pewresearch.org/fact-tank/2016/04/14/mexico-us-border-apprehensions/

Greenberg, J. (2014, July 24). *Deirdre Imus: More illegal immigrants "pouring in" now than under Reagan*. Punditfact. St. Petersburg, FL: Politifact.com. Retrieved from http://www.politifact.com/punditfact/statements/2014/jul/24/deirdre-imus/deirdre-imus-more-illegal-immigrants-pouring-now-u/

Herridge, C. (2014, July 16). Misperceptions about U.S. immigration policy behind surge of illegal children, report says. FoxNews.com. Retrieved from http://www.foxnews.com/politics/2014/07/16/misperceptions-about-us-immigration-policy-behind-surge-illegal-children-report.html

H.R. 399. (2015, January 16). Secure our borders first act of 2015. 114th Congress (2015–2016). Retrieved from https://www.congress.gov/bill/114th-congress/house-bill/399

Johnson, J. C. (2015, January 22). *Statement by Secretary Jeh C. Johnson concerning H.R. 399, the Secure Our Border First Act of 2015*. Washington, DC: Department of Homeland Security. Retrieved from https://www.dhs.gov/news/2015/01/22/statement-secretary-jeh-c-johnson-concerning-hr-399-secure-our-border-first-act-2015

Johnson, J. C. (2015, June 8). *Immigration: Perception versus reality* [Remarks and PowerPoint presentation by U.S. Secretary of Homeland Security at Rice University] [Transcript]. Houston, TX: Rice University. Retrieved from http://www.dhs.gov/news/2015/06/08/remarks-secretary-johnson-immigration-perception-versus-reality

Markon, J. (2015, May 27). Fewer immigrants are entering the U.S. illegally, and that's changed the border security debate. *The Washington Post*. Retrieved from https://www.washingtonpost.com/politics/flow-of-illegal-immigration-slows-as-us-mexico-border-dynamics-evolve/2015/05/27/c5caf02c-006b-11e5-833c-a2de05b6b2a4_story.html

McCaul, M. (2015). *Summary of the Secure Our Borders First Act*. Washington, DC: Committee on Homeland Security. Retrieved from https://homeland.house.gov/files/documents/012215-HR399-Bill-Summary_0.pdf

Meissner, D., Kerwin D. M., Chishti, M., & Bergeron, C. (2013, January). *Immigration enforcement in the United States: The rise of a formidable machinery*. Washington, DC: The Migration Policy Institute. Retrieved from http://www.migrationpolicy.org/research/immigration-enforcement-united-states-rise-formidable-machinery

Nowrasteh, A. (2015, June 11). *What explains the flow of unlawful immigration?* CATO at Liberty. Washington, DC: CATO Institute. Retrieved from http://www.cato.org/blog/what-explains-flow-unlawful-immigration

Pappas, A. (2015, January 24). Ben Carson: Next president should pledge to seal border within 1 year. *The Daily Caller*. Retrieved from http://dailycaller.com/2015/01/24/ben-carson-next-president-should-pledge-to-seal-border-within-1-year/

Passel, J. S., & Cohn, D. (2015, July 22). *Unauthorized immigrant population stable for half a decade*. Washington, DC: Pew Research Center. Retrieved from http://www.pewresearch.org/fact-tank/2015/07/22/unauthorized-immigrant-population-stable-for-half-a-decade/

Passel, J. S., Cohn, D., & Gonzalez-Barrera A. (2013, September 23). *Population decline of unauthorized immigrants stalls, may have reversed*. Washington, DC: Pew Research Center. Retrieved from http://www.pewhispanic.org/2013/09/23/population-decline-of-unauthorized-immigrants-stalls-may-have-reversed/

PBS.org. (2016, February 7). How accurate were the GOP candidates at the New Hampshire debate? PBS Newshour. Retrieved from http://www.pbs.org/newshour/bb/how-accurate-were-the-gop-candidates-at-the-new-hampshire-debate/

Rosenblum, M. R., & Ball, I. (2016, January). *Trends in unaccompanied child and family migration from Central America*. Washington, DC: Migration Policy Institute. Retrieved from http://www.migrationpolicy.org/research/trends-unaccompanied-child-and-family-migration-central-america

Seghetti, L., & Bjelopera, J. P. (2015, January 27). *H.R. 399, the Secure Our Borders First Act of 2015: Report in brief (R43879)*. Washington, DC: Congressional Research Service. Retrieved from http://fas.org/sgp/crs/homesec/R43879.pdf

Selby, W. G. (2013, September 6). John Carter claim that 40 percent of nation's illegal residents came by plane and overstayed visas draws on 2006 estimate. Politifact.com. Retrieved from http://www.politifact.com/texas/statements/2013/sep/06/john-carter/john-carter-claim-40-percent-nations-illegal-resid/

U.S. Border Patrol. (2015a). *Border Patrol agent staffing by fiscal year (as of September 19, 2015)*. Washington, DC: Department of Homeland Security, Customs and Border Protection. Retrieved from https://www.cbp.gov/sites/default/files/documents/BP%20Staffing%20FY1992-FY2015.pdf

U.S. Border Patrol. (2015b). *United States Border Patrol: Total illegal alien apprehensions by month—FY 2000*. Washington, DC: Department of Homeland Security, Customs and Border Protection. Retrieved from https://www.cbp.gov/sites/default/files/documents/BP%20Total%20 Monthly%20Apps%20by%20Sector%20and%20Area%2C%20FY 2000-FY2015.pdf

U.S. Border Patrol. (2015c). *United States Border Patrol: Enacted Border Patrol program budget by fiscal year*. Washington DC: Department of Homeland Security, Customs and Border Protection. Retrieved from https://www.cbp.gov/sites/default/files/documents/BP%20Budget%20 History%201990-2015.pdf

U.S. Congress. (2014, June 30). H.R. 5014 (113th): Illegal Entry Accountability Act of 2014. Govtrack.us. Retrieved from https://www .govtrack.us/congress/bills/113/hr5014

U.S. Department of Homeland Security (DHS). (2015, February 2). *Annual performance report for fiscal years 2014–2016*. Washington, DC: Department of Homeland Security. Retrieved from https://www .dhs.gov/sites/default/files/publications/DHS-FY-2014-FY-2016-APR_ 1_0.pdf

U.S. Department of Homeland Security (DHS). (2016, February 9). *Annual performance report for fiscal years 2015–2017*. Washington, DC: Department of Homeland Security. Retrieved from https://preview .dhs.gov/sites/default/files/publications/15-17-APR_0.pdf

U.S. Immigration and Customs Enforcement (ICE). (2014, December 19). ICE enforcement and removal operations report. U.S. Immigration and Customs Enforcement: Department of Homeland Security. Retrievedfromhttps://www.ice.gov/doclib/about/offices/ero/pdf/2014- ice-immigration-removals.pdf

U.S. Immigration and Customs Enforcement (ICE). (2015, December 22). *DHS releases end of fiscal year 2015 statistics*. Washington, DC: Department of Homeland Security. Retrieved from https://www.ice .gov/news/releases/dhs-releases-end-fiscal-year-2015-statistics

Van Susteren, G. (2016, February 20). *Trump: I don't lie, I'm too truthful—it gets me in trouble* [Television interview]. New York, NY: Fox News. Retrieved from https://www.donaldjtrump.com/media/trump-pope- did-not-understand-illegal-immigration-crime-problem

Warren, R., & Kerwin, D. (2015). Beyond DAPA and DACA: Revisiting legislative reform in light of long-term trends in unauthorized immigration to the United States. *Journal on Migration and Human Society*, 3(1), 80–108. New York: Center for Migration Studies. Retrieved from http://jmhs.cmsny.org/index.php/jmhs/article/view/45

Wasem, R. E. (2013, February 27). *Brief history of comprehensive immigration reform efforts in the 109th and 110th Congresses to inform policy discussions in the 113th Congress* (R42980). Washington, DC: Congressional Research Service. Retrieved from http://fas.org/sgp/crs/homesec/R42980.pdf

Q31. IS A FENCE ALONG THE BORDER THE MOST EFFECTIVE WAY TO ADDRESS UNAUTHORIZED IMMIGRATION INTO THE UNITED STATES?

Answer: No. The border is one aspect of a much larger issue of immigration policy. A number of researchers, pundits, Democrats, and even some conservatives have called proposals to build a fence/wall along the border unrealistic because of the cost, length, geographical terrain over which the wall would need to be built, and the fact that a wall does not address broader immigration concerns, including approximately 40 percent of unauthorized persons who entered legally but overstayed their visas.

The Facts: The idea of erecting a physical wall or fence between the United States and Mexico has garnered interest for many years, particularly among political conservatives. Republican Representative Duncan Hunter of California was an early supporter of a fence, crafting the first plan for fence construction in 2005. As of 2016, roughly 700 miles of fence or barriers had been constructed. Since that time, however, numerous politicians and activists have called for completion of the fence across the entire border. During a 2011 campaign rally in Tennessee, presidential candidate Herman Cain proposed a massive wall to secure the southern U.S. border. "It's going to be 20 feet high," he said. "It's going to have barbed wire on the top. It's going to be electrified. And there's going to be a sign on the other side saying, 'It will kill you—Warning'" (Wyatt, 2011). During the 2016 presidential campaign cycle, Ted Cruz promised on his Web site to "build a wall that works" (Cruz, 2016), Marco Rubio stated, "We must secure our border, the physical border, with a wall, absolutely" (Associated Press, 2016), and John Kasich said he would use "a wall or other technologies" to secure the southern border (Torry, 2016).

But the candidate who has catapulted the notion of a wall into the public spotlight most fervently is Donald Trump, who in 2015–2016 made building the wall the pillar of his Republican presidential campaign.

"We're gonna get the wall built . . . and Mexico's gonna pay for the wall," Trump said in August 2015, "and they're gonna be happy about it . . . because the cost of the wall is peanuts compared to the kind of money they're making. Mexico is becoming the new China" (Miller, 2015).

To support his idea for a U.S.-Mexico border wall and tougher immigration policies, Trump launched a television ad in early 2016 that showed grainy footage of a mass of migrants jumping a border fence and scattering into the territory on the other side of it. The ad claims that Trump will "stop illegal immigration by building a wall on our southern border that Mexico will pay for" (Trump, 2016). However, while implying that the footage was of the U.S.-Mexico border, it was later discovered that the video footage was actually taken 5,000 miles away on the border between Morocco and the Spanish enclave of Melilla (Emery Jr. & Jacobson, 2016). After Politifact published a report revealing the source of the video, Trump's campaign manager told *NBC News*, "No s*** it's not the Mexican border, but that's what our country is going to look like. This was 1,000 percent on purpose" (Vitali, Tur, & Terrell, 2016).

Public reaction to the idea of a U.S.-Mexico border wall is varied, but opinions closely follow political alliances. Among registered voters in the United States, just 38 percent support the idea of building a wall between the United States and Mexico, while 83 percent of Trump supporters favor the wall (Pew Research Center, 2016). Although the notion may be popular among certain segments of the population, a number of prominent authorities have spoken out against the idea because of cost, feasibility, and economic impact on the border region. Sheriff Larry Dever of Cochise County, Arizona (which sits on the U.S.-Mexico border), told NBCNEWS.com, "I think [the fence] is well intentioned, but you can build all the fence you want to build and unless it's the right kind of fence and unless you have the manpower to watch it, it's of very little or no value. The federal government has built a lot of fence and most of it has been inadequate in terms of actually stopping people from crossing" (Johnson, 2011). Senior U.S. Senator John Cornyn of Texas said a physical wall was not the answer to border security, but "what we need is a virtual border" (Shadwick, 2016). Pete Saenz, mayor of Laredo, Texas, whose county is 96 percent Hispanic, stated, "Absolutely, definitively, I'm opposed to the border wall. I don't think it's good business and I've told Trump clearly when he was here" (Gonzalez, 2016).

Law enforcement officers have also voiced strong opinions about construction of physical barriers separating the United States from Mexico. Río Grande Valley Border Patrol agent Chris Cabrera, who has been openly critical of federal border policies under the Obama administration, dismissed the idea that a wall will solve the problem of illegal immigration. "You can't just put up a fence and hope that it's going to stem the flow," Cabrera said. "We put an 18-foot wall and they came with a 19-foot ladder" (Hernandez, 2016).

In addition to practical and ideological concerns, the cost of the proposed wall has drawn major criticism. According to a *CNN* report, experts say the wall would cost over $10 billion and take at least four years to construct (Carroll et al., 2016). This figure includes the cost of materials only, not labor or enforcement expenses. A *Washington Post* fact-check investigation estimated the cost of Trump's described wall could be closer to $25 billion, and completion would require 40,000 workers for at least four years, if not more (Kessler, 2016).

To put costs in perspective, the price tag for the 633 miles of U.S.-Mexico border fencing constructed by June 2009 was $2.4 billion, with an estimated cost of $6.5 billion over the next 20 years just to maintain the fence, which had already been breached more than 3,363 times (Government Accountability Office, 2009, September). And costs vary widely depending on the type of terrain being covered and the types of materials necessary to effectively inhibit passage through that area. According to the Government Accountability Office (GAO), in 2009 the average cost of pedestrian fencing was $3.9 million per mile, and the average price of vehicle fencing was $1 million per mile (Government Accountability Office, 2009, January). The triple-layer barrier constructed near San Diego (which required massive movement of earth to fill in a gulch) was roughly $9 million per mile, or $127 million for the 14-mile fence (Nuñez-Neto & Kim, 2008). As of 2016, nearly 1,300 miles of border lack fencing, much of it in areas much more difficult to access and build on than the original 650 plus miles of fencing.

Although Trump has stated he would bill Mexico for the cost of the wall, the Mexican government has made it clear it will not pay. When asked about Trump's claim that Mexico will foot the bill for the proposed project, a spokesperson for Mexican President Enrique Peña Nieto said, "Of course it's false. It reflects an enormous ignorance for what Mexico represents, and also the irresponsibility of the candidate who's saying it" (Martin, 2015). Portions of the fence already constructed over the past decade have done little to promote goodwill between the United States and its southern neighbor. The 14-mile section of fence built between San Diego, California, and Tijuana, Mexico, was dubbed "The Iron Curtain" by Mexicans (Andreas, 2009).

Trump has pointed to the more than $50 billion U.S. trade deficit with Mexico as proof that Mexico has sufficient funds to pay for the wall. However, experts point out that most trade takes place between corporations or private individuals, not the government, and in reality the trade deficit has nothing to do with the Mexican government's ability to pay for a wall. According to one analyst, "The Mexican government does not have adequate funds to pay for health, education or roads—much less build a wall" (Sherman, 2016).

Trump has also proposed raising visa fees and blocking remittance payments to Mexico to fund the border wall (Trump, 2016). In 2015, immigrants in the United States sent an estimated $24.77 billion to Mexico in remittances (Li Ng & Salgado, 2016). However, Trump's plan relies on the assumption that the majority of remittance senders are undocumented immigrants. Experts say it is impossible to know just how much remittance money is sent by undocumented versus established immigrants, but one study suggests that the figure is only 48 percent (Cave, 2016). Additionally, analysts argue that blocking remittances to Mexico would not only encourage money laundering and other illicit smuggling of funds but also devastate Mexico's poorest populations for whom remittances are a lifeline, potentially increasing outmigration to the United States (Hinojosa, 2015; Klein, 2016).

The greatest obstacles to construction of a border wall, however, may be legal and geographical ones. Much of the U.S.-Mexico border passes through privately held land that ranchers have been unwilling to sell; other sections pass through Native American reservations or protected wildlife refuges. Acquiring the land and/or the right to place a physical barrier on these lands would be both costly and difficult to achieve. Topography also provides a challenge. Portions of the border where the proposed wall would be constructed include rugged mountains, remote valleys, and deep canyons, all of which are largely inaccessible by motorized vehicles needed to transport materials. Once completed, the remoteness of these sections would make them difficult to patrol. Also, the Río Grande River forms 1,255 miles of natural border (International Boundary and Water Commission, n.d.). Constructing a wall in the middle of this river where the actual boundary lies would not only be a physically dubious task but would also violate the terms of a 1970 treaty prohibiting any impediments to the natural flow of the river (Nixon, 1970).

Environmental groups have also decried the construction of a border fence or wall, citing the devastating impact on wildlife whose natural ranges span both sides of the border. Of specific concern is the recovery of two endangered species found along the southwestern border: the ocelot and jaguarondi, for which the border wall "would almost certainly expedite the disappearance of these species from the U.S. and could essentially nullify decades of cost- and labor-intensive planning, restoration, and recovery efforts" (Eriksson & Taylor, 2010). Scientists who have identified numerous other species at risk along the length of the border cite not only the detrimental effects of the wall itself but the secondary effects of noise, artificial lights, and other aspects of the physical barrier that disrupt natural migration and life cycles (Lasky, Jetz, & Keitt, 2011; Oregon State University, 2009).

Even where walls are already in place, determined border-crossers have breached them. Human and drug smugglers have used ladders to climb over them, built tunnels to pass under them, or have avoided them altogether by hiding illicit cargo in vehicles passing through legal ports of entry (Dear, 2013). Since 2008, authorities have discovered over 70 tunnels connecting Mexico to the United States, including an elaborate half-mile Mexico–California tunnel discovered in April 2016 (Dear, 2013; Graham, 2016). As previously mentioned, by May 14, 2009, the border fence had already been breached 3,363 times at an average cost of $1,300 for each repair (Government Accountability Office, 2009, September). Perhaps even more significantly, walls have no impact on the many unauthorized in the United States who enter legally. It is estimated that 40 percent of the unauthorized population in the country came through legal channels and then overstayed the terms of their visas (PBS.org, 2016; Selby, 2013).

Finally, construction of a border wall may have the unintended effect of increasing unauthorized populations in the United States. Princeton sociology professor Douglas Massey argues that border militarization, including construction of a border fence along certain stretches of border, was not only unsuccessful, but that "it backfired in the sense that it transformed what had been a circular migration of male workers to three states [California, Texas, and Illinois] into a much larger, settled population of families living in 50 states" (Bernstein, 2012). A more heavily patrolled border means those who lack the legal means to enter the United States will likely stay put if they successfully make the crossing, rather than following more traditional circular migration patterns (Massey, Durand, & Pren, 2016). Analysts point to the need for comprehensive immigration reform that acknowledges push factors such as inequality and poverty in sending countries, conforms to U.S. labor needs, and emphasizes immigration management (as opposed to reduction) as the most effective means of addressing unauthorized migration (Massey, Durand, & Pren, 2016; Payan & de la Garza, 2014; Reyes, 2007).

In terms of cost, topographical challenges, environmental concerns, and undesirable consequences, construction of a wall (or fence) across the entire border is neither practical nor plausible. Instead, a more comprehensive approach that emphasizes reform and management of existing immigration policies may prove more cost-effective and successful for long-term reduction of unauthorized populations.

FURTHER READING

Andreas, P. (2009). *Border games: Policing the U.S.-Mexico divide* (2nd ed.). Ithaca, NY, and London: Cornell University Press.

Associated Press. (2016, January 1). *Presidential candidates differ on border wall with Mexico*. New York, NY: The Associated Press. Retrieved from https://www.yahoo.com/news/presidential-candidates-differ-border-wall-mexico-150722185.html

Bernstein, M. F. (2012, April 25). Crisis contrived. *Princeton Alumni Weekly*. Princeton, NJ: Princeton University. Retrieved from http://paw.princeton.edu/article/crisis-contrived

Campo-Flores, A. (2016, February 28). Jeff Sessions, leading GOP Senate voice on immigration, endorses Trump. *The Wall Street Journal*. Retrieved from http://blogs.wsj.com/washwire/2016/02/28/jeff-sessions-leading-gop-senate-voice-on-immigration-endorses-trump/

Carroll, J., Urbany, B., Cummings, J., Pisano, M., Watkins, E., & Reyes, J. (2016, February 17). Trump says he'd build a wall along the Mexican border. We tried to figure out how. CNN.com. Retrieved from http://www.cnn.com/2016/02/17/politics/donald-trump-mexico-wall/index.html

Cave, A. (2016, April 8). Donald Trump claims most wire transfers to Mexico are from undocumented immigrants. Politifact Arizona. Retrieved from http://www.politifact.com/arizona/statements/2016/apr/08/donald-trump/donald-trump-claims-most-wire-transfers-mexico-are/

Cruz, T. (2016). Secure the border [Official Web site—issues]. Retrieved from https://www.tedcruz.org/issues/secure-the-border/

Dear, M. (2013, February). *Why walls won't work: Repairing the US-Mexico divide*. New York: Oxford University Press.

Emery Jr., C. E., & Jacobson, L. (2016, January 4). Donald Trump's first TV ad shows migrants "at the southern border," but they're actually in Morocco. Politifact.com. Retrieved from http://www.politifact.com/truth-o-meter/statements/2016/jan/04/donald-trump/donald-trumps-first-tv-ad-shows-migrants-southern-/

Eriksson, L., & Taylor, M. (2010). *The environmental impacts of the border wall between Texas and Mexico* [Briefing]. Austin, TX: University of

Texas Law School. Retrieved from https://law.utexas.edu/humanrights/
borderwall/analysis/briefing-The-Environmental-Impacts-of-the-
Border-Wall.pdf

Gonzalez, V. (2016, March 3). Laredo mayor opposes Trump's idea of border
wall. *kgns.tv*. Retrieved from http://www.kgns.tv/home/headlines/mayor-
on-fox-370960941.html

Government Accountability Office (GAO). (2009, January 29). *Secure
border initiative fence construction costs* [GAO-09-244R]. Washington,
DC: GAO. Retrieved from http://www.gao.gov/assets/100/95951
.pdf

Government Accountability Office (GAO). (2009, September). *Secure
Border Initiative: Technology deployment delays persist and the impact of
border fencing has not been assessed* [GAO 09-896]. Washington, DC:
GAO. Retrieved from http://www.gao.gov/assets/300/294982.pdf

Graham, M. (2016, April 21). Longest drug tunnel under U.S.-Mexico
border unearthed. *Reuters*. Retrieved from http://www.huffingtonpost
.com/entry/california-mexico-drug-tunnel_us_5718d380e4b0c92
44a7af11f?utm_hp_ref=us-mexico-border

Hernandez, K. (2016, April 2). BP Council says "catch and release"
policy continues fueling illegal immigration. *The Monitor* (McAllen,
TX). Retrieved from http://www.themonitor.com/news/local/bp-coun
cil-says-catch-and-release-policy-continues-fueling-illegal/article_
b48caa0c-f92c-11e5-914a-671ec164babb.html

Hinojosa, R. (2015, September 16). *Six HUGE numbers which should
automatically disqualify Trump from being president*. Los Angeles: University of California North American Integration and Development Center.
Retrieved from http://www.naid.ucla.edu/publications/six-huge-num
bers-which-should-automatically-disqualify-trump-from-being-
president

International Boundary and Water Commission (IBWC). (n.d.). *About
the Río Grande*. El Paso, TX: IBWC. Retrieved from http://ibwc.state
.gov/Contact_Us/Contact_us.html

Johnson, G. (2011, July 18). Arizona launching fundraising website for
border fence. NBCNEWS.com. Retrieved from http://www.nbcnews
.com/id/43796960/ns/us_news-security/t/arizona-launching-fundrais
ing-website-border-fence/#.VwHarl-cHmS

Johnson, J. C. (2015, June 8). *Immigration: Perception versus reality*
[Remarks and PowerPoint by U.S. Secretary of Homeland Security at
Rice University] [Transcript]. Houston, TX: Rice University. Retrieved
from http://www.dhs.gov/news/2015/06/08/remarks-secretary-johnson-
immigration-perception-versus-reality

Kessler, G. (2016, February 11). Trump's dubious claim that his border wall would cost $8 billion. *The Washington Post* [Fact checker]. Retrieved from https://www.washingtonpost.com/news/fact-checker/wp/2016/02/11/ trumps-dubious-claim-that-his-border-wall-would-cost-8-billion/

Klein, A. (2016, April 7). Donald Trump's plan to build a wall is actually really dangerous. *Fortune*. Retrieved from http://fortune.com/2016/ 04/07/donald-trump-mexico-wall/

Lasky, J. R., Jetz, W., & Keitt, T. H. (2011, May 3). Conservation biogeography of the U.S.-Mexico border: A transcontinental risk assessment of barriers to animal dispersal. *Diversity and Distributions, 17*(4), 673–687.

Li Ng, J. J., & Salgado, A. (2016, February 3). Remittances reached U.S.$24.77 billion in 2015, 4.8% up on the previous year. BBVA, Bank of Mexico. Retrieved from https://www.bbvaresearch.com/wp-content/ uploads/2016/02/160203_ObsMigracionMexico_eng.pdf

Martin, E. (2015, August 12). Sorry Donald Trump, Mexico says it will not pay for border wall. Bloomberg.com. Retrieved from https:// www.bloomberg.com/politics/articles/2015-08-13/sorry-donald-trump-mexico-says-it-will-not-pay-for-wall-on-border

Massey, D. S., Durand, J., & Pren, K. A. (2016, March). Why border enforcement backfired. *American Journal of Sociology, 121*(5), 1557–1600.

Miller, J. (2015, August 13). Mexico: No, Donald Trump, we won't pay for a border wall. CBSnews.com. Retrieved from http://www.cbsnews .com/news/mexico-no-donald-trump-we-wont-pay-for-a-border-wall/

Nixon, R. (1970, November 23). *Treaty to resolve pending boundary differences and maintain the Río Grande and Colorado River as the international boundary*. (Treaty between the United States and Mexico). Washington, DC: Author. Retrieved from http://www.ibwc.gov/Files/1970_Treaty .pdf

Nuñez-Neto, B., & Kim, Y. (2008, May 13). *Border security: Barriers along the U.S. international border*. Washington, DC: Congressional Research Service. Retrieved from http://congressionalresearch.com/RL33659/ document.php

Oregon State University. (2009, July 8). U.S.-Mexico border wall could threaten wildlife species. *ScienceDaily*. Retrieved from https://www .sciencedaily.com/releases/2009/07/090707171002.htm

Passel, J. S., Cohn, D., & Gonzalez-Barrera, A. (2012, April 23). *Net migration from Mexico falls to zero—and perhaps less*. Washington, DC: Pew Research Center. Retrieved from http://www.pewhispanic.org/2012/04/23/net-migration-from-mexico-falls-to-zero-and-perhaps-less/

Passel, J. S., Cohn, D., & Gonzalez-Barrera, A. (2013, September 23). *Population decline of unauthorized immigrants stalls, may have reversed.*

Washington, DC: Pew Research Center. Retrieved from http://www
.pewhispanic.org/2013/09/23/population-decline-of-unauthorized-
immigrants-stalls-may-have-reversed/

Payan, T., & de la Garza, E. (Eds.). (2014). *Undecided nation: Political
gridlock and the immigration crisis. Cham*, Switzerland: Springer International Publishing.

PBS.org. (2016, February 7). How accurate were the GOP candidates
at the New Hampshire debate? PBS Newshour. Retrieved from
http://www.pbs.org/newshour/bb/how-accurate-were-the-gop-
candidates-at-the-new-hampshire-debate/

Pew Research Center. (2016, March). *Campaign exposes fissures over
issues, values and how life has changed in the U.S.* Washington, DC:
Pew Research Center. Retrieved from http://www.people-press.org/
files/2016/03/3-31-16-March-Political-release-1.pdf

Reyes, B. I. (2007). The impact of U.S. immigration policy on Mexican
unauthorized immigration. *The University of Chicago Legal Forum*, 1(6),
131–155. Retrieved from http://chicagounbound.uchicago.edu/uclf/
vol2007/iss1/6

Selby, W. G. (2013, September 6). John Carter claim that 40 percent
of nation's illegal residents came by plane and overstayed visas draws
on 2006 estimate. Politifact.com. Retrieved from http://www.politi
fact.com/texas/statements/2013/sep/06/john-carter/john-carter-claim-
40-percent-nations-illegal-resid/

Shadwick, L. (2016, March 31). Cornyn: No border wall needed
between Texas and Mexico. *Breitbart News*. Retrieved from http://
www.breitbart.com/texas/2016/03/31/cornyn-no-border-wall-needed-
between-texas-and-mexico/

Sherman, A. (2016, January 26). Donald Trump says of course Mexico can
pay for wall—because of trade deficit. Politifact Florida. Retrieved from
http://www.politifact.com/florida/statements/2016/jan/26/donald-
trump/donald-trump-says-course-mexico-can-pay-wall-becau/

Torry, J. (2016, February 18). Kasich says U.S. has right to build a wall;
defends pope against Trump. *Dayton Daily News*. Retrieved from http://
www.daytondailynews.com/news/news/state-regional-govt-politics/
john-kasich-donald-trump-jeb-bush-on-cnn-town-hall/nqSXm/

Trump, D. (2016). Compelling Mexico to pay for the wall [Web site—
positions]. Retrieved from https://www.donaldjtrump.com/positions/
pay-for-the-wall

Trump, D. (2016, January). Donald Trump AD first commercial TV
AD campaign [Campaign advertisement]. YouTube. Retrieved from
http://www.bing.com/videos/search?q=trump+%27s+first+television+

ad&view=detail&mid=3F6DDE6BADFF1C2B06E13F6DDE6BAD
FF1C2B06E1&FORM=VIRE

Van Susteren, G. (2016, February 20). *Trump: I don't lie, I'm too truthful—
it gets me in trouble* [Television interview]. New York, NY: Fox News.
Retrieved from http://www.foxnews.com/on-air/on-the-record/index
.html

Vitali, A., Tur, K., & Terrell, A. (2016, January 5). Trump ad fact checked
for border footage, campaign says "No s***." *NBC News*. Retrieved
from http://www.nbcnews.com/politics/2016-election/trump-ad-fact-
checked-mexican-border-footage-campaign-says-no-n489981

Wyatt, E. (2011, October 15). Cain proposed electrified border fence.
The New York Times. Retrieved from http://thecaucus.blogs.nytimes
.com/2011/10/15/cain-proposes-electrified-border-fence/?_r=0

Q32. IS NATIONAL SECURITY THE PRIMARY ISSUE OF CONCERN ALONG THE U.S.-MEXICO BORDER?

Answer: Yes and no. Security is the issue that has received the most attention. However, humanitarian concerns related to migrant deaths, unlawful detentions, and mistreatment of migrants have also drawn local, national, and international attention to the southern U.S. border.

The Facts: Border security has become one of the most widely addressed immigration topics of recent decades, and particularly so since the terror-ist attacks of 2011. However, even before 9/11, national security was often tied to the U.S.-Mexico border. In 1986 Ronald Reagan warned congres-sional leaders that failure to support his aid package for the Nicaraguan Contra forces could result in a terrorist haven "just two days' driving time from Harlingen, Texas" (Chardy, 1986).

Recent years, however, have produced an unprecedented flurry of "security first" dialogue. Marco Rubio, for example, stated, "There are at least three sectors of the border, one in particular, that are just completely insecure" (Contorno, 2015). This claim was investigated and deemed mostly false by Politifact.com (ibid.). California U.S. Representative Duncan Hunter along with Texas Governor Rick Perry, Pennsylvania U.S. Representative Lou Barletta, and Florida Senator Marco Rubio claimed in 2014 that ISIS militants already had entered or could be planning to enter the United States through the southern border (Hart, 2014), to which DHS testified before Congress that "to date we have not had credible reporting that either Hezbollah or any other terrorist group has been taking advantage of our borders to move individuals in and out" (C-SPAN, 2014). One official added, "We have been projecting our anxiety about threats to the United States on the U.S.-Mexico border for as long as I have been alive. It does not mean we should not be vigilant. Does not mean we should not take the threats seriously. We should only traffic in the facts and the data and we should only raise these kinds of fears and anxieties when there are facts to support them" (ibid.).

Some scholars surmise the ongoing emphasis on enforcement has continued "because the Mexico-U.S. border has become the preeminent symbolic line separating Americans from any and all external threats" (Massey, Durand, & Pren, 2016, p. 1563). Other scholarship has also analyzed the border's role as a symbol of security, order, power, and national identity (Ackleson, 2005; Andreas, 2009; Payan, 2006; Wilson & Donnan, 2012).

However, in spite of the prominence of the security discussion, border matters of a different nature have sparked concern among politicians, residents of southwestern United States, and members of civic organizations. The number of migrant deaths occurring along the U.S.-Mexico border has skyrocketed since the mid-1990s, largely due to multiple push factors from the south and tougher U.S. border enforcement measures that rechanneled migrant flows into more remote and dangerous crossing areas.

Once a quiet desert landscape with no more than a handful of unauthorized migrants passing through, the Sonoran desert of southern Arizona drew international attention in the mid-1990s when bodies of migrants began to appear—first by the dozens and later by the hundreds. As the new "Prevention through Deterrence" U.S. immigration policies of the mid-1990s focused on securitization of traditional border-crossing areas such as Tijuana/San Diego and Ciudad Juárez/El Paso (U.S. Border Patrol, 1994), would-be migrants shifted their crossing routes to the more remote and dangerous stretches of desert in northern Sonora and southern Arizona. This "funnel effect" (Rubio-Goldsmith et al., 2006) proved deadly. Those whose remains were found most often died of exposure— hypothermia or hyperthermia often coupled with dehydration (Martínez et al., 2013). Some of those fatalities were migrants who were unable to keep up with the group because of injury or sickness, and were left behind by *coyotes* (human smugglers)—a probable death sentence in the vast, dry desert (Regan, 2010; Romeri, 2014). The United States Customs and Border Protection (CBP) reported 6,571 deaths along the southwestern U.S. border between 1998 and 2015 (U.S. Customs and Border Protection, 2015). While large, these official numbers are usually

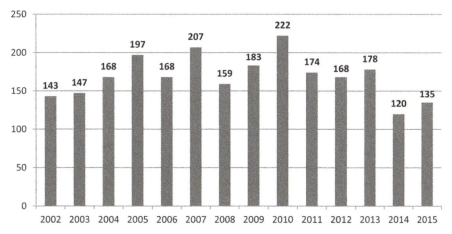

Figure 7.1 Unidentified border-crosser (UBC) recoveries in the U.S. Border Patrol Tucson Sector (FY 2002–2015)

Source: Pima County Office of the Medical Examiner—Annual Report 2015.

smaller than the death counts compiled by human rights organizations who have tracked migrant fatalities. In Arizona's Tucson Sector alone, more than 2,200 deaths occurred between 1990 and 2012 (Martínez et al., 2013). As reflected in figure 7.1 data, the Pima County Medical Examiner's Office, which handles bodies discovered in the Tucson border sector and surrounding areas, averaged 177 cases of unidentified border-crosser deaths each year from 2002 to 2013 (Pima County Office of the Medical Examiner, 2014). At one point the office had to rent a refrigerated trailer to store the backlog of bodies yet to be examined (Rubio-Goldsmith et al., 2006).

By 2007 the number of migrant-crossing deaths led scholars and activists to label the situation as a "humanitarian crisis" (Jimenez, 2009; Rubio-Goldsmith et al., 2007). In 2009, the American Public Health Association (APHA) also called for the recognition of border-crossing deaths as a public health crisis and furthermore directly linked such deaths to militarization of the border, the demand for inexpensive, low-skill labor, and "haphazard and ineffective border and immigration policies that do not address the root causes of migration" (American Public Health Association, 2009). The APHA also recommended that immigration policy prioritize the prevention of border-crossing deaths and stated that such efforts "should target the social and economic underpinnings of migration and the need for effective and just immigration policies and the protection of humanitarian aid efforts" (American Public Health Association, 2009).

However, in the years that have ensued, financial support for prevention strategies have resoundingly focused on increasing border enforcement and strengthening security on the U.S. side of the border. In spite of its cost in human lives and in spite of the fact that net undocumented migration since 2008 has remained at or fallen below zero (Passel 2015; Passel & Cohn, 2015), the precepts of the "prevention through deterrence" strategy are still in place more than two decades after they were first implemented (Massey, Durand, & Pren, 2016).

As a result, the risk of death among migrants has actually increased. According to a Binational Migration Institute study, "Border militarization has redistributed migration flow into remote areas increasing the risk of death associated with attempting an unauthorized border crossing" (Martínez et al., 2013). By pushing migrants into more remote and dangerous crossing areas, border enforcement measures have increased the probability that those who attempt unauthorized entry die in the process. When comparing the number of deaths to the number of apprehensions made, the death rate in Arizona's Tucson Sector tripled between 2008 and 2013 (Martínez, 2015) and has quintupled since 2005 (Blust, 2016). The highest death rate to date, however, was in 2015, when there were 21 deaths per 10,000 apprehensions in the Tucson Sector. That was double the death rate of 2010, which remains the deadliest year on record for total number of migrant deaths (ibid.).

Since 2015 the Río Grande Valley (RGV) of Texas has become one of the deadliest Border Patrol Sectors. That year, according to Customs and Border Protection (CBP) reports, 97 bodies were recovered in the RGV compared with 63 in the Tucson Sector (U.S. Customs and Border Protection, 2015). (It is worth noting that figures from the CBP are traditionally lower than other agencies and humanitarian groups, partly because of the methods used to determine place and cause of death. In 2015, the Pima County Medical Examiner's Office recovered 138 bodies of suspected unauthorized border-crossers, making the Tucson Sector the most deadly corridor. Nevertheless, death rates in the RGV have spiked to unprecedented levels.) Recorded deaths, while alarming, do not account for the many remains that are never found, nor those that are recovered in Mexico. Texas border counties have faced the additional problem of insufficient funds to properly handle and identify the remains of those who have perished (Washington Office on Latin America, 2015). Missing migrants in Texas have become known as the "new disappeared," a term borrowed from the 1970s and 1980s when civil conflicts and oppressive military regimes in Central and South America led to the disappearance of many civilians (Kovic, 2013).

One reason for the increased death rate in the RGV is a spike in border-crossers entering through that sector over the past five years. Beginning in roughly 2011, the numbers of unaccompanied children and family units crossing the Texas border began to rise dramatically. The vast majority of these individuals were from Guatemala, Honduras, and El Salvador, and unlike the motivations of previous migrants, many of these border-crossers were asylum seekers fleeing extreme poverty and violence in their home countries (Bersin, 2015; Donato & Sisk, 2015; Robles, 2014; Rosenblum & Ball, 2016; United Nations High Commissioner for Refugees, 2014; Wasem, 2013). (For more about this topic, please see Chapter 6—Immigration and Children).

The recent surge in Central American border-crossers, particularly unaccompanied children, has been described by President Obama, members of Congress, scholars, and activists as a humanitarian crisis (Cohen, Payne, & Ford, 2014; International Rescue Committee, 2015; Kandel & Seghetti, 2015; Negroponte, 2014; Obama, 2014). Democratic U.S. Representative Henry Cuellar of Texas, while calling for the president to visit the border to see the extent of the problems, said: "The kids that I've talked to, little innocent little boys and girls that have come across and have traveled over 1,000 miles, that one-third of the girls have been abused and raped on the way up here. The last young kid was an 11-year-old little boy from Guatemala that died of dehydration. That is the face that I want him to see" (Cohen, Payne, & Ford, 2014).

Additional problems created by and related to the arrival and treatment of children and families through Texas and Arizona borders have contributed to this "crisis" described by officials:

- Recent Central American and Mexican border-crossers have overwhelmed detention facilities and created an enormous backlog of cases in federal immigration courts (Dominguez Villegas & Rietig, 2015). For the government, this crisis has been largely defined by insufficient facilities, while human rights activists have decried the nature of the facilities, abuses of detainees, and the indefinite holding of asylum seekers in detention facilities as the larger concern (American Civil Liberties Union, 2011; Human Rights Watch, 2015).
- Because U.S. immigration law does not provide for legal representation, those seeking protection (including children and toddlers) are left to represent themselves in immigration courts (*The Economist*, 2016). Records show that 9 out of 10 children who appeared in court alone without representation were ordered deported (Transactional

Records Access Clearinghouse, 2014), placing them back in the environments they sought to escape.

- Humanitarian groups have also raised concern that Customs and Border Protection agents are not adequately screening those apprehended for "credible fear" interviews—the first step in seeking asylum—thus resulting in individuals being deported back into life-threatening situations in their home countries (Campos & Friedland, 2014; Human Rights Watch, 2014).

- While U.S. immigration law dictates that children from noncontiguous countries cannot be immediately deported (and instead are housed, evaluated, and presented with legal options for relief), those from Mexico (and Canada) can be promptly sent back to their home countries. Advocates argue that because of this, many Mexican children (and adults) are being deported back into harmful circumstances without being offered the opportunity for asylum (Campos & Friedland, 2014; United Nations High Commissioner for Refugees, 2014).

- Central American migrants passing through Mexico, including children, are subject to violence, are less likely to be granted asylum or other types of relief if apprehended, and are far more likely to be quickly deported—particularly after Mexico implemented its Southern Border Program with support from the U.S. government (Meyer, Boggs, & Córdova, 2014). In fact, according to Mexico's National Immigration Institute, between 2012 and 2014 the kidnapping of foreigners in Mexico increased by 800% (La Policiaca, 2015). Although U.S. apprehensions of unaccompanied children fell between FY 2014 and FY 2015, apprehensions in Mexico doubled during that same time period (Rosenblum & Ball, 2016). Also in 2014, for every 100 minors apprehended Mexico deported 77 and the United States deported 3, raising questions about insufficient humanitarian screening and application of due-process protections in Mexico (Dominguez Villegas & Rietig, 2015).

Finally, cases of abuse by officials, particularly misuse of authority resulting in migrant deaths, have been a source of decades' worth of distrust and strained relations in communities where people of Mexican descent have been considered with suspicion. Descendants of those killed in the Porvenir Massacre and similar early 1900s incidences in Texas, for example, talk about how Rangers and other authorities "evaporated" both Mexicans and Tejanos who caused problems or were just suspected of wrongdoing (Johnson, 2005, p.119).

More recently, treatment of migrants, immigrants, refugees, and asylum seekers has been called into question by humanitarian groups citing infractions including coercion, unlawfully taking personal belongings including money, sexual abuse of women in custody and even murder (manslaughter) of border-crossers. Between January 2009 and January 2012, there were 809 complaints filed that alleged abuse at the hands of Border Patrol agents (Martínez, Cantor, & Ewing, 2014). Two recent studies have focused on deportation practices (termed "dispossession through deportation") involving the confiscation of migrants' personal belongings while they are in custody (Martínez, Slack, & Heyman, 2013; No More Deaths, 2014). This practice leaves the migrants particularly vulnerable to gangs and criminal factions when they are deported to Mexico without money, identification, phone numbers, or other critical personal information (ibid.). (For more information on this topic, see Chapter 3, question 16.)

In another recent study by the University of Arizona, recent Mexican deportees were interviewed about their treatment by U.S. officials. While 31 percent reported that all officials treated them with respect, others reported various types and degrees of abuse: 11 percent of respondents reported physical abuse at the hands of U.S. authorities, 23 percent reported verbal abuse, 45 percent reported insufficient food while being held in custody, 39 percent reported personal possessions being taken by U.S. authorities and not returned, and 26 percent reported having identifying documents taken and not returned (Slack et al., 2013). These researchers also documented cases of migrants with severe injuries who were denied medical attention by authorities. Among the interviewees, 37 percent of those who requested medical attention from authorities did not receive it (ibid.).

Excessive use of force by U.S. Border Patrol officials has also been called into question by numerous researchers and civil groups. According to the Department of Homeland Security guidelines, use of deadly force is justified only when officers believe the subject issuing the threat "poses an imminent danger of death or serious physical injury to the officer or to another person" (U.S. Department of Homeland Security, 2004). A 2013 *Arizona Republic* report found that 42 individuals, including 13 U.S. citizens, had been killed by on-duty U.S. Border Patrol agents and Customs and Border Protection officers since 2005 (Ortega & O'Dell, 2013). This number includes a teenager who died after being shot 10 times in the back and head by Border Patrol agents firing into Mexico through holes in the border fence. None of the officers involved in the 42 killings was known to have faced consequences other than a short administrative leave (ibid.).

Groups such as the Southern Border Communities Coalition continue to track Border Patrol use of force incidents in an effort to inform the public of abuses and hold authorities accountable in cases where the use of force is questionable (Southern Border Communities Coalition, 2016).

In summary, while national security remains a major issue along the U.S.-Mexico border, issues such as migrant deaths, the nature and the treatment of border-crossers, and application of due process are additional concerns that have drawn attention to the southern border and demanded action among lawmakers and public alike. The depth and scope of issues such as these provide further evidence that border security alone is not the answer to reducing unauthorized migration into the United States.

FURTHER READING

Ackleson, J. (2005, February). Constructing security on the U.S.-Mexico border. *Political Geography*, 24(2), 165–184.

American Civil Liberties Union (ACLU). (2011). Sexual abuse in immigration detention facilities (interactive map). Retrieved from https://www.aclu.org/map/sexual-abuse-immigration-detention-facilities

American Public Health Association. (2009, November 10). Border crossing deaths: A public health crisis along the U.S.-Mexico border (Policy Number 20092). APHA Policy Statement Database. Retrieved from http://www.apha.org/policies-and-advocacy/public-health-policy-statements/policy-database/2014/07/24/08/56/border-crossing-deaths-a-public-health-crisis-along-the-us-mexico-border

Andreas, P. (2009). *Border games: Policing the U.S.-Mexico divide* (2nd ed.). Ithaca and London: Cornell University Press.

Bersin, A. (2015, April 30). Written testimony of PLCY Office of International Affairs Assistant Secretary and Chief Diplomatic Officer Alan Bersin for a House Committee on Foreign Affairs, Subcommittee on Western Hemisphere hearing titled "Migration Crisis: Oversight of the Administration's Proposed $1 Billion Request for Central America." Washington, DC: U.S. Department of Homeland Security. Retrieved from https://www.dhs.gov/news/2015/04/30/written-testimony-plcy-house-foreign-affairs-subcommittee-western-hemisphere-hearing

Blust, K. (2016, May 22). Deaths per 10,000 border crossers are up 5 times from a decade ago. *The Arizona Daily Star*. Retrieved from http://tucson.com/news/local/border/deaths-per-border-crossers-are-up-times-from-a-decade/article_c1279aaf-4ad8-51c9-82d8-3143b836f52e.html

Campos, S., & Friedland, J. (2014, May). *Mexican and Central American asylum and credible fear claims: Background and context.* Washington, DC: American Immigration Council. Retrieved from http://www.immi grationpolicy.org/sites/default/files/docs/asylum_and_credible_fear_ claims_final.pdf

Chardy, A. (1986, March 4). Reagan warns of a "second Cuba" meets Nicaraguan rebel leaders, presses Congress on aid. Philly.com. Retrieved from http://articles.philly.com/1986-03-04/news/26082381_1_contra-forces-contra-leaders-larry-speakes

Cohen, T., Payne, E., & Ford, D. (2014, July 10). Texas governor lashes out at Obama over immigration crisis. CNN.com. Retrieved from http://www.cnn.com/2014/07/09/politics/obama-texas-immigration-visit/index.html

Contorno, S. (2015, March 5). Marco Rubio: At least three sectors of the border are "completely insecure." *Tampa Bay Times.* Politifact.com. Retrieved from http://www.politifact.com/truth-o-meter/statements/ 2015/mar/05/marco-rubio/marco-rubio-least-three-sectors-border-are-complet/

C-SPAN. (2014, September 10). Domestic threat by western terrorists [U.S. House Homeland Security subcommittee hearing on the threat posed by ISIL terrorists with western passports]. Retrieved from http:// www.c-span.org/video/?321387-1/hearing-isis-terrorists-western-pass ports

Dominguez Villegas, R., & Rietig, V. (2015, September). *Migrants deported from the United States and Mexico to the Northern Triangle: A statistical and socioeconomic profile.* Washington, DC: The Migration Policy Institute. Retrieved from http://www.migrationpolicy.org/research/ migrants-deported-united-states-and-mexico-northern-triangle-statis tical-and-socioeconomic

Donato, K. M., & Sisk, B. (2015). Children's migration to the United States from Mexico and Central America: Evidence from the Mexican and Latin American migration projects. *Journal on Migration and Human Security, 3*(1), 58–79. Retrieved from http://jmhs.cmsny.org/index.php/ jmhs/article/view/43

The Economist. (2016, March 26). Self-defence: Can toddlers represent themselves in court? At the moment, yes. The Economist.com. Retrieved from http://www.economist.com/news/united-states/21695572-can-toddlers-represent-themselves-court-moment-yes-self-defence

Hart, A. (2014, September 30). The 9 biggest myths about ISIS debunked. *The Huffington Post.* Retrieved from http://www.huffingtonpost.com/ 2014/09/30/isis-myths-debunked_n_5875050.html

Human Rights Watch. (2014, October 16). "You don't have rights here": U.S. border screening and returns of Central Americans to risk of serious harm. Retrieved from https://www.hrw.org/report/2014/10/16/you-dont-have-rights-here/us-border-screening-and-returns-central-americans-risk

Human Rights Watch. (2015, March 2). Statement to the U.S. Commission on Civil Rights on Immigration Detention Facilities. Retrieved from https://www.hrw.org/news/2015/03/02/statement-us-commission-civil-rights-immigration-detention-facilities

International Rescue Committee. (2015, March 31). Humanitarian crisis on the border: The plight of unaccompanied children [Blog]. Retrieved from http://www.rescue.org/blog/humanitarian-crisis-border-plight-unaccompanied-children

Jimenez, M. (2009, October 1). Humanitarian crisis: Migrant deaths at the U.S.-Mexico border. American Civil Liberties Union of San Diego and Imperial Counties & Mexico's National Commission of Human Rights. Retrieved from https://www.aclu.org/sites/default/files/field_document/humanitariancrisisreport.pdf

Johnson, B. H. (2005). *Revolution in Texas: How a forgotten rebellion and its bloody suppression turned Mexicans into Americans*. New Haven, CT: Yale University Press.

Kandel, W. A., & Seghetti, L. (2015, August 18). *Unaccompanied alien children: An overview* (CRS R43599). Congressional Research Service Report. Washington, DC: Congressional Research Service. Retrieved from http://www.refworld.org/pdfid/55eebcfd4.pdf

Kovic, C. (2013, July 15). *Searching for the living, the dead, and the new disappeared on the migrant trail in Texas*. Houston: Texas Civil Rights Project. Retrieved from http://texaslawhelp.org/files/685E99A9-A3EB-6584-CA74-137E0474AE2C/attachments/BB0D8C09-9011-40D2-98E7-24C1E87B0B6E/report-on-migrant-deaths-in-south-texas-(3).pdf

La Policiaca. (2015, April 27). *Se disparan en el país secuestros de extranjeros* (Redacción). (Kidnappings of foreigners are shooting upward) (Draft). Lapoliciaca.net. Retrieved from http://www.lapoliciaca.com/nota-roja/se-disparan-en-el-pais-secuestros-de-extranjeros/

Martínez, D. E. (2015, July 19). Structural violence and migrant deaths in southern Arizona: Data from the Pima County Office of the Medical Examiner, 1990–2013. *Journal on Migration and Human Security*, 2(4), 257–286. Retrieved from https://www.researchgate.net/publication/280133495_Structural_Violence_and_Migrant_Deaths_in_Southern_Arizona_Data_from_the_Pima_County_Office_of_the_Medical_Examiner_1990-2013

Martínez, D. E., Cantor, G., & Ewing, W. A. (2014, May). *No action taken: Lack of CBP accountability in responding to complaints of abuse.* Washington, DC: American Immigration Council. Retrieved from http://www.americanimmigrationcouncil.org/sites/default/files/No percent20Action percent20Taken_Final.pdf

Martínez, D. E., Reineke, R. C., Rubio-Goldsmith, R., Anderson, B. E., Hess, G. I., & Parks, B. O. (2013, June). *A continued humanitarian crisis at the border: Undocumented border crosser deaths recorded by the Pima County Office of the Medical Examiner, 1990–2012.* Tucson, AZ: Binational Migration Institute, Mexican American Studies and Research Center, University of Arizona. Retrieved from http://bmi.arizona.edu/sites/default/files/border_deaths_final_web.pdf

Martínez, D. E., Slack, J., & Heyman, J. (2013, December). *Bordering on criminal: The routine abuse of migrants in the removal system.* Washington, DC: The Immigration Policy Center. Retrieved from https://www.americanimmigrationcouncil.org/sites/default/files/research/bordering_on_criminal.pdf

Massey, D. S., Durand J., & Pren, K. A. (2016, March). Why border enforcement backfired. *The American Journal of Sociology, 121*(5), 1557–1600.

Meyer, M., Boggs, C., & Córdova, R. (2014). *Mexico's government deploys additional forces and requests funds for southern border program.* Washington, DC: Washington Office on Latin America. Retrieved from https://www.wola.org/analysis/new-developments-along-mexicos-southern-border/

Negroponte, D. V. (2014, July 2). *The surge in unaccompanied children from Central America: A humanitarian crisis at our border.* Washington, DC: The Brookings Institution. Retrieved from http://www.brookings.edu/blogs/up-front/posts/2014/07/02-unaccompanied-children-central-america-negroponte

No More Deaths. (2014). *Shakedown: How deportation robs immigrants of their money and belongings* [Report]. Tucson, AZ: No More Deaths. Retrieved from http://forms.nomoredeaths.org/abuse-documentation/shakedown/

Obama, B. (2014, June 30). *Remarks by the president on border security and immigration reform.* Washington, DC: White House Office of the Press Secretary. Retrieved from https://www.whitehouse.gov/the-press-office/2014/06/30/remarks-president-border-security-and-immigration-reform

Ortega, B. & O'Dell, R. (2013, December 16). Deadly border agent incidents cloaked in silence. *AZCentral.* Retrieved from http://archive.azcentral.com/news/politics/articles/20131212arizona-border-patrol-deadly-force-investigation.html

Passel, J. S. (2015, March 26). *Testimony of Jeffrey S. Passel—Unauthorized immigrant population: National and state trends industries, and occupations.* Washington, DC: Pew Research Center Hispanic Trends. Retrieved from http://www.pewhispanic.org/2015/03/26/testimony-of-jeffrey-s-passel-unauthorized-immigrant-population/

Passel, J. S., & Cohn, D. (2015, July 22). *Unauthorized immigrant population stable for half a decade.* Washington, DC: Pew Research Center Fact Tank. Retrieved from http://www.pewresearch.org/fact-tank/2015/07/22/unau thorized-immigrant-population-stable-for-half-a-decade/

Payan, T. (2006). The three U.S.-Mexico border wars: Drugs, immigration, and homeland security. Westport, CT, and London: Praeger Security International.

Pima County Office of the Medical Examiner (PCOME). (2014, March 31). *Annual report 2013.* Tucson, AZ: PCOME. Retrieved from http://web cms.pima.gov/UserFiles/Servers/Server_6/File/Health/Medicalpercen t20Examiner/2013_AnnualReport_PCOME.pdf

Regan, M. (2010). *The death of Josseline: Immigration stories from the Arizona borderlands.* Boston, MA: Beacon Press.

Robles, F. (2014, July 9). Fleeing gangs, children head to U.S. border. *The New York Times.* Retrieved from http://mobile.nytimes.com/2014/07/10/world/americas/fleeing-gangs-children-head-to-us-border.html

Romeri, G. (2014, December). *Left behind to die—rescued by volunteers.* No More Deaths December Newsletter. Tucson, AZ: No More Deaths. Retrieved from http://forms.nomoredeaths.org/wp-content/uploads/2014/12/Dec-2014-NMD-letter-for-digital.pdf

Rosenblum, M. R., & Ball, I. (2016, January). *Trends in unaccompanied child and family migration from Central America.* Retrieved from http://www.migrationpolicy.org/research/trends-unaccompanied-child-and-family-migration-central-america

Rubio-Goldsmith, R., McCormick, M. M., Martínez, D., & Duarte, I. M. (2006, October). *The "Funnel Effect" and recovered bodies of unauthorized migrants processed by the Pima County Office of the Medical Examiner, 1990–2005.* Tucson, AZ: Binational Migration Institute, Mexican American Studies and Research Center, University of Arizona. Retrieved from http://www.derechoshumanosaz.net/images/pdfs/bmi%20report.pdf

Rubio-Goldsmith, R., McCormick, M. M., Martínez, D., & Duarte, I. M. (2007, February). *A humanitarian crisis at the border: New estimates of deaths among unauthorized immigrants.* Washington, DC: Immigration Policy Center, American Immigration Council. Retrieved from http://

www.immigrationpolicy.org/sites/default/files/docs/Crisis%20at%20 the%20Border.pdf

Slack, J., Martínez, D. E., Whiteford, S., & Peiffer, E. (2013, March). *In the shadow of the wall; Family separation, immigration enforcement and security.* Tucson, AZ: University of Arizona, The Center for Latin American Studies. Retrieved from http://las.arizona.edu/sites/las .arizona.edu/files/UA_Immigration_Report2013web.pdf

Southern Border Communities Coalition. (2016). Border Patrol abuse since 2010 [Web site]. Retrieved from http://southernborder.org/ border-patrol-brutality-since-2010/

Transactional Records Access Clearinghouse (TRAC). (2014, July 15). *New data on unaccompanied children in immigration court.* Syracuse, NY: Syracuse University. Retrieved from http://trac.syr.edu/immigration/ reports/359/

United Nations High Commissioner for Refugees (UNHCR). (2014, March). *Children on the run.* Washington, DC: UNHCR Regional Office for the United States and the Caribbean. Retrieved from http:// www.unhcrwashington.org/children

U.S. Border Patrol (USBP). (1994, July). *Border Patrol strategic plan, 1994 and beyond: National strategy* [Government document]. Washington, DC: USBP. Retrieved from http://cw.routledge.com/textbooks/ 9780415996945/gov-docs/1994.pdf

U.S. Customs and Border Protection. (2015). *United States Border Patrol Southwest Border Sectors; Southwest Border Deaths by Fiscal Year (Oct. 1st through Sept. 30th).* Washington, DC: Department of Homeland Security. Retrieved from http://www.cbp.gov/sites/default/files/documents/ BP%20Southwest%20Border%20Sector%20Deaths%20FY1998% 20-%20FY2015.pdf

U.S. Customs and Border Protection. (2015, April). *On a typical day in Fiscal Year 2014, CBP.* Washington, DC: Department of Homeland Security. Retrieved from http://www.cbp.gov/newsroom/stats/ typical-day-fy2014

U.S. Department of Homeland Security (DHS). (2004, June 25). *Department of Homeland Security policy on the use of deadly force.* Washington, DC: DHS. Retrieved from https://www.dhs.gov/sites/default/files/ publications/dhs-use-of-force-policy.pdf

Wasem, R. E. (2013, December 12). *U.S. House of Representatives Committee on the Judiciary Hearing on "Asylum Abuse: Is It Overwhelming Our Borders?"* Washington, DC: U.S. House of Representatives Judiciary Committee. Retrieved from https://judiciary.house.gov/hearing/asylum-abuse-is-it-overwhelming-our-borders-0/

Washington Office on Latin America (WOLA). (2015, January 26). The U.S. fails to respond to shifting migration patterns and the urgent humanitarian need at the border. Washington, DC: WOLA. Retrieved from http://www.wola.org/publications/us_failing_to_respond_to_shifting_migration_patterns_urgent_humanitarian_need_at_the_bo

Wilson, T. M., & Donnan, H. (Eds.). (2012). *A companion to border studies*. West Sussex, UK: Wiley Blackwell Publishing.

8

❖

Policies and Politics of Immigration

Q33. DO POLITICIANS SEE THE GROWTH OF IMMIGRANT POPULATIONS (AND ESPECIALLY IMMIGRANTS OF HISPANIC DESCENT) IN THE UNITED STATES AS A MAJOR INFLUENCE ON BOTH PRESENT AND FUTURE ELECTIONS?

Answer: Yes, for varying reasons. Immigration became a defining topic within the two major political parties, particularly during the 2016 presidential campaign season. Some politicians and political parties view the growth of immigrant populations positively, while others view such growth as a threat to traditional cultural and political norms. Regardless of how it is perceived, the significant growth of immigrant populations over the past 50 years means that immigrants are likely to have an impact on elections for many generations to come.

The Facts: It is well known that the United States was founded by immigrants, but the arrival of today's newcomers continues to shape the country's demographics in new ways. Over the past 50 years, 59 million immigrants have arrived on U.S. shores (Pew Research Center, 2015). In fact, nearly 20 percent of the globe's immigrants live in the United States, making the United States host of the world's largest immigrant population (Conner, Cohn, & Gonzalez-Barrera, 2013).

Between 1965 and 2015, over 55 percent of the United States' population growth came from immigrants, their children, and their grandchildren (Pew Research Center, 2015). These immigrant families, largely from Latin America and Asia, have contributed to a shifting demographic and cultural composition of the United States (ibid.). In 2014, Hispanics made up 17.3 percent of the total population of the country, compared to just 6.5 percent in 1980 and 3.5 percent in 1960 (Stepler & Brown, 2016). Presently, nearly 80 percent of U.S.-born Asians and almost half of U.S.-born Latinos are children of immigrants (Patten, 2016). African immigrant populations, although still small, have also risen—jumping from 80,000 in 1970 to 1.8 million in 2013 (Anderson, 2015).

The growth of immigrant populations in the United States, particularly that of Hispanics which have traditionally been the largest foreign-born population, means the makeup of voters in future elections will likely shift from a primarily white base to an increasingly diverse, multiethnic voter pool. In response, many candidates have widened their focus to include the views and concerns of groups previously not considered statistically significant in election outcomes.

Politicians in recent years have worked particularly hard to garner support among Latinos, the largest minority group in the United States. In 2016 over 17 percent of the overall U.S. population comprised Latinos; by 2060 that figure is projected to reach 28.6 percent (Stepler & Brown, 2016). Because of the rapid growth of Hispanic populations, it is projected that in 2016 the Latino electorate (at 11.9 percent of all eligible U.S. voters) will be almost as large as the black electorate (12.4 percent of all eligible U.S. voters) (Krogstad et al., 2016). As of 2016, there were 27.3 million people of Latino origin in the United States eligible to vote— roughly 12 percent of the country's population (ibid.).

The largest source of growth for the Hispanic electorate comes from its youth. Almost half (47 percent) of U.S.-born Latinos are under the age of 18 (Patten, 2016), underscoring the significance of the Latino impact as those children reach voting age. But the impact of Latino youth is not just a phenomenon of the future. Of the 27 million eligible Hispanic voters, nearly half of them are Millennials (born between 1981 and 1996) (Krogstad et al., 2016). This group of Hispanic millennials is more likely than older Hispanics to be comprised of U.S. citizens and to speak English proficiently (ibid.).

The impact of the Latino vote, however, will depend on the success of voter mobilization and participation. In 2012, only 48 percent of eligible Hispanic voters went to the polls (Lopez & Gonzalez-Barrera, 2013). That same year, only about half of Latino millennial eligible voters registered to vote (Krogstad et al., 2016). The impact of Latinos at the ballot box in 2016 and beyond will depend largely on turnout of *all* eligible Latino voters.

One factor that may boost overall Latino voter participation is the increasing number of Hispanic immigrants, legally present in the country, who have decided to become U.S. citizens. This accounts for the second-largest source of growth for the Hispanic electorate, just behind Latino youth (Krogstad et al., 2016). At the beginning of 2013, there were an estimated 13.1 million legal permanent residents (LPRs, or "green card" holders) living in the United States, one-quarter of whom were of Mexican origin. Of these LPRs, 8.8 million were qualified to naturalize (Baker & Rytina, 2014). And since 2012, more than 1.2 million Hispanics have become U.S. citizens (ibid.). According to Pew researcher Jens Manuel Krogstad, "When Latino immigrants become naturalized U.S. citizens, they exercise their right to vote in higher proportions than U.S.-born Latinos" (Lee, 2016). Accordingly, voter participation among naturalized immigrant Latinos was higher than that of U.S.-born Latinos in both 2008 and 2012 (Krogstad et al., 2016).

But interest in political reform is not limited to Hispanic voters. American Muslims have also called for members of their communities to vote in the 2016 presidential election. The United States Council of Muslim Organizations plans to register a million Muslim voters in response to candidate Donald Trump's proposed ban on Muslims entering the country (Pogash, 2016). One Muslim leader compared the fears modern Muslims face to those of Japanese Americans after the attack on Pearl Harbor. "Just because you share an ethnic group or religion, you shouldn't have to pass a loyalty oath to be considered a loyal American," he said (ibid.).

Statistics also indicate that the overall number of green card holders interested in applying for citizenship has increased since the start of the 2016 presidential campaign cycle. The average number of citizenship (N-400) applications received from August 2015 to January 2016 was 14 percent higher than the number of applications received during the same time period one year earlier (United States Citizenship and Immigration Services, 2016).

LATINOS AND THE GOP

Politicians are well aware that this increase in Latino voters could have a significant impact on the 2016 elections (Lee, 2016), and both Democrats and Republicans have acknowledged the need to gain Hispanic votes. However, as the country's electorate has become increasingly diversified, the GOP has struggled to appeal to and attract minority voters—Hispanics in particular. For years, Republican leaders have struggled to pacify a vocal, anti-immigrant faction within their party while reiterating the importance of reaching out to Latinos for the future of the party.

Although proposals to crack down on unauthorized immigration have appealed to a particular segment of Republican voters, a number of efforts to appease the far Right on issues related to Hispanics (specifically unauthorized immigrants) have backfired for the GOP. For example, California's Republican support of Proposition 187 in 1994 played a major role in galvanizing the state's growing share of Latino voters and shaping California into a blue state. Although Proposition 187 was declared unconstitutional and never became law, its intent to deny public services such as education and health care to people in the country illegally, along with anti-immigrant rhetoric that accompanied the proposal, alienated California Latinos and Anglos alike (Damore & Pantoja, 2013).

In response, California Latinos organized citizenship drives that mobilized political participation of Hispanics, primarily as Democrats (Grenier, 2014). Between March 1996 and March 1997, nearly 500,000 of California's immigrants naturalized and became U.S. citizens (Public Policy Institute of California, 1999), and the total number of Latino registered voters jumped from 2 million in the mid-1990s to 3.7 million in 2014 (Grenier, 2014). This increase is not totally attributed to the effects of Proposition 187; much of it is due to a corresponding increase in the state's Latino population. However, the fact that voter participation among Latinos surged in 1994 and has remained high since is one example of how the legislation negatively affected the state's Republicans long term. Latinos made up 7 percent of California's electorate in 1992, 14 percent in 2000, and 28 percent in 2016 (Pew Research Center, 2016; Ramírez, 2013). Once considered a swing state, by 2015 less than 28 percent of California's electorate was registered Republican (Padilla, 2015).

Republicans also struggled to identify with Hispanics during the 2012 presidential election, in which Barack Obama received 71 percent of the Hispanic vote compared to Mitt Romney's 27 percent (Lopez & Taylor, 2012). Senator Ted Cruz commented after the election, "If Republicans want to do better in the Hispanic community, and it's critical that we do better in the Hispanic community, we have got to be the party that champions opportunity, champions policies that work and that help people climb the economic ladder" (Beamon & Walter, 2013). Ironically, when Cruz (a Hispanic) ran as a Republican presidential candidate in 2015–2016, he struggled to gain Latino support in part because of his hard-Right stances on issues such as immigration reform.

Shortly after Romney's defeat in 2012, the Republican National Committee devised a new strategic plan, the Growth and Opportunity Project Report, which prioritized building trust with Hispanic and other minority populations as one of the party's primary goals (Republican National Committee, 2013). In spite of these efforts, the GOP continued to struggle to find common ground on immigration and Hispanic issues. The nomination of Donald Trump as the GOP's 2016 presidential candidate did not help. Trump, who began his campaign by proposing mass deportations of unauthorized immigrants and the building of a wall between the United States and Mexico to prevent Mexico from sending "rapists and criminals" across the border (2015), has repeatedly offended Hispanics and other minority groups with what many even in his own party call extreme positions and racist remarks (CNN, 2016; Raju, 2016). Polls indicate Trump's message resonates most soundly with those who feel growing numbers of newcomers threaten U.S. values and who believe a majority minority population will be bad for the country (Jones & Kiley, 2016).

POLITICS AND VIEWS OF IMMIGRANTS

Ultimately, the success of any political party in attracting the votes of immigrants depends on how its members view and approach immigrant populations. Research over two decades shows that while Democrats' and Republicans' views of immigrants were quite similar between 1994 and 2005, they have grown apart substantially since then (Jones, 2016). The number of Democrats who feel that immigrants strengthen the country through their hard work and talents steadily increased from 49 to 78 percent, while the number of Republicans who feel immigrants strengthen the country has remained relatively low, at just 34 and 35 percent (ibid.).

The growth and increasing political participation among immigrant populations will make their votes increasingly important in future elections. How those votes will be cast will depend on the willingness of Democrats and Republicans to hear their concerns and acknowledge their contributions as members of an increasingly multicultural society.

FURTHER READING

Anderson, M. (2015, November 2). *African immigrant population in U.S. steadily climbs*. Washington, DC: Pew Research Center. Retrieved from http://www.pewresearch.org/fact-tank/2015/11/02/african-immi grant-population-in-u-s-steadily-climbs/

Baker, B., & Rytina, N. (2014, September). *Estimates of the lawful permanent resident population in the United States: January 2013*. Office of Immigration Statistics. Washington, DC: Department of Homeland Security. Retrieved from https://www.dhs.gov/sites/default/files/publications/ois_lpr_pe_2013_0.pdf

Beamon, T., & Walter, K. (2013, January 26). Ted Cruz: Real immigration reform requires "securing the borders." Newsmax.com. Retrieved from http://www.newsmax.com/Headline/SenTed-Cruz-US-Must-Get-Serious-About-Securing-the-Borders/2013/01/26/id/487514/

Conner, P., Cohn, D., & Gonzalez-Barrera, A. (2013, December 17). *Changing patterns of global migration and remittances*. Washington, DC: Pew Research Center. Retrieved from http://www.pewsocialtrends.org/2013/12/17/changing-patterns-of-global-migration-and-remittances/

CNN. (2016, June 7). Paul Ryan: Trump's judge comments are "textbook" racism. cnn.com. Retrieved from http://www.cnn.com/videos/politics/2016/06/07/paul-ryan-presser-trump-judge-comments-sot.cnn

Damore, D., & Pantoja, A. (2013). Anti-immigrant politics and lessons for the GOP from California [Blog]. Latino Decisions. Retrieved from http://www.latinodecisions.com/blog/wp-content/uploads/2013/10/Prop187Effect.pdf

Grenier, A. (2014, November 7). 20 years later, California still feels effects of anti-immigrant measure. *Immigration Impact*. Washington, DC: American Immigration Council. Retrieved from http://immigrationimpact.com/2014/11/07/20-years-later-california-still-feels-effects-anti-immigrant-measure/

Jones, B. (2016, April 15). *Americans' view of immigrants marked by widening partisan, generational divides*. Washington, DC: Pew Research Center, Fact Tank. Retrieved from http://www.pewresearch.org/fact-tank/2016/04/15/americans-views-of-immigrants-marked-by-widening-partisan-generational-divides/

Jones, B., & Kiley, J. (2016, June 2). *More "warmth" for Trump among GOP voters concerned by immigrants, diversity*. Washington, DC: Pew Research Center, Fact Tank. Retrieved from http://www.pewresearch.org/fact-tank/2016/06/02/more-warmth-for-trump-among-gop-voters-concerned-by-immigrants-diversity/

Krogstad, J. M., Lopez, M. H., López, G., Passel, J. S., & Patten, E. (2016, January 19). *Millennials make up almost half of Latino eligible voters in 2016*. Washington, DC: Pew Research Center, Hispanic Trends. Retrieved from http://www.pewhispanic.org/2016/01/19/millennials-make-up-almost-half-of-latino-eligible-voters-in-2016/#

Lee, W. (2016, June 2). Latino voters potentially a "game changer" in U.S. presidential elections. Voice of America, VOA News. Retrieved from http://m.voanews.com/a/latino-voters-potentially-a-game-changer-in-the-us-presidential-elections/3357394.html

Lopez, M. H., & Gonzalez-Barrera, A. (2013, June 3). *Inside the 2012 Latino electorate*. Washington, DC: Pew Research Center, Hispanic Trends. Retrieved from http://www.pewhispanic.org/2013/06/03/inside-the-2012-latino-electorate/

Lopez, M. H., & Taylor, P. (2012, November 7). *Latino voters in the 2012 election*. Washington, DC: Pew Research Center, Hispanic Trends. Retrieved from http://www.pewhispanic.org/2012/11/07/latino-voters-in-the-2012-election/

Padilla, A. (2015, February 10). *Report of registration: Registration by county*. Sacramento, CA: California Secretary of State. Retrieved from http://www.sos.ca.gov/elections/voter-registration/voter-registration-statistics/ror-odd-year-2015

Patten, E. (2016, April 20). *The nation's Latino population is defined by its youth*. Washington, DC: Pew Research Center. Retrieved from http://www.pewhispanic.org/2016/04/20/the-nations-latino-population-is-defined-by-its-youth/

Pew Research Center. (2015, September 28). *Modern immigration wave brings 59 million to U.S., driving population growth and change through 2065*. Washington, DC: Pew Research Center, Hispanic Trends. Retrieved from http://www.pewhispanic.org/2015/09/28/modern-immigration-wave-brings-59-million-to-u-s-driving-population-growth-and-change-through-2065/

Pew Research Center. (2016, January 19). *Mapping the Latino electorate by state*. Washington, DC: Pew Research Center, Hispanic Trends. Retrieved from http://www.pewhispanic.org/interactives/mapping-the-latino-electorate-by-state/

Pogash, C. (2016, June 1). Unsettling U.S. political climate galvanizes Muslims to vote. *The New York Times*. Retrieved from http://www.nytimes.com/2016/06/02/us/unsettling-political-climate-galvanizes-muslims-to-vote.html?_r=0

Public Policy Institute of California (PPIC). (1999, September 14). *Naturalization rates surged in mid 1990s, study finds* [Press release]. San Francisco: PPIC. Retrieved from http://www.ppic.org/main/pressrelease.asp?i=344

Raju, M. (2016, June 8). GOP congressman: Trump "likely a racist." cnn.com. Retrieved from http://www.cnn.com/2016/06/08/politics/reid-ribble-donald-trump-racist/index.html

Ramírez, R. (2013). *Mobilizing opportunities: The evolving Latino electorate and the future of American politics*. Charlottesville: University of Virginia Press.

Republican National Committee. (2013). Growth & opportunity project. Republican National Committee. Retrieved from http://goproject.gop .com/RNC_Growth_Opportunity_Book_2013.pdf

Stepler, R., & Brown, A. (2016, April 19). *Statistical portrait of Hispanics in the United States*. Washington, DC: Pew Research Center, Hispanic TrendsProject.Retrievedfromhttp://www.pewhispanic.org/2016/04/19/ statistical-portrait-of-hispanics-in-the-united-states-key-charts/

Trump, D. (2015, June 16). Donald Trump presidential campaign announcement. C-SPAN. Retrieved from http://www.c-span.org/video/? 326473-1/donald-trump-presidential-campaign-announcement

United States Citizenship and Immigration Services (USCIS). (2016, January). *N-400 receipts and oaths*. Washington, DC: USCIS. Retrieved from https://www.uscis.gov/sites/default/files/USCIS/About%20Us/Elec tronic%20Reading%20Room/Statistics_and_Data/Monthly_Natz_ Stats.pdf

Q34. ARE STATE AUTHORITIES OR FEDERAL AUTHORITIES IN CHARGE OF IMMIGRATION LAW AND ITS ENFORCEMENT?

Answer: Primarily and historically, federal. However, in recent years numerous states have challenged the authority of federal officials by creating and enforcing their own immigration laws.

The Facts: On April 23, 2010, Arizona Governor Jan Brewer signed into law the controversial Support [Our] Law Enforcement and Safe Neighborhoods Act, better known as Senate Bill 1070. At the time, it was said to be the country's toughest state law against illegal immigration (Gonzalez, 2011). In explaining her decision to sign the bill, Brewer stated, "We in Arizona have been more than patient waiting for Washington to act, but decades of federal inaction and misguided policy have created a dangerous and unacceptable situation" (2010). The bill was immediately challenged in court, but in spite of its uncertain future, numerous other states followed suit and passed similar bills, some even more restrictive than Arizona's (Wessler, 2011).

CAN STATES TAKE ISSUES RELATED TO IMMIGRATION INTO THEIR OWN HANDS?

Article 1, section 8, clause 4, of the United States Constitution grants Congress the power to "establish a uniform Rule of Naturalization," thus making the question of how and when someone may become a citizen of the United States a federal issue (Archives.org, 1787). However, immigration concerns include much more than just becoming a citizen, and for nearly 100 years after the signing of the Constitution, many states passed their own immigration laws to regulate the entry and treatment of specific populations (Chacón, 2014).

Then, in the late 1800s, Congress began to pass broad immigration legislation (first, to restrict entry of the Chinese, and later to control the inflow of other racial and ethnic groups). At the same time, the Supreme Court began restricting the powers of states to create their own immigration regulations. From this point forward, congressional decisions and regulations basically guided immigration policy in the United States (Chacón, 2014).

Few of these decisions were challenged for yet another century. As the number of unauthorized immigrants began to rise to unprecedented levels in the 1990s and early 2000s, however, states and cities began to push back by once again crafting their own regulations regarding the entry and treatment of unauthorized noncitizens inside their borders.

Some state laws were anti-immigrant in nature, restricting access (particularly by unauthorized immigrants) to social services, health care, and education. One of the most controversial of these early laws was California's Proposition 187, which denied state-funded services such as education and health care to people in the country illegally (Eig, n.d.). Later came Arizona's S.B. 1070 and numerous copycat laws in other states that were inspired by its provisions (Cannon, 2011; Morse, 2011).

Not all state laws regarding immigration, however, were negative in tone. Numerous pieces of state legislation have been pro-immigrant in nature, allowing unauthorized immigrants to buy health insurance on a state exchange (Reuters, 2016), obtain driver's licenses (Mendoza, 2015), qualify for in-state tuition at colleges and universities (National Conference of State Legislatures, 2014), and benefit from English-language and citizenship classes (Morse et al., 2015) among other things. In 2015 alone, 391 immigration-related laws and resolutions of various types were enacted by state legislatures around the country (ibid.). Some of these laws have been challenged in court and others have not. As an example, in 2015 18 states allowed undocumented students to pay in-state tuition rates and 6 states allowed those students to receive state financial aid (National Conference of State Legislatures, 2015). In 2008, a California appeals court ruled this benefit unconstitutional, but the state Supreme Court later reversed that ruling, stating that providing in-state tuition does not violate federal law and therefore is permissible (Keller, 2010).

A good number of other state-sponsored immigration laws, both restrictive and friendly, were also challenged in court. The result was a judicial tug-of-war. States argued that federal authorities were either incapable or unwilling to control immigration and address states' financial and social concerns, with unauthorized immigrants in particular. The federal government argued that states had no right to regulate immigration and therefore could not pass laws that usurped federal power.

Arizona's S.B. 1070 was one of those bills that ended up in court. The law made it a state crime for immigrants to work or seek work in Arizona and to fail to carry with them proper documentation. The legislation also gave law enforcement officials authorization to arrest someone without a warrant if they suspected that person was in the country illegally, and the legislation required law enforcement to check an individual's immigration status after a lawful arrest if there was "reasonable suspicion" that the person in question was unauthorized (Howe, 2012).

Three of the four main provisions of S.B. 1070 were struck down by the U.S. Supreme Court because, the Court ruled, they are preempted by existing federal immigration laws (*Arizona et al. v. United States*, 2012; Howe, 2012). The only provision allowed to stand was the one requiring officers to check a person's immigration status after a lawful stop if they have reasonable suspicion that the person is in the country illegally. Immigrant advocates and scholars, however, have argued that the "reasonable suspicion" clause leads to racial profiling (Campbell, 2012).

The Supreme Court's ruling on *Arizona et al. v. United States* (a decision about S.B. 1070) in 2012 made clear that the federal government is in charge of immigration-related matters, not state governments, and that no state law can override or infringe on federal policy. The Court specifically said that in regard to immigration, "Federal governance is extensive and complex" (p. 1) and its regulation "so pervasive" that it precludes even state laws that supplement it (p. 2). However, the Court allowed provision 2(b) to stand because it explained that "consultation between federal and state officials is an important feature of the immigration system" (p. 4).

Although the Supreme Court ruling defined the extent to which states can exercise power over immigration-related matters, it did not prevent states from looking for new ways to gain greater control over immigration issues. For example, federal law does authorize states to withhold certain state benefits from noncitizens, and as a result some provide only the most basic emergency services to those who are undocumented (Chacón, 2014). Others protest by targeting noncitizens in the enforcement of general criminal law or by resisting federal immigration directives (ibid.).

Cities have also stood up to federal immigration laws by refusing to participate in programs like Secure Communities or by acting as "sanctuary cities" and refusing Immigration and Customs Enforcement requests to further detain unauthorized immigrants in local police custody (Chacón, 2014; Gamboa, 2011). Both types of defiance have landed participating cities in hot water with the federal government. However, until federal policies are substantially reformed, cities and states will likely continue to find ways to protest or circumvent what they feel are unjust laws.

FURTHER READING

Archives.org. (1787, September 17). The Constitution of the United States: A transcription. Retrieved from http://www.archives.gov/exhib its/charters/constitution_transcript.html

Arizona et al. v. United States. 567 U.S. Supreme Court of the United States. 2012, June 25. Retrieved from http://www.fronterasdesk.org/ sites/default/files/SCOTUS_SB1070.pdf

Brewer, J. (2010, April 23). Governor Jan Brewer address upon signing Arizona Senate Bill 1070. Retrieved from http://www.americanrheto ric.com/speeches/janbrewersenatebill1070speech.htm

Campbell, K. M. (2012, August 9). (Un)reasonable suspicion: Racial profiling in immigration enforcement after *Arizona v. United States.* *Wake Forest Journal of Law & Policy*, 3(2), 367–395. Retrieved from http:// ssrn.com/abstract=2127926

Cannon, L. (2011, July/August). *Right turn.* Denver, CO; Washington, DC: National Conference of State Legislatures. Retrieved from http:// www.ncsl.org/Portals/1/Documents/magazine/articles/2011/SL_0711-Right.pdf

Chacón, J. (2014, Spring). Who is responsible for U.S. immigration policy? *Insights on Law & Society*, 14(3). Retrieved from http://www.amer icanbar.org/publications/insights_on_law_andsociety/14/spring-2014/ who-is-responsible-for-u-s--immigration-policy-.html

Eig, L. M. (n.d.). *California's Proposition 187: A brief overview.* Washington, DC: Congressional Research Service (Report for Congress). Retrieved from http://www.congressionalresearch.com/97-543/docu ment.php

Gamboa, S. (2011, February 16). "Voluntary" immigration program not so voluntary. The Associated Press. Retrieved from https://www .yahoo.com/news/voluntary-immigration-program-not-voluntary-20 110216-001024-427.html

Gonzalez, D. (2011, April 23). Arizona's immigration law: A look at bill's impact 1 year later. *The Arizona Republic.* Retrieved from http://www.azcentral.com/news/election/azelections/articles/2011/04/23/20110423arizona-immigration-law-impact-year-later.html

Howe, A. (2012, June 25). *S.B. 1070:* In plain English. SCOTUS-blog. Retrieved from http://www.scotusblog.com/2012/06/s-b-1070-in-plain-english/

Keller, J. (2010, November 15). California Supreme Court upholds law giving in-state tuition to illegal immigrants. *The Chronicle of Higher Education.* Retrieved from http://chronicle.com/article/California-Supreme-Court/125398/

Mendoza, G. (2015, July 8). *States offering driver's licenses to immigrants.* Denver, CO, and Washington, DC: National Conference of State Legislatures. Retrieved from http://www.ncsl.org/research/immigration/states-offering-driver-s-licenses-to-immigrants.aspx

Morse, A. (2011, July 28). *Arizona's immigration enforcement laws.* Denver, CO, and Washington, DC: National Conference of State Legislatures. Retrieved from http://www.ncsl.org/research/immigration/analysis-of-arizonas-immigration-law.aspx

Morse, A., Mendoza, G. S., Malow, L., & Weigle, H. (2015, August 3). *2015 immigration report.* Denver, CO; Washington, DC: National Conference of State Legislatures. Retrieved from http://www.ncsl.org/research/immigration/2015-immigration-report.aspx

National Conference of State Legislatures (NCSL). (2014, February 19). *In-state tuition and unauthorized immigrant students.* Denver, CO; Washington, DC: NCSL. Retrieved from http://www.ncsl.org/research/immigration/in-state-tuition-and-unauthorized-immigrants.aspx

National Conference of State Legislatures (NCSL). (2015, October 29). *Undocumented student tuition: Overview.* Denver, CO; Washington, DC: NCSL. Retrieved from http://www.ncsl.org/research/education/undocumented-student-tuition-overview.aspx

Reuters. (2016, June 10). California governor signs bill letting undocumented immigrants buy insurance. *Reuters.* Retrieved from http://news.trust.org/item/20160611051315-ayjdc/

State of Arizona. (2010). Senate Bill 1070 (Full text of bill). Arizona legislature. Retrieved from http://www.azleg.gov/legtext/49leg/2r/bills/sb1070s.pdf

Wessler, S. F. (2011, March 2). Bills modeled after Arizona's SB 1070 spread through states. *Colorlines.* Retrieved from http://www.colorlines.com/content/bills-modeled-after-arizonas-sb-1070-spread-through-states

Q35. HOW DO MAINLINE RELIGIONS AND RELIGIOUS DENOMINATIONS IN THE UNITED STATES FEEL ABOUT COMPREHENSIVE IMMIGRATION REFORM MEASURES SUCH AS THE "GANG OF 8" LEGISLATION PROPOSED IN 2013?

Answer: Representatives of all the largest faith communities in the United States have spoken out about the need for comprehensive immigration reform.

The Facts: Religious groups are not newcomers to the immigration debate. For years, faith-based organizations have engaged in efforts to educate and influence public understanding of immigration-related issues at hand. The work of the Catholic Church in assisting immigrants in the United States and promoting acceptance of noncitizens, for example, dates back to the 19th century (Byrne, n.d.).

Over the past few decades, however, as changing demographics and mounting public discontent with failed immigration policies produced a firestorm of controversy, faith groups have adopted more active roles in promoting the idea of immigration reform. Perhaps most significantly, certain branches of traditionally fundamental denominations and religions have now joined the call for comprehensive reform. Groups once hesitant to take a political stance have made public proclamations of their support for humanitarian-based legislation that acknowledges the well-being of migrants and their families as a central concern. Other groups, historically opposed to similar comprehensive immigration reform proposals, have modified their platforms to advocate for more inclusive changes to the current immigration system, including legal pathways for individuals in the United States without documentation. Reverend Tony Suarez, vice president of the National Hispanic Christian Leadership Conference, commented that "immigration reform created an incredible, unified coalition of people that don't normally work together" (Gomez, 2014).

Why is the role of faith-based groups so important to the immigration debate? Religious individuals hold a large degree of influence partly because their numbers are so significant. More than three-quarters of the country's population (77 percent) adheres to some type of religious group. A Pew Research Study found that in 2014, 70.6 percent of the U.S. population identified as Christian (2015, May 12). Within that category, 25.4 percent of the population was evangelical Protestant, 22.8 percent was unaffiliated, 20.8 percent was Catholic, 14.7 percent was mainline

Protestant, and 5.9 percent was made up of non-Christian faiths such as Jewish, Muslim, Hindu, and Buddhist (ibid.). Among members of the U.S. Congress, 92 percent identified as Christian, 5 percent are Jewish, just over 1 percent belong to non-Christian faiths, 1.7 percent did not answer the question, and only one member of Congress claimed no religious affiliation (Pew Research Center, 2015, January 2).

A 2013 Brookings Institution and Public Religion Research Institute survey, one of the largest surveys on immigration ever conducted, found vast support for comprehensive immigration reform among the American public that cut across all political and religious lines (Jones et al., 2013). The study found that "majorities of all religious groups, including Hispanic Catholics (74 percent), Hispanic Protestants (71 percent), black Protestants (70 percent), Jewish Americans (67 percent), Mormons (63 percent), white Catholics (62 percent), white mainline Protestants (61 percent), and white evangelical Protestants (56 percent), agree that the immigration system should allow immigrants currently living in the U.S. illegally to become citizens provided they meet certain requirements" (ibid.).

Faith groups' support of migrants, immigrants, and the policies that affect them often stems from the fact that many religious organizations consist of large minority populations. Since 1965, half of the legal immigrant population in the United States has come from Latin America (Taylor, 2014), a part of the world where today, 69 percent of adults identify as Catholic and 19 percent are Protestant (Pew Research Center, 2014, November 13). Thirty-four percent of all U.S. Catholics are Hispanic (while 15 percent of all U.S. adults are Hispanic) and more than a quarter of U.S. Catholic adults were born outside the United States, the majority coming from other parts of the Americas (Lipka, 2015). In contrast, only 15 percent of U.S. adults overall were born in other countries (ibid.).

In other cases, religious groups tend to lend support to immigrants because of their own experiences with oppression and marginalization. They relate to the struggles of migrants fleeing poverty or persecution in their home countries who come to the United States looking for a better life. This was certainly the case of Catholics in the mid-1800s, as Irish farmers wiped out by the potato famine searched for new opportunities in America, only to be attacked and treated with disdain by groups such as the nativist American Party (Library of Congress, n.d.).

But most faith groups profess to speak out on behalf of comprehensive immigration reform (CIR) because of inherent teachings and doctrines of their religions, not because of the makeup of their membership or histories. The vast majority of Christian churches active in the CIR movement cite biblical mandates to care for the sojourner just as God did (Deuteronomy 10:17–19), to treat neighbors with love and kindness just like the Good Samaritan (Luke 10:30–37), and to show compassion and love for the "stranger" (Matthew 25), to cite a few commonly quoted passages. Church leaders also remind followers that God's people were mistreated as slaves and foreigners in Egypt (Exodus 23:9; Leviticus 19:33–34), and that Jesus began his life as a refugee (Matthew 2) (Carroll, 2012).

CATHOLIC CHURCH

The Catholic Church has been one of the most active and vocal religious organizations advocating on behalf of migrants in the United States. As early as 2001 the Catholic Church issued a pastoral statement titled "Welcoming the Stranger among Us: Unity in Diversity," urging congregational members to embrace newcomers and immigrants (United States Catholic Conference, 2000). In 2003 the United States Conference of Catholic Bishops (USCCB) and Catholic bishops from Mexico jointly published "Strangers No Longer: Together on a Journey of Hope," which offered specific recommendations for immigration reform (United States Conference of Catholic Bishops, Inc., and Conferencia del Episcopado Mexicano, 2003). The church's "Justice for Immigrants" campaign, initiated in May 2005 and launched in 2008, combined educational efforts and public policy campaigns promoting CIR (Jones, 2008; USCCB, 2012).

Through its Migration and Refugee Services branch, the Catholic Church is engaged in extensive political activity aimed at passing CIR and educating Catholics about the church's teaching about migration, among other things (USCCB, 2013). In addition to promoting an obligation of rich nations to take on a moral responsibility for poorer nations, the church implores that "[m]ore powerful economic nations which have the ability to protect and feed their residents, have a stronger obligation to accommodate migration flows" (United States Conference of Catholic Bishops, Inc., and Conferencia del Episcopado Mexicano, 2003, p. 15).

In 2013, the year when the "Gang of 8" CIR bill was being considered, the U.S. Conference of Catholic Bishops issued a press release informing parishioners that "nearly eighty percent of Catholics support earned citizenship" and urging them to "engage their elected officials on behalf of immigration reform" (USCCB, 2013, April 19).

Finally, Pope Francis has been an adamant supporter of migrants and refugees, bringing awareness of their struggles and the need for more humane treatment of the world's displaced persons. When he became the first pope to address a joint session of Congress in September 2015, Pope Francis did not address comprehensive immigration reform by name. He did, however, call on lawmakers to embrace immigrants and reject "a mindset of hostility," stating "We are not fearful of foreigners, because most of us were once foreigners" and "Let us treat others with the same passion and compassion with which we want to be treated" (U.S. News, 2015).

RESPONSES OF PROTESTANTS AND OTHER FAITH COMMUNITIES

Protestants from various denominations have also been active in calling for CIR for well over a decade, as have members of other religions or faith-based communities. While evangelicals are discussed separately, major efforts of some of the largest and/or most active non-evangelical denominations are described in this section.

Support for immigration reform is nothing new for the United Methodist Church, the second-largest Protestant denomination in the United States. In 2008 Methodist leadership passed a resolution calling for CIR at the General Conference (United Methodist Church, 2008), and in 2010 Methodist bishops pledged support to a campaign for humane changes to immigration policy the following year (Hahn, 2010). Bishop Minerva Carcaño, the first female Hispanic bishop elected in the church, was one of the 14 faith leaders invited to the White House in 2013 to discuss how to overhaul the nation's immigration system and encourage Republican lawmakers to join reform efforts (Rampersad, 2013). She was also one of 32 people of faith arrested outside the White House in 2014 while participating in a peaceful demonstration protesting immigration deportations (Gilbert, 2014), and she has testified on Capitol Hill on behalf of families hurt by current immigration policy (Carcaño, 2016).

Various branches of the Lutheran Church have also been active in promoting acceptance of the migrant and CIR. Lutheran Immigration and Refugee Service, working on behalf of uprooted people since 1939, has called for a just and humane approach to migration that provides a path to earned citizenship, ensures humane enforcement of U.S. immigration laws, keeps families together, protects both U.S. citizen and immigrant workers, and provides adequate resources for the integration of refugees and other vulnerable persons (Lutheran Immigration and Refugee Service, 2012). Church leaders in 2009 published a book titled *They Are Us*, a call to exercise radical hospitality and welcome and embrace immigrants (Bouman & Deffenbaugh, 2009).

The Presbyterian Church has been politically active on the topic of immigration since at least 1994. In 1999 and 2004 General Assembly actions were directed toward both Presbyterians and the government to work for just laws for immigrants living and working in the United States and for welcoming of immigrants into U.S. communities. In April 2010 church leadership sent a letter to Congress urging the passage of CIR (VanMarter, 2010). Presbyterian efforts also include accompaniment programs, "sanctuary responses" at church camp and conference centers, and development of educational resources outlining immigration policy history and analyzing current legislation (Presbyterian Church USA, n.d.).

Perhaps because of their own historical persecution or struggle for belonging, members of "minority" religions tend to display more tolerance toward immigrants and less anti-immigrant sentiment than members of mainline faiths (Knoll, 2009). The Muslim Public Affairs Council, for instance, issued a policy report in 2010 that focused on reform of the legal immigration system, advocating for earned legalization of individuals without documentation, and stressing the importance of effective immigration enforcement (Beutel, Hasan, & Hathout, 2010). Jewish leaders have also expressed support for comprehensive reform, calling for both enforcement of current laws and creation of a path to citizenship (Ginsberg, 2013). Immigration was the primary issue of discussion by the Jewish Social Justice Roundtable in 2013. "The Torah is very clear about how we ought to treat immigrants," wrote one rabbi (ibid.).

Prior to 2011, the Church of Jesus Christ of Latter-Day Saints (Mormons, or LDS) refused to take a public stance on immigration reform. In 2010, however, LDS leadership voiced public support of the *Utah Compact* on immigration which calls for federal immigration solutions that show compassion for undocumented persons in the country (The Church of Jesus Christ of Latter-Day Saints, 2010). The official LDS statement on immigration, released in 2011, discourages individuals from entering the country without authorization and calls on the federal government to resolve the issue, but also promotes the idea of earned legal status (not necessarily leading to citizenship) that would allow migrants in the United States without authorization to continue to work (The Church of Jesus Christ of Latter-Day Saints, 2011). In 2013, however, the church appeared to lean more heavily in favor of comprehensive reform after LDS authority Dieter F. Uchtdorf and 13 other faith leaders met with President Obama to discuss immigration reform. Uchtdorf later stated that the principles discussed by Obama were "totally in line with our values" (Canham, 2013).

RESPONSE OF EVANGELICALS AND
INTERFAITH EFFORTS

Historically, churches in the U.S. South (the heart of evangelical Prot-
estantism) have chosen to avoid social or political campaigns concerned
with immigrants (Winders, 2011, p. 610). Over the past two decades,
however, well-known evangelical leaders have become some of the most
prominent voices speaking out in favor of humane CIR, often as part of
interfaith efforts. In 2007, after the defeat of CIR legislation, Sojourners
Ministries director Jim Wallis launched a broad "Christians for Comprehensive Immigration Reform" campaign that included both educational
tools and calls to political action. This was followed by the publication
of *Christians at the Border* by evangelical professor M. Daniel Carroll R.
in 2008 and the Matthew Soerens and Jenny Hwang book *Welcoming
the Stranger* in 2009. Both books offered a starting point for conversation
about immigration among persons of faith and were endorsed by a number
of prominent evangelical leaders.

In 2009 the National Association of Evangelicals (NAE) representing more than 40 denominations, 45,000 congregations, and millions of
constituents passed a resolution calling for reform that included a path to
earned legal status (National Association of Evangelicals, 2009). Conservatives for Comprehensive Immigration Reform was formed in 2010
to address anti-immigrant rhetoric and promote a "heart of righteousness
and justice" in reform proposals (Conservatives for CIR, 2012). Then in
June 2012, more than 150 of the most influential evangelical Christian
leaders and organizations formed the Evangelical Immigration Table,
made up of groups including the NAE, the Southern Baptist Ethics and
Religious Liberty Commission, the National Hispanic Christian Leadership Conference, the Council for Christian Colleges and Universities,
World Relief, and World Vision. In addition to engaging in political and
educational immigration efforts, this coalition launched a 40-day scrip-
ture and prayer-based "I Was a Stranger" campaign (National Association
of Evangelicals, 2012). Finally, in March 2013, a large evangelical presence was felt during the White House gathering of faith leaders called to
discuss CIR (Dwoskin, 2013).

In spite of the efforts and gains made by evangelical leadership, white
evangelicals continue to be the religious group most opposed to CIR
(Kellstedt & Melkonian-Hoover, 2015). This resistance has been partly
attributed to a disconnect between reform efforts by evangelical elites and
actual preaching on immigration by evangelical clergy, but researchers
have found that evangelicals' identification with conservative positions

and the Republican Party play a greater role (ibid.). Evangelical constituents tend to follow the lead of their conservative lawmakers regarding attitudes toward immigration and Hispanics—a tendency that would explain the struggle of evangelical leaders to recruit support amidst the highly negative and polarizing atmosphere toward immigrants that has pervaded the 2016 presidential elections.

FURTHER EXPRESSIONS OF FAITH

While this is not a comprehensive list, it does give an indication of the involvement of diverse churches and faith communities in advocating for CIR. As they continue to work toward reform in the United States, many of these churches (as well as faith groups not already mentioned) have extended their outreach beyond U.S. borders to assist migrants and immigrants in Europe (Church of the Nazarene, 2015; Episcopal Relief & Development, 2016; Tanis, 2016).

Given that historically, religious differences have likely created more divisions than alliances, the fact that such a broad range of religious groups and denominations agree on the basic tenants of CIR is remarkable. As Mark Tooley of the Institute on Religion and Democracy remarked, "That the representatives of most of American religion are agreed on CIR maybe should herald either the Second Coming or the Apocalypse" (Tooley, 2013).

FURTHER READING

Beutel, A. J., Hasan, A., & Hathout, M. (2010, November). *Ineffective & unjust: Fixing our nation's broken immigration system.* Washington, DC: Muslim Public Affairs Council.

Bouman, S., & Deffenbaugh, R. (2009). *They are us.* Minneapolis, MN: Augsburg Fortress.

Byrne, J. (n.d.). *Roman Catholics and immigration in nineteenth-century America.* Research Triangle Park, NC: National Humanities Center. Retrieved from http://www.nationalhumanitiescenter.org/tserve/nine teen/nkeyinfo/nromcath.htm

Canham, M. (2013, March 9). Mormon leader: Obama's immigration plan matches LDS values. *The Salt Lake Tribune*, p. A1

Carcaño, M. G. (2016, April 19). The real victims of a reckless and lawless immigration policy: Families and survivors speak out on the real cost of this administration's policies [Testimony by Bishop Minerva G. Carcaño before the Subcommittee on Immigration and Border Security, Committee on the Judiciary of the U.S. House of Representatives], Washington, DC. Retrieved from https://judiciary.house.gov/wp-con tent/uploads/2016/04/Bishop-Minerva-Carcano-Testimony-HJC-04.19.pdf

Carroll, R.M.D. (2012, June 28). Immigration: What does the Bible say? *Christian Standard.* Retrieved from http://christianstandard.com/ 2012/06/immigration-what-does-the-bible-say/

The Church of Jesus Christ of Latter-Day Saints. (2010, November 11). Church supports principles of *Utah Compact* on immigration [Official statement]. Retrieved from http://www.mormonnewsroom.org/article/ church-supports-principles-of-utah-compact-on-immigration

The Church of Jesus Christ of Latter-Day Saints. (2011, June 10). Immigration: Church issues new statement [Policy statement]. Retrieved from http://www.mormonnewsroom.org/article/immigration-church-issues-new-statement

Church of the Nazarene. (2015, September 17). Board of General Superintendents urges church response to refugee crisis. Retrieved from http://nazarene.org/article/board-general-superintendents-urges-church-response-refugee-crisis

Conservatives for CIR. (2012, January 6). The Conservatives for Comprehensive Immigration Reform Coalition Applauds the Proposed Administrative fix to our Nation's Immigration Procedures. Retrieved from http://www.prnewswire.com/news-releases/the-conservatives-for-com prehensive-immigration-reform-coalition-applauds-the-proposed-administrative-fix-to-our-nations-immigration-procedures-1368449 23.html

Dwoskin, E. (2013, March 21). Why Evangelicals now favor immigration reform. *Bloomberg Businessweek.* Retrieved from http://www .businessweek.com/articles/2013-03-21/why-evangelicals-are-now-for-immigration-reform

Episcopal Relief & Development. (2016). Syria crisis response updates. Retrieved from http://www.episcopalrelief.org/press-and-resources/ press-releases/2016-press-releases/syria-crisis-response-updates

Evangelical Immigration Table. (n.d.). Evangelical statement of principles for immigration reform. Retrieved from http://evangelicalimmi grationtable.com/

Gilbert, K.L. (2014, February 18). *Out of jail, but concerns over deportations remain.* Washington, DC: United Methodist News Service. Retrieved from http://www.umc.org/news-and-media/united-methodist-d.c.-pray-in-for-immigration-reform

Ginsberg, J. (2013, February 13). Immigration returns to communal agenda. New Jersey Jewish News, American Jewish Committee. Retrieved from http://www.ajc.org/site/apps/nlnet/content3.aspx?c=7 oJILSPwFfJSG&b=8482997&ct=12966337&notoc=1

Gomez, A. (2014, November 28). Obama immigration action may split religious coalition. *USA Today*. Retrieved from http://www.usatoday.com/story/news/politics/2014/11/28/obama-immigration-executive-action-religious-groups-division/70099916/

Hahn, H. (2010). Bishops oppose racism, back immigration reform. United Methodist News Service. Retrieved from http://www.umc.org/news-and-media/bishops-oppose-racism-back-immigration-reform

Jones, R. P., Cox, D., Navarro-Rivera, J., Dionne Jr., E. J., & Galston, W. A. (2013, March 21). *Citizenship, values, and cultural concerns: What Americans want from immigration reform*. Washington, DC: Public Religion Research Institute and The Brookings Institution. Retrieved from http://www.brookings.edu/research/reports/2013/03/21-immigration-survey-jones-dionne-galston

Jones, S. (2008, July 7). Catholic leaders launch "Justice for Immigrants" campaign. cnsnews.com. Retrieved from http://cnsnews.com/news/article/catholic-leaders-launch-justice-immigrants-campaign

Kellstedt, L. A., & Melkonian-Hoover, R. (2015, February 6). White evangelicals and immigration reform. *The Christian Post*. Retrieved from http://www.christianpost.com/news/white-evangelicals-and-immigration-reform-133687/

Knoll, B. R. (2009). "And Who Is My Neighbor?" Religion and immigration policy attitudes. *Journal for the Scientific Study of Religion, 48*(2), 313–331.

Library of Congress. (n.d.). *Immigration: Religious conflict and discrimination*. Washington, DC: Library of Congress. Retrieved from http://www.loc.gov/teachers/classroommaterials/presentationsandactivities/presentations/immigration/irish5.html

Lipka, M. (2015, September 14). *A closer look at Catholic America*. Pew Research Center. Washington, DC: Pew. Retrieved from http://www.pewresearch.org/fact-tank/2015/09/14/a-closer-look-at-catholic-america/

Lutheran Immigration and Refugee Service. (2012, May). Lutherans and immigration reform: Frequently asked questions [Fact sheet]. Retrieved from http://lirs.org/wp-content/uploads/2012/05/LUTHERAN-IMMIGRATION-AND-REFUGEE-SERVICE-FAQS.pdf

National Association of Evangelicals. (2009). Immigration 2009 [Policy resolution]. Retrieved from http://www.cmalliance.org/news/2009/10/09/nae-immigration-2009-resolution/

National Association of Evangelicals. (2012, November 13). Open letter on immigration reform [Endorsed document]. Retrieved from http://nae.net/open-letter-on-immigration-reform/

Pew Research Center. (2014, November 13). *Religion in Latin America.* Washington, DC: Pew, Religion and Public Life. Retrieved from http://www.pewforum.org/2014/11/13/religion-in-latin-america/

Pew Research Center. (2015, January 2). *Faith on the Hill: How the 114th Congress compares with the general public.* Washington, DC: Pew, Religion and Public Life. Retrieved from http://www.pewforum.org/2015/01/05/faith-on-the-hill/pr_15-01-05_religioncongress-01-new/

Pew Research Center. (2015, May 12). *America's changing religious land-scape.* Washington, DC: Pew, Religion and Public Life. Retrieved from http://www.pewforum.org/2015/05/12/americas-changing-religious-landscape/

Presbyterian Church USA. (n.d.). Immigration resources. Retrieved from https://www.pcusa.org/browse/resources-resource/departments/immigration/

Rampersad, L. (2013, March 13). UMC Bishop Carcaño meets with Pres. Obama. United Methodist Church, Justice for our Neighbors, West Michigan. Retrieved from http://jfonwestmichigan.org/general/umc-bishop-carcao-meets-president-obama/

Tanis, P. (2016, May 3). North Americans welcome refugees, immigrants. World Communion of Reformed Churches. Retrieved from http://wcrc.ch/news/north-americans-welcome-refugees-immigrants

Taylor, P. (2014, April 10). *The next America.* Washington, DC: Pew Research Center. Retrieved from http://www.pewresearch.org/next-america/#Two-Dramas-in-Slow-Motion

Tooley, M. (2013, March 11). For evangelicals, the temptation of CIR [Web log entry]. Retrieved from http://www.patheos.com/blogs/philosophicalfragments/2013/03/11/evangelical-temptation-comprehensive-immigration-reform-tooley/

United Methodist Church (UMC). (2008). Book of resolutions: Call for comprehensive immigration reform. United Methodist Publishing House. Retrieved from http://www.umc.org/what-we-believe/call-for-comprehensive-immigration-reform

United States Catholic Conference (USCC). (2000). *Welcoming the stranger among us: Unity in diversity* [Pastoral letter]. Washington, DC: USCC. Retrieved from http://www.usccb.org/issues-and-action/cultural-diversity/pastoral-care-of-migrants-refugees-and-travelers/resources/welcoming-the-stranger-among-us-unity-in-diversity.cfm

United States Conference of Catholic Bishops (USCCB). (2012). *A parish outreach, education, and organizing manual in support of the Justice for Immigrants campaign of the United States Conference of Catholic Bishops.* Washington, DC: USCCB.

United States Conference of Catholic Bishops (USCCB). (2013). *Migration policy* [Policy position]. Retrieved from http://www.usccb.org/about/migration-policy/index.cfm

United States Conference of Catholic Bishops (USCCB). (2013, April 19). *Survey shows strong Catholic support for immigration reform.* Washington, DC: USCCB. Retrieved from http://www.usccb.org/news/2013/13-073.cfm

United States Conference of Catholic Bishops, Inc., and Conferencia del Episcopado Mexicano. (2003, January 22). *Strangers no longer: Together on the journey of hope.* Retrieved from http://www.usccb.org/mrs/stranger.shtml

U.S. News. (2015, September 24). READ: Pope Francis' Address to Joint Session of Congress. usnews.com. Retrieved from http://www.usnews.com/news/articles/2015/09/24/text-of-pope-francis-address-to-congress

VanMarter, J. L. (2010, May 3). PC(USA) leaders press for immediate immigration reform. *Presbyterian News Service.* Retrieved from http://www.pcusa.org/news/2010/5/3/pcusa-leaders-press-immediate-immigration-reform/

Winders, J. (2011). Representing the immigrant: Social movements, political discourse, and immigration in the U.S. South. *Southeastern Geographer*, 51(4), 596–614.

Q36. ARE CONGRESSIONAL ATTITUDES TOWARD COMPREHENSIVE IMMIGRATION REFORM, INCLUDING A PATH TO LEGALIZATION FOR UNAUTHORIZED IMMIGRANTS, DIVIDED ALONG PARTY LINES?

Answer: Yes and no. Both Democrats and Republicans, in Congress and in the general public, have supported comprehensive immigration reform efforts over the past decade. The two parties differ, however, in the way they would structure that reform and the priorities they would give to various elements of reform. Leaders of both parties have also agreed that a path toward legalization is necessary, but Republicans have generally demanded that the U.S.-Mexico border be secured first before a path toward legalization is provided, while Democrats have said total securitization may not even be possible and providing a means toward legalization should be among the top reform priorities.

The Facts: Since the early 2000s, members of both political parties have made efforts to pass various types of immigration reform, but disagreements within or between the parties prevented any major legislation from passing through Congress. Consider the following partial list of failed attempts at reform since 2005:

- May 2005—The Secure America and Orderly Immigration Act (S. 1033) proposed by Senators Ted Kennedy (D-MA) and John McCain (R-AZ)
- July 2005—The Comprehensive Enforcement and Immigration Reform Act of 2005 (S. 1438) proposed by Senators John Cornyn (R-TX) and Jon Kyl (R-AZ)
- December 2005—The Border Protection, Antiterrorism and Illegal Immigration Control Act of 2005 (H.R. 4437) sponsored by Rep. James Sensenbrenner (R-WI) and Rep. Peter King (R-NY)
- May 2006—The Comprehensive Immigration Reform Act of 2006 (S. 2611) sponsored by Sen. Arlen Specter (R-PA)
- May 2007—Secure Borders, Economic Opportunity and Immigration Reform Act of 2007 (S. 1348) sponsored by Sen. Harry Reid (D-NV)
- December 2009—The Comprehensive Immigration Reform for America's Security and Prosperity Act of 2009 (H.R. 4321) sponsored by Rep. Solomon P. Ortiz (D-TX)
- September 2010—Comprehensive Immigration Reform Act of 2010 (S. 3932) sponsored by Sen. Robert Menendez (D-NJ)
- June 2011—Comprehensive Immigration Reform Act of 2011 (S. 1258) sponsored by Sen. Robert Menendez (D-NJ)
- January 2013—Border Security, Economic Opportunity, and Immigration Modernization Act of 2013 (S. 744) sponsored by the Sen. Charles Schumer (D-NY) and "Gang of 8" (see later in chapter)
- January 2015—Save America Comprehensive Immigration Act of 2015 (H.R. 52) sponsored by Rep. Sheila Jackson Lee (D-TX)

As the list attests, members of both political parties have tried in earnest to pass comprehensive immigration reform, but none of these attempts was successful because of differing opinions on just how the reform should be structured. Comments made by 2016 presidential candidates about comprehensive immigration reform reflect a continuance of the deep divide between and within the two parties:

> When politicians talk about "immigration reform" they mean: amnesty, cheap labor and open borders. The Schumer-Rubio immigration bill was nothing more than a giveaway to the corporate patrons who run both parties—*Republican presidential candidate Donald Trump* (Trump, 2015)
>
> I think if instead the bill includes elements that are deeply divisive—and I would note that I don't think there is any issue in this entire debate that is more divisive than a path to citizenship for those who are here illegally—in my view, any bill that insists upon that jeopardizes the likelihood of passing any immigration reform bill—*Republican presidential candidate Ted Cruz* (Hunter, 2013)
>
> The American people support comprehensive immigration reform not just because it's the right thing to do—and it is—but because it will strengthen families, strengthen our economy, and strengthen our country. That's why we can't wait any longer, we can't wait any longer for a path to full and equal citizenship—*Democratic presidential candidate Hillary Clinton* (Clinton, 2015)
>
> It is incomprehensible that the U.S. House has not yet taken up the comprehensive immigration reform bill passed by the Senate with my support. We need legislation which takes 11 million undocumented people living in the United States out of the shadows and puts them on a path to citizenship—*Democratic presidential candidate Bernie Sanders* (Sanders, 2015)

While Democratic and Republican leaders have worked to promote specific principles of reform within their respective parties, the Republican Party made the adoption of comprehensive immigration reform part of its new agenda. After the defeat of presidential candidate Mitt Romney in 2012 the GOP recognized the need to attract and address the concerns of Hispanic voters, and doing so meant supporting immigration reform efforts. In March 2013, the Republican National Committee released a list of recommendations for the party titled the "Growth and Opportunity Project," which specifically stated the following:

> Among the steps Republicans take in the Hispanic community and beyond we must embrace and champion comprehensive immigration reform. If we do not, our Party's appeal will continue to shrink to its core constituencies only. We also believe that comprehensive

immigration reform is consistent with Republican economic policies that promote job growth and opportunity for all. (Republican
National Committee, 2013, p. 76)

Soon after, in Congress, politicians on both sides of the political aisle
embraced the idea of comprehensive immigration reform (CIR). The
Gang of 8 that crafted the proposed 2013 CIR legislation was made up of
four Democratic Senators (Chuck Schumer—NY, Robert Menendez—NJ,
Michael Bennet—CO, and Richard Durbin—IL) and four Republican
Senators (Marco Rubio—FL, John McCain—AZ, Lindsey Graham—SC,
and Jeff Flake—AZ). After months of wrangling and compromising, the
Gang of 8 came forth with the biggest potential overhaul of the immigration system in decades—S. 744. Even though the four Republican Gang of
8 senators had all previously stated that a path toward legalization should
only come about after the border with Mexico is more secure, the group
was able to develop a reform plan that provided enough compromise to
attract followers from both parties. Legislators from both sides of the aisle
spoke out in favor of the bill and encouraged its passage, although it also
drew criticism from a number of conservatives who did not agree with the
path to legalization provisions (McGuire, 2013). Although the work of
the bipartisan Gang of 8 elicited great hope that comprehensive reform
would finally be passed, the 2013 CIR bill was eventually defeated. The
Senate approved it with a vote of 68–32 (including 14 Republican senators), but the bill died when House leadership refused to bring it to a vote.

The defeat of the Gang of 8 bill was followed by more than two years
of congressional inaction on the issue of comprehensive immigration
reform, with no such legislation given serious consideration in Congress.

PATH TOWARD LEGALIZATION

Disagreement among GOP leaders, particularly over the issue of a path to
legalization, was one of the key elements that contributed to the defeat
of the 2013 Gang of 8 CIR bill. Republican constituents, unlike their
congressional leaders, were not overwhelmingly opposed to the idea of
legalization. A March 2016 Pew Research poll found that overall, 76 percent of registered voters in the United States think undocumented immigrants who meet specific requirements should be allowed to stay legally.
When broken down into party affiliation, 57 percent of Republican voters favored this legalization, as well as 88 percent of Democrats (Pew
Research Center, 2016). This support among the majority of Republican
voters stands in stark contrast to the anti-amnesty rhetoric that pervaded

discussion surrounding efforts to pass comprehensive immigration reform in 2013 and has been prominent in presidential primary discourse among Republicans in 2015–2016.

Perhaps more surprising is the extent of the divide between party leadership and its constituents. In spite of the fact that studies and public opinion polls show the majority of registered voters have supported the idea of a path to legalization for undocumented immigrants since at least 2013 (Camarota, 2013; Motel, 2014; Newport & Wilke, 2013; Pew Research Center, 2015; Steinhauser, 2014), anti-amnesty rhetoric has enough of a following that it has continued to dominate political discussions about immigration for years.

Public opinions, though, are partially dependent on the language used to describe the idea of legalization for unauthorized persons. A 2007 survey revealed that use of the word "amnesty" in polls resulted in a much more negative opinion toward offering a chance at legalization than did the phrase "opportunity to eventually become citizens" even though both phrases referred to the same action (Merolla, Karthick Ramakrishnan, & Haynes, 2013). Thus, public opinion can be construed differently depending on the language used when polls are conducted.

For the time being, the divide between congressional Democrats and Republicans on key elements of comprehensive immigration reform is too great to produce any significant changes. President Obama's efforts to use his executive powers to initiate specific elements of reform have also been hampered by court challenges (U.S. Citizenship and Immigration Services, 2015). Although both political parties agree immigration reform is crucial, major change will have to wait a bit longer.

FURTHER READING

Camarota, S. A. (2013, April 5). *Legalization vs. enforcement.* Washington, DC: Center for Immigration Studies. Retrieved from http://cis.org/legalization-vs-enforcement-what-the-american-people-think

Clinton, H. (2015). America needs comprehensive immigration reform with a pathway to citizenship [Campaign Web site]. Retrieved from https://www.hillaryclinton.com/issues/immigration-reform/

Hunter, M. (2013, April 22). Sen. Cruz: Pathway to citizenship would kill immigration reform bill. cnsnews.com. Retrieved from http://cnsnews.com/news/article/sen-cruz-pathway-citizenship-would-kill-immigration-reform-bill-0

McGuire, M. (2013, January 30). Who are the Gang of 8 in Senate immigration debate? abcnews.com. Retrieved from http://abcnews.go.com/

Politics/OTUS/meet-gang-senators-immigration-reform-include-mar
co-rubio/story?id=18348317

Merolla, J., Karthick Ramakrishnan, S., & Haynes, C. (2013, September).
"Illegal," "Undocumented," or "Unauthorized": Equivalency frames,
issue frames, and public opinion on immigration. *Perspectives on Politics*, 11(3), 789–807.

Motel, S. (2014, January 28). *On immigration, Republicans favor path to legal
status, but differ over citizenship*. Washington, DC: Pew Research Center. Retrieved from http://www.pewresearch.org/fact-tank/2014/01/28/
on-immigration-republicans-favor-path-to-legal-status-but-differ-
over-citizenship/

Newport, F., & Wilke, J. (2013, June 19). *Immigration reform proposals garner broad support in U.S.* Gallup.com. Retrieved from http://www.gallup
.com/poll/163169/immigration-reform-proposals-garner-broad-support
.aspx

Pew Research Center. (2015, June 4). *Broad public support for legal status
for undocumented immigrants*. Washington, DC: Pew Research Center. Retrieved from http://www.people-press.org/2015/06/04/broad-
public-support-for-legal-status-for-undocumented-immigrants/

Pew Research Center. (2016, March). *Campaign exposes fissures over
issues, values, and how life has changed in the U.S.* Washington, DC: Pew
Research Center. Retrieved from http://www.people-press.org/files/
2016/03/3-31-16-March-Political-release-1.pdf

Republican National Committee. (2013). Growth & opportunity project.
Republican National Committee. Retrieved from http://goproject.gop
.com/RNC_Growth_Opportunity_Book_2013.pdf

Sanders, B. (2015, September 4). Sanders calls for immigration reform,
rips Trump attacks on immigrants [Campaign Web site press release].
Retrieved from https://berniesanders.com/press-release/sanders-calls-
for-immigration-reform-rips-trump-attacks-on-immigrants/

Steinhauser, P. (2014, February 6). CNN poll: Pathway to citizenship
trumps border security. CNNcom. Retrieved from http://political
ticker.blogs.cnn.com/2014/02/06/cnn-poll-pathway-to-citizenship-
trumps-border-security/

Trump, D. (2015). Immigration reform that will make America great
again. Donald J. Trump political Web site. Retrieved from https://www
.donaldjtrump.com/positions/immigration-reform

U.S. Citizenship and Immigration Services (USCIS). (2015, April 15).
Executive actions on immigration. Washington, DC: USCIS. Retrieved
from https://www.uscis.gov/immigrationaction

Q37. HAS IMMIGRATION ENFORCEMENT BEEN NEGLECTED DURING THE OBAMA ADMINISTRATION?

Answer: Primarily, no, although numbers can potentially support both critics and advocates of Obama administration policies regarding prosecutions and removal of unauthorized persons. Growth of for-profit prisons and detention facilities has also formed a part of Obama's immigration enforcement legacy.

The Facts: In addition to unprecedented funding and growth of border enforcement agencies and personnel during the Obama administration (discussed in Chapter 7), more unauthorized immigrants have been deported under Obama than under any previous president. President Obama, while touting his role as a champion of immigration, has also distinguished himself as the president who has deported more unauthorized immigrants than any other president in history. Deportations under the Obama administration reached 2 million in 2014, averaging over 1,000 deportations a day. This record has earned Obama the designation among some pro-immigrant groups as "deporter-in-chief" (Krogstad, 2014) and has inspired hunger strikes, demonstrations, and social media campaigns among those who demand a reduction in deportations (Kamp, 2015; Krogstad, 2014; Torres, 2014).

While the total number of individuals expelled from the United States under the Bush administration is actually larger than the number expelled under the Obama administration, the number of *formal* deportations (removals) was far higher during Obama's years in office. (The Department of Homeland Security uses the term "removal" rather than "deportation" to describe both deportations and expedited removals of foreign nationals from the United States by Immigration and Customs Enforcement and Customs and Border Protection) (Passel, Cohn, & Gonzalez-Barrera, 2013).

The difference between returns and removals is critical when evaluating immigration enforcement data. When an unauthorized border-crosser is apprehended, Border Patrol agents have the discretionary capability to do one of three things: (1) release (often called a voluntary return and only an option for citizens of Canada or Mexico), (2) deport (often called an expedited removal, in which the deportation process takes about a month and during which time the detainee is held in Border Patrol facilities), or (3) criminally charge the individual (the detainee is charged with

Entry Without Inspection and held in federal detention facilities until arraignment) (Sheldon, 2013).

During the first half of the George W. Bush administration, the vast majority of unauthorized persons sent out of the United States were simply returned, meaning they were sent back across the border without going through formal removal proceedings. Prior to 2006, these returns were referred to as "voluntary departures." Returns do not carry with them harsh consequences, such as ineligibility to apply for legal entry, and are not a part of formal record-keeping. Thus, someone who has been returned either can apply to enter the United States legally or may retry an unauthorized entry.

Removals, on the other hand, are included in formal record-keeping practices and carry much harsher criminal or administrative penalties. Persons who have been removed are subject to fines, may face temporary or permanent ineligibility for legal entry, and can be charged with a felony if they are apprehended during a reentry attempt. Certain forms of removal also do not require hearings before an immigration judge (Elmi & McCabe, 2011).

In 2005, the initiation of Operation Streamline changed the way the Department of Homeland Security handled the departure of unauthorized persons. This Bush-era enforcement program (that was continued under the Obama administration) aimed to criminally prosecute border-crossers and thus *require* their removal by federal authorities instead of allowing unauthorized persons to voluntarily return home with no permanent marks on their immigration records. Formal deportations under the Obama administration include more unauthorized individuals than ever before being removed for reasons *other than* criminal convictions (Gonzalez-Barrera & Krogstad, 2014; Torres, 2014), consistent with the guidelines of Operation Streamline. Also, the largest category of criminal deportations is currently made up of people whose only conviction was an immigration-related offense (Migration Policy Institute, 2014).

Under U.S. immigration law, first-time illegal entry is a misdemeanor punishable by up to six months in prison (8 U.S.C. Section 1325), and illegal reentries are felonies punishable by up to 20 years in prison (8 U.S.C. Section 1326). Prior to Operation Streamline, first-time unauthorized border-crossers were usually either voluntarily removed or processed under formal removal proceedings through the civil (not criminal) immigration system. Generally, only border-crossers with repeated entry attempts or those with criminal records were criminally prosecuted. Under Operation Streamline, prosecutorial discretion was removed and agents were required to place all unauthorized border-crossers in criminal prosecution proceedings, regardless of their crossing or criminal history (Lydgate, 2010). Thus, many border-crossers who were counted as voluntary returns prior to 2005 were now officially deported and included in formal removal statistics. Formal deportation under Operation Streamline carries with it a five-year bar on readmission (a civil sanction under 8 U.S.C. § 1182(a)(9)(A)) and a criminal charge of Entry Without Inspection (Sheldon, 2013).

Intended as a means of decreasing unauthorized border crossings and reentries, Operation Streamline has raised concerns and created new problems. Critics decry lack of due process resulting from rapidly conducted mass hearings, during which 40–80 persons may appear and enter pleas at the same time, often without having an opportunity to consult a lawyer or fully understand the consequences of pleading guilty. Decisions by the judge are generally rendered within "seconds or minutes" (American Immigration Lawyers Association, 2015). Operation Streamline has also flooded federal courts with illegal entry cases. By 2011 illegal entry and illegal reentry were the most common charges brought by federal prosecutors (Transactional Records Access Clearinghouse, 2011). From 2004 to 2013, illegal entry convictions made up 65 percent of all immigration convictions and illegal reentry accounted for 26 percent (Transactional Records Access Clearinghouse, 2014).

In regard to Obama's immigration enforcement record, then, under the guidelines of Operation Streamline formal deportations did rise under Obama's watch. The president's commitment to "quickly return unlawful migrants to their home countries" (2014) is evident in the fact that more removals came from the interior of the United States than from border areas during his first three years in office, indicating a concerted effort to remove not only recent border-crossers but also those already established further into the country (U.S. Immigration and Customs Enforcement, 2015). During ensuing years, these interior removals placed increasing emphasis on individuals with criminal convictions as opposed to non-criminals (Rosenblum & McCabe, 2014). From FY 2009 to FY 2014, over 1 million unauthorized individuals were removed from the interior of the United States (U.S. Immigration and Customs Enforcement, 2015) and 2 million removed overall (U.S. Department of Homeland Security, 2014). That is twice as many as were deported during the last six years of the Bush administration (ibid.).

Obama's resolve to remove unauthorized persons was also apparent during the last five years of his administration, when 99 percent of total DHS removals and 97 percent of interior removals fell under the Department of Homeland Security's three priority categories: recent unauthorized entrants, those in violation of immigration court orders, and those with a criminal conviction—including immigration convictions (Rosenblum & McCabe, 2014). The focus on recent unauthorized entrants included the thousands of Central American border-crossers who began arriving en masse in 2012, resulting in criticism that the administration was not giving due process to those who sought and qualified for asylum (Pelosi, 2016; Tzamaras & Feliz, 2015).

In regard to how Obama's immigrant prosecution record compares with previous administrations, it is very difficult to compare records side by side. In addition to the fact that DHS changed its tactics during the second half of the Bush administration to increase the number of formal removals, other factors make such comparisons challenging. For instance, statistics indicate the number of returns or removals, but not the number of *separate individuals* returned or removed. That is to say, it is unknown how many of those who were returned *or* removed attempted subsequent reentries. Individuals who were simply returned under informal record-keeping practices would likely not be identified in subsequent reentry attempts, and could be counted multiple times in statistics even though just one person attempted reentry. Also, formal removals require more time and manpower than simple returns, resulting in a large backlog of immigration cases that may result in deportation but have not yet been decided. These statistics, too, will shape the legacy of the Obama administration's immigration enforcement and prosecution record (Caplan-Bricker, 2014). Finally, lower numbers of unauthorized migration attempts, changing push and pull factors that affect migratory flows, and voluntary departures of unauthorized persons in the United States also affect the overall circumstances within which immigration-related prosecutorial decisions take place. Therefore, as one reporter stated, "In this light, any apples-to-apples comparison of Bush's policies with Obama's is meaningless" (ibid.).

One additional aspect of immigration enforcement that has expanded under the Obama administration is the for-profit prison industry. While not a direct product of immigration law, this expansion has major implications for the direction of current and future immigration enforcement legislation, which has favored incarceration as contracts with private prison corporations have grown. The number of noncitizens detained in U.S. facilities doubled from roughly 230,000 in FY 2005 to roughly 440,600 in FY 2013 (Government Accountability Office, 2014), and in 2011, 49 percent of immigration detention beds for Immigration and Customs Enforcement (ICE) were managed by private corporations (Detention Watch Network, 2011). An analysis of government records by a Texas nonprofit put the 2015 figure at 62 percent (Carson & Diaz, 2015).

For profit-motivated private prison companies whose revenues depend on incarcerations, growth of immigration-related incarcerations has resulted in huge revenues (Ackerman & Furman, 2013). In 2010 alone, the combined profits of the two largest private prison corporations totaled nearly $3 billion overall, with immigration-related incarcerations making up a substantial portion of that total (Ashton & Petteruti, 2011). One way the corporations assure profits is to maintain full prisons. For example, a number of contracts that Corrections Corporation of America (CCA) has entered into with various states require bed quotas. The states are required to pay penalty taxes to CCA if their occupancy rates fall below 90 percent (In the Public Interest, 2013). In Arizona, a state with one of the highest incarcerated noncitizen populations in the nation, three such contracts require 100 percent occupancy rates (ibid.).

The combination of the criminalization of immigration and the privatization of detention facilities, however, has raised concerns about the creation of an immigration industrial complex that discourages efforts toward systemic reform (Doty & Wheatley, 2013). Critics contend that increased federal support of private prisons does nothing to address public policy goals of reducing crime, but instead encourages harsher penalties for crimes that otherwise would not have warranted prison sentences. A report filed by CCA, the largest of the for-profit prison corporations, says as much: "The demand for our facilities and services could be adversely affected by the relaxation of enforcement efforts, leniency in conviction or parole standards and sentencing practices or through the decriminalization of certain activities that are currently proscribed by criminal laws" (2010, p. 19).

Reports have also revealed private prison companies' attempts to influence legislation through extensive lobbying and campaign contributions to candidates and legislators who support their motives (Ashton & Petteruti, 2011; Diaz & Keen, 2015; Leow, 2010). These efforts included campaign donations to the sponsors of Arizona's controversial S.B. 1070, which at the time was considered the country's toughest immigration law (Sullivan, 2010). Thus, according to a Justice Policy Institute report, while the companies claim to simply be meeting the demand for prisons, they intentionally work to create the demand for their services (Ashton & Petteruti, 2011).

As Immigration and Customs Enforcement (ICE) has continued to criminalize unauthorized entry, its facilities have become increasingly overcrowded. In response, the Department of Homeland Security has turned to private prison corporations to provide additional facilities and detention centers. One of the more controversial aspects of this relationship has been the government's decision to detain families (or more often women) with children, many of whom are asylum seekers (Human Rights Watch, 2014). Although the Obama administration had closed the largest immigration family detention facility in 2009 over concerns of abuses and a lawsuit, it later approved the construction or expansion of additional facilities to house growing family migrant populations and awarded the contracts to private prison firms. GEO group, one of the largest such corporations, attributed the expansion of a residential center in Karnes, Texas, as a major reason for its $83 million revenue increase over the prior year (Seeking Alpha, 2016). Likewise, a family detention facility in Dilley, Texas, completed in 2015 and run by CCA generated over $70 million in revenue during the first quarter of 2016 (Globe Newswire, 2016). The facility in Dilley alone costs the federal government $720,000 a day, or almost $263 million a year (Preston, 2014).

For some, the rise in incarcerations of unauthorized persons and the expansion of for-profit prisons to hold them is an example of government efforts to curb illegal immigration and improve national security. Others see these changes as being beneficial to prison corporations but of little utility in addressing underlying factors that push individuals to attempt unauthorized entries into the United States. While increased support of for-profit private detention corporations began before Obama came into office, his support and continuance of private prison contracts is also part of his administration's immigration enforcement legacy.

FURTHER READING

Ackerman, A. R., & Furman, R. (2013). The criminalization of immigration and the privatization of the immigration detention: Implications for justice. *Contemporary Justice Review: Issues in Criminal, Social, and Restorative Justice, 16*(2), 251–263.

American Immigration Lawyers Association (AILA). (2015, June 19). *AILA's take on Operation Streamline* [AILA Doc. No. 15061930]. Washington, DC: AILA. Retrieved from http://www.aila.org/infonet/aila-take-on-operation-streamline

Ashton, P., & Petteruti, A. (2011, June). *Gaming the system: How the political strategies of private prison companies promote ineffective incarceration policies.* Washington, DC: Justice Policy Institute. Retrieved from http://www.justicepolicy.org/uploads/justicepolicy/documents/gaming_the_system.pdf

Caplan-Bricker, N. (2014, April 17). Who's the real deporter-in-chief: Bush or Obama? *New Republic.* Retrieved from https://newrepublic.com/

article/117412/deportations-under-obama-vs-bush-who-deported-more-immigrants

Carson, B., & Diaz, E. (2015, April). Payoff: How Congress ensures private prison profit with an immigration detention quota. Grassroots Leadership. Retrieved from http://grassrootsleadership.org/reports/pay off-how-congress-ensures-private-prison-profit-immigrant-deten tion-quota#1

Corrections Corporation of America (CCA). (2010). Annual report on form 10-K. United States Security and Exchange Commission Report. Retrieved from http://ir.correctionscorp.com/phoenix .zhtml?c=117983&p=irol-reportsannual

Detention Watch Network. (2011, May). *The influence of the private prison industry in the immigration detention business.* Washington, DC: Detention Watch Network. Retrieved from http://www.detentionwatchnet work.org/pressroom/reports/2011/private-prisons

Diaz, M., & Keen, T. (2015, May 12). *How US private prisons profit from immigrant detention.* Washington, DC: Council on Hemispheric Affairs. Retrieved from http://www.coha.org/how-us-private-prisons-profit-from-immigrant-detention/

Doty, R. L., & Wheatley, E. S. (2013, December 12). Private detention and the immigration industrial complex. *International Political Sociology, 7*(4), 426–443.

Elmi, S., & McCabe, K. (2011, October 25). *Immigration enforcement in the United States.* Washington, DC: Migration Policy Institute. Retrieved from http://www.migrationpolicy.org/article/immigration-enforcement-united-states#19

Globe Newswire. (2016, May 4). CCA reports first quarter 2016 financial results. Nashville, TN: CCA. Retrieved from https://globenewswire .com/news-release/2016/05/04/836807/0/en/CCA-Reports-First-Quar ter-2016-Financial-Results.html

Gonzalez-Barrera, A., & Krogstad, J. M. (2014, October 2). *U.S. deportations of immigrants reach record high in 2013.* Washington, DC: Pew Research Center. Retrieved from http://www.pewresearch.org/ fact-tank/2014/10/02/u-s-deportations-of-immigrants-reach-record-high-in-2013/

Government Accountability Office (GAO). (2014, October 10). *Immigration detention: Additional actions needed to strengthen management and oversight of facility costs and standards.* Washington, DC: U.S. GAO. Retrieved from http://www.gao.gov/products/GAO-15-153

Human Rights Watch. (2014, July 29). *US: Halt expansion of immigrant family detention.* Washington, DC: Human Rights Watch. Retrieved from https://www.hrw.org/news/2014/07/29/us-halt-expansion-immi grant-family-detention

In the Public Interest. (2013, September). *Criminal: How lockup quotas and "low-crime taxes" guarantee profits for private prison corporations.* Washington, DC: In the Public Interest. Retrieved from https://www .inthepublicinterest.org/wp-content/uploads/Criminal-Lockup-Quota-Report.pdf

Kamp, A. (2015, October 28). Breaking: Hutto detainees begin hunger strike. *The Austin Chronicle*. Retrieved from http://www.austinchronicle .com/daily/news/2015-10-28/breaking-hutto-detainees-begin-hunger-strike/

Kirkham, C. (2012, June 7). Private prisons profit from immigration crackdown; federal and local law enforcement partnerships. *Huffington Post Business*. Retrieved from http://www.huffingtonpost.com/2012/06/ 07/private-prisons-immigration-federal-law-enforcement_n_1569219 .html

Krogstad, J. M. (2014, March 11). *Americans split on deportations as Latinos press Obama on issue.* Washington, DC: Pew Research Center. Retrieved from http://www.pewresearch.org/fact-tank/2014/03/11/americans-split-on-deportations-as-latinos-press-obama-on-issue/

Leow, M. (2010, September 1). Brewer linked to private prisons housing illegal immigrants. cbs5az. Retrieved from http://www.cbs5az .com/story/14791252/brewer-linked-to-private-prisons-housing-illegal-immigrants-9-01-2010

Lydgate, J. (2010, January). *Assembly-line justice: A review of Operation Streamline* [Policy brief]. Berkeley, CA: University of California, Berkeley Law School. Retrieved from https://www.law.berkeley.edu/files/Opera tion_Streamline_Policy_Brief.pdf

Migration Policy Institute (MPI). (2014, October 16). *MPI report offers most detailed analysis yet of U.S. deportation system under DHS; Examines criminality, origin, gender & more of deportees.* Washington, DC: MPI. Retrieved from http://www.migrationpolicy.org/news/mpi-report-of fers-most-detailed-analysis-yet-us-deportation-system-under-dhs-examines

Obama, B. (2014, June 30). *Letter from the president—Efforts to address the humanitarian situation in the Río Grande Valley areas of our nation's south-west border.* Washington, DC: The White House Office of the Press Sec-retary. Retrieved from https://www.whitehouse.gov/the-press-office/ 2014/06/30/letter-president-efforts-address-humanitarian-situation-rio-grande-valle

Passel, J. S., Cohn, D., & Gonzalez-Barrera A. (2013, September 23). *Population decline of unauthorized immigrants stalls, may have reversed.* Washington, DC: Pew Research Center. Retrieved from http://www .pewhispanic.org/2013/09/23/population-decline-of-unauthorized-im migrants-stalls-may-have-reversed/

Pelosi, N. (2016, May 17). *Pelosi statement on ICE deportation actions.* Washington, DC: Democratic Leader Web site. Retrieved from http:// www.democraticleader.gov/newsroom/pelosi-statement-on-ice-deportation-actions/

Preston, J. (2014, December 15). Detention center presented as deterrent to border crossings. *The New York Times.* Retrieved from http:// www.nytimes.com/2014/12/16/us/homeland-security-chief-opens-larg est-immigration-detention-center-in-us.html?_r=0

Rosenblum, M. R., & McCabe, K. (2014, October). *Deportation and discretion: Reviewing the record and options for change.* Washington, DC: Migration Policy Institute. Retrieved from http://www.migrationpolicy.org/ research/deportation-and-discretion-reviewing-record-and-options-change

Seeking Alpha. (2016, April 28). The GEO Group's (GEO) CEO George Zoley on Q1 2016 Results—Earnings Call Transcript (Q1 2016 Earnings Conference Call). Retrieved from http://seekingalpha.com/article/ 3969107-geo-groups-geo-ceo-george-zoley-q1-2016-results-earnings-call-transcript?part=single

Sheldon, H. A. (2013). Operation Streamline: The Border Patrol prosecutions initiative. *The Public Purpose*, 11, 89–114.

Sullivan, L. (2010, October 28). Prison economics help drive Ariz. immigration law. *National Public Radio.* Retrieved from http://www .npr.org/2010/10/28/130833741/prison-economics-help-drive-ariz-immigration-law

Torres, L. (2014). Dismantling the deportation nation [Editorial]. *Latino Studies*, 12, 169–171. Retrieved from http://www.palgrave-journals .com/lst/journal/v12/n2/pdf/lst201433a.pdf

Transactional Records Access Clearinghouse (TRAC). (2011, July 19). *Immigration continues to top federal prosecutions.* Syracuse, NY: Syracuse University. Retrieved from http://trac.syr.edu/whatsnew/email.110719 .html

Transactional Records Access Clearinghouse (TRAC). (2014, June 26). *Despite rise in felony charges, most immigration convictions remain misdemeanors.* Syracuse, NY: Syracuse University. Retrieved from http:// trac.syr.edu/immigration/reports/356/

Tzamaras, G., & Feliz, W. (2016, January 6). *After successfully delaying the deportations of four Central American families, groups demand meeting with DHS Secretary Johnson.* Washington, DC: American Immigration Council and American Immigration Lawyer's Association. Retrieved from http://aila.org/advo-media/press-releases/2016/groups-demand-meeting-with-dhs-secretary-johnson

U.S. Department of Homeland Security (DHS). (2014, August). *2013 Yearbook of Immigration Statistics.* Washington, DC: Office of Immigration Statistics. Retrieved from https://www.dhs.gov/sites/default/files/publications/ois_yb_2013_0.pdf

U.S. Immigration and Customs Enforcement (ICE). (2015, December 22). *ICE enforcement and removal operations report.* Washington, DC: Department of Homeland Security. Retrieved from https://www.ice.gov/sites/default/files/documents/Report/2016/fy2015removalStats.pdf

Index

About the Author

Cari Lee Skogberg Eastman, PhD, is an independent scholar studying border and immigration issues. She is the author of *Shaping the Immigration Debate: Contending Civil Societies on the U.S.-Mexico Border.*